Practical
FORENSIC DIGITAL IMAGING
Applications and Techniques

CRC SERIES IN
**PRACTICAL ASPECTS OF CRIMINAL
AND FORENSIC INVESTIGATIONS**

VERNON J. GEBERTH, BBA, MPS, FBINA *Series Editor*

Practical Homicide Investigation: Tactics, Procedures, and Forensic Techniques, Fourth Edition
Vernon J. Geberth

The Counterterrorism Handbook: Tactics, Procedures, and Techniques, Third Edition
Frank Bolz, Jr., Kenneth J. Dudonis, and David P. Schulz

Forensic Pathology, Second Edition
Dominick J. Di Maio and Vincent J. M. Di Maio

Interpretation of Bloodstain Evidence at Crime Scenes, Second Edition
William G. Eckert and Stuart H. James

Tire Imprint Evidence
Peter McDonald

Practical Drug Enforcement, Third Edition
Michael D. Lyman

Practical Aspects of Rape Investigation: A Multidisciplinary Approach, Fourth Edition
Robert R. Hazelwood and Ann Wolbert Burgess

The Sexual Exploitation of Children: A Practical Guide to Assessment, Investigation, and Intervention, Second Edition
Seth L. Goldstein

Gunshot Wounds: Practical Aspects of Firearms, Ballistics, and Forensic Techniques, Second Edition
Vincent J. M. Di Maio

Friction Ridge Skin: Comparison and Identification of Fingerprints
James F. Cowger

Footwear Impression Evidence: Detection, Recovery and Examination, Second Edition
William J. Bodziak

Principles of Kinesic Interview and Interrogation, Second Edition
Stan Walters

Practical Fire and Arson Investigation, Second Edition
David R. Redsicker and John J. O'Connor

The Practical Methodology of Forensic Photography, Second Edition
David R. Redsicker

Practical Aspects of Interview and Interrogation, Second Edition
David E. Zulawski and Douglas E. Wicklander

Investigating Computer Crime
Franklin Clark and Ken Diliberto

Practical
FORENSIC
DIGITAL IMAGING
Applications and Techniques

Patrick Jones

CRC Press
Taylor & Francis Group
Boca Raton London New York

CRC Press is an imprint of the
Taylor & Francis Group, an **informa** business

Cover image details: The gun is a 9mm Ruger, semi automatic pistol. There is blood/tissue "blow-back" from a contact wound with a victim. It is lit with a halogen, fiber optic light at 1/2 power. Photographed with a Nikon D-80 camera with a Nikon 60mm f/2.8D AF Micro-Nikkor Lens. The macro photo of a gold colored wedding type ring shows the engraving: 10K and "TW" in a circle. The ring is lit with "tent" lighting with two 60 watt incandescent light sources. Photographed with a Nikon D-80 camera with a Nikon 60mm f/2.8D AF Micro-Nikkor Lens. The pill is a caplet which has had a latent fingerprint developed by use of fluorescent powder and the "Jones Brush System". The image was lit with a halogen fiber optic light source at full power. Photographed with a Nikon D-80 camera with a Nikon 60mm f/2.8D AF Micro-Nikkor Lens.

CRC Press
Taylor & Francis Group
6000 Broken Sound Parkway NW, Suite 300
Boca Raton, FL 33487-2742

© 2011 by Taylor and Francis Group, LLC
CRC Press is an imprint of Taylor & Francis Group, an Informa business

No claim to original U.S. Government works

Printed in the United States of America on acid-free paper
10 9 8 7 6 5 4 3 2 1

International Standard Book Number: 978-1-4200-6012-6 (Hardback)

Library of Congress Cataloging-in-Publication Data

Jones, Patrick, 1946-
    Practical forensic digital imaging : applications and techniques / Patrick Jones.
       p. cm. -- (CRC series in practical aspects of criminal and forensic investigations)
    "A CRC title."
    Includes bibliographical references and index.
    ISBN 978-1-4200-6012-6
    1. Legal photography. 2. Photography--Digital techniques. 3. Crime scenes. I. Title.

TR822.J66 2011
778.9'936325--dc22

2010031768

Visit the Taylor & Francis Web site at
http://www.taylorandfrancis.com

and the CRC Press Web site at
http://www.crcpress.com

Dedication

I dedicate this book to my wife, Beverly, for her understanding, support, encouragement, and love. To my children, Brandy and Ryan, who give me great joy. To my grandchildren, Quinn and Ethan, who teach me to be young. To Patrick Farrell, who was always there for me for computer support. Finally to my friend, I consider a sister, Jan Jakubiak, for her encouragement to write.

Table of Contents

Series Editor's Note

This book is part of a series entitled *Practical Aspects of Criminal and Forensic Investigation*. This series was created by Vernon J. Geberth, New York City Police Department Lieutenant Commander (Retired), who is an author, educator, and consultant on homocide and forensic investigations. This series, written by authors who are nationally recognized experts in their respective fields, has been designed to provide contemporary, comprehensive, and pragmatic information to the practitioner involved in criminal and forensic investigations.

Foreword

MARCUS K. ROGERS

"Oh no, not another book on forensics!" This is often the refrain I hear from my students. With the mass appeal of *CSI* and its numerous offshoots, it seems as though we are being inundated with all things forensic science related. As a forensic scientist, teacher, and practitioner, I often feel that the popularity of forensic sciences has gotten in the way of the science itself. However, with the increase in popularity there has been increased scrutiny of the scientific fields that comprise the domain of forensic sciences. At times, the results or findings of this scrutiny have been less than kind. The National Academies of Sciences (NAS) report to the U.S. Congress (2009) jumps to mind. The NAS report shone a light on many of the shortcomings, gaps, and growing pains from which the forensic sciences in the United States suffer. It was somewhat painful to read about many of the issues on which we in research, academia, government, and the private sector have observed and commented for years. To see the amalgamation of concerns captured in one document truly ignited a passion in many of us to address some of these fundamental concerns.

Patrick is one such individual who has risen to address one of the largest issues we face, a common body of quality resources and reference materials. Patrick is part of a rare but growing breed of forensic scientists and academics, practitioners from the law enforcement domain who have entered academia with a fabulous grasp of the applied and appreciation for the necessities of theory. Patrick and I share a common background; we both cut our teeth in the field of law enforcement and have spent countless hours on real cases and at real crime scenes, dealing with real problems affecting real people. Patrick is now a fellow colleague at Purdue University and has played an invaluable role in the development and success of the undergraduate minor degree in forensic sciences at Purdue. He is a much-sought-after teacher, researcher, and consultant. The success of the graduates of the degree is a testament to the quality of the curricula and the dedicated folks teaching the program.

I need to return to my initial comments regarding yet another book on forensic sciences. I can honestly say that this is "not just another forensic sciences book." Patrick's diverse background and his experiences in the field and the classroom have been translated into a work that not only gets the essential information into the hands of the reader but also does so in a way that readers will find refreshing and intuitive. The book and its sections balance practical considerations with scientific and standards-based requirements. The coverage of the topics in each section is clear and concise, and the breadth of coverage of the book is inclusive of what one needs to know about the fundamentals of digital imaging as it relates to forensics.

To those of you like my students who worry about being inundated by often-retreaded or pedantic works that really add no value to your reference library, I say take heart; here is an example of what real-world knowledge combined with years of experience produces.

This book will no doubt be an invaluable reference source whether you are just beginning your journey in the field or are a seasoned veteran looking for a source of information to help inform future generations of forensic scientists and practitioners. I already have a special place set aside on my crowded library bookshelf for Patrick's book and expect it to become dog-eared and rather ragged looking in no time.

Acknowledgments

I would like to acknowledge the many friends and colleagues who gave me assistance and support:

Ralph E. Williams, professor, Purdue University; Marcus Rogers, professor, Purdue University; Vernon J. Geberth, colleague and friend; Paul Huff, detective, Lafayette Indiana Police Department; Jason Thompson, coroner, White County, Indiana; Tom Gersbeck, EOD; Captain Rosanne Radavich, U.S. Army; Beverly Jones; Kristi Bugajski, PhD candidate, Purdue University; Marissa McDonough, PhD candidate, Purdue University; Clayton Nolting, master's candidate, Purdue University; Venumadhav Margam, research associate, Purdue University; Douglas Maish, clinical support manager, Purdue University; Dayson Smith, undergraduate student, Purdue University; Brad Spray, undergraduate student, Purdue University; Cheri Lemon, undergraduate student, Purdue University; Michael Burgess, undergraduate student, Purdue University; Summer Wagner-Walker, undergraduate student, Purdue University; Ryan Jones, number 1 son; Paula Layden, office manager, Purdue University.

Introduction

Tell me, I forget;
show me, I remember;
involve me, I understand.

—Confucius

I teach a graduate course on forensic digital photo imaging. One of the necessary things for a course is a good textbook, a book that the students could read in preparation for lectures. I had much difficulty in attempting to find such a text.

When I was learning forensic photo imaging, back in the dark ages (no, we did not use pictograms), we used film cameras. There were books available, but those available did not relate to technical or forensic photography but rather creative imaging, such as scenery or portraits.

I learned by a different method than today. I was assigned a "mentor," and we worked together, I as his "apprentice" and he as the "master." He would tell me about a particular facet of photography, then demonstrate it, and finally had me try. Sometimes, I "got it," and we moved on, and sometimes I failed. If I did fail, he would make me repeat it until I had learned it and could demonstrate to him that I understood.

We did not have colleges or universities that taught criminalistics or forensic or investigative sciences. There were occasional seminars given, but the departments and agency were slow to allocate funds for training. It was believed that, because we did a good job, we did not need the training.

I sometimes go into detail about what to look for or explain the collection of some evidence types. This is because I believe that you cannot adequately photo document a crime scene without understanding the crime scene. We teach "forensic science" as a subject. The word *forensic* means "as pertains to a court of law." Science is *science*. It is not only death investigation, fingerprints, trace, DNA, microscopy, entomology, soil, casting, anthropology, osteology, chemistry, biology, toxicology, odontology, radiology, computers, tool marks, measuring, drawing diagrams, firearms, explosive, accident reconstruction, blood spatter, serology, investigation, and so on, but it is a combination of all of these scientific disciplines. If we are true forensic scientists, we need to know and understand these disciplines, not as an expert in each but, at the very least, a practitioner.

I also require my students to call me Patrick. Not professor. Not doctor. When I instructed my first students when I was still on the job as a criminalistics investigator, I was "Patrick," their mentor. A student may have difficulty asking a question of a superior. He may not want to sound foolish or be embarrassed. Asking a "partner" a question does not evoke the same type of feelings. The student can make a mistake in front of a partner—it is okay. Partners are good like that. They want you to succeed. After all, they are your backup. I do not say that this works in all cases, but in this career path, I have had much success. The student is more apt to ask questions and therefore learn more.

I believe in hands-on work in my classes. This is the way of true learning. Confucius said "Tell me, I forget; show me and I remember; involve me and I understand." This is my philosophy of teaching.

Back to the book: I wanted this book to have some technical information. You have to understand the tool with which you are working. But, the book I wanted would also be a "how to" book. It would tell how to photograph fingerprints, wounds, bodies, blood spatter, footwear impressions, and more. It would describe how to use lighting to capture the image that you want and need to tell the story of the crime scene or evidence because the book is about forensic photo imaging.

You will note throughout the book that when describing the location of a wound or a body part that I use "left front" or "lower right back" rather that "distal," "medial," "anterior," or the like. This is because of who will read your reports. In all probability, it will be the detective, the jurors, or others who do not have the training to understand the technical descriptions. You have to write, you have to document, so that your audience, the reader, understands what you are trying to describe.

Not only should our photography be technically correct, but also it needs to be acceptable in the courts. We must abide by the law and court decisions such as *Daubert v. Merrell Dow Pharmaceuticals* (1993) and *Frye v. United States* (1923). We must also conform to the recommendations of the Scientific Working Group on Imaging Technology (SWGIT).

It came down to the fact that if I wanted a book that did all of this, and more, I would have to write the book myself. Fortunately, the people at Taylor & Francis, more specifically, Becky Masterman, and my good friend Vern Geberth, agreed. So, I began writing this book. I learned that it is not easy to write a book, but thanks to their support, it is finally finished (for now). Technology is changing almost on a daily basis. There will be new techniques based on new technology and new discoveries.

The book is based on my learning from my mentors, trials and errors (many trials and errors), and the 35 years that I have been involved in law enforcement, criminalistics, and forensic photography.

Enjoy, learn, and experiment. Please feel free to make many mistakes on your own. If you learn from your mistakes, you will be a great success. *Experiential docent*: This is a Latin phrase meaning "experience teaches."

About the Author

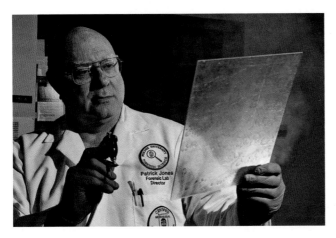

Photo courtesy of *The Purdue Exponent*

Patrick Jones is the Forensic Science Laboratory director at Purdue University. In addition to managing two laboratories, he teaches Crime Scene Investigation, Introduction to Forensic Science, Criminalistics Lab, and Advanced Criminalistics Lab. He has been named to the graduate faculty by the dean of the Graduate School and teaches graduate level courses in Advanced Forensic Studies (Sex-Related Homicide and Death Investigation) and Forensic Digital Imaging. He has mentored one master's and two doctoral candidates.

Mr. Jones has more than 34 years of experience in law enforcement, forensics investigation, security, and training. As a Crime Scene Investigator (CSI), he has worked on the John Wayne Gacy case, the Larry Eyler case (both serial killers), and the Ed Ling case among many others. He lectures and presents these cases for students and interested groups. Patrick Jones is also currently a White County Indiana Deputy Coroner and is an Indiana State Certified Medicolegal Death Investigator.

A former Cook County (Illinois) Sheriff Police Investigator, Jones retired with 21 years of service, which included 11 years as a CSI involved in more than 5000 death investigations and present at over 750 autopsies. He was also an undercover narcotics team leader and narcotics unit commander, a tactical investigator, prosecutor's investigator, and general assignment investigator. He earned one Sheriffs Medal, 13 Departmental Commendations, the J. Edgar Hoover Medal, and numerous other awards for service and excellence.

Jones has also been a staff faculty member of the National Intelligence Academy, instructing government personnel, military members, and law enforcement personnel in audio and video surveillance techniques. He was a staff instructor at the Cook County Sheriff's Police Academy and is a Certified Police Science Instructor, Illinois. He was named a District Director of the Illinois Crime Commission (1995–1996). He is a graduate of the National Law Enforcement Academy (DEA) and has attended over 67 law enforcement and security related seminars. He has been qualified and accepted as an expert witness in the area of forensic photo imaging and evidence collection.

Research and Professional Interests

Jones is currently conducting research with forensic lasers in the areas of trace evidence and latent fingerprint recovery. He has also invented the Jones Brush System, a new method to recover latent fingerprints without cross contamination of DNA. He has developed a method for recovering latent fingerprints from very small objects such as pills, capsules and coins. He is also working with a new camera sensitive only in the UV and IR wavelengths. The camera can photo image subcutaneously (under the skin) and see deep tissue bruising.

Patrick Jones collaborated with Ralph E. Williams to coauthor *Crime Scene Processing and Laboratory Workbook* (CRC Press, 2009). He also contributed a chapter, "Forensic Digital Photo Imaging," in *Forensic Science*, edited by Stuart H. James and Jon J. Nordby (CRC Press, 2009).

Jones is also affiliated with or certified by the following professional organizations:

- Certified Medicolegal Death Investigator (CMDI), State of Indiana
- SWGIT, Scientific Working Group on Imaging Technology—member
- International Association for Identification (IAI), Division—board member
- Indiana Homicide and Violent Crimes Investigator's Association—charter member
- American Society for Industrial Security (ASIS), Chapter—past chairman
- DEA Alumni Association—member
- Faculty and Staff (NIA), 1984–1989
- International Law Enforcement Educators and Trainers Association—member
- International Association of Crime Scene Investigators (IACSI)—member
- International Homicide Investigators Association (IHIA)—member
- Indiana Coroner's Association (ICA)—member

Documentation

1

Digital Imaging

The terms *digital imaging* and *photography* are in fact synonymous. They have the same meaning. They both can be defined as the act of recording light or reflected light from an object or group of objects. Rarely do we directly record light for this would require us to point the camera directly at a light source such as the sun, a lightbulb, or other visible spectrum light-emitting source. While there may be a need for it in some specific instances, such as recording sunspots, the great preponderance of what we do in forensic digital imaging is record reflected light.

Light from a source, a flash, light beam, or ambient light strikes an object and is reflected off the object and into our lens. The camera then "sees" the light though its lens and allows it to continue through its aperture to the media on which the image will be recorded on digital media or film.

The only real difference is the recording medium. Film cameras record on film, and digital cameras record on magnetic media, CDs, DVDs, and memory cards. Memory cards are probably the most common. Memory cards are actually computer chips that use flash memory to record the digital images. This type of memory, unlike the RAM (random access memory) in your computer, does not lose data when current is disconnected. It maintains the image files until they are moved or erased.

These memory cards are manufactured in many different configurations, depending on what the manufacturer has decided to build into the camera design (Figure 1.1). The memory cards are not interchangeable (if different types are used), however, so to share the images taken by cameras with different type memory cards, you must first upload them to a computer. This is similar to the example of two law enforcement officers carrying different handguns, one a .38-caliber handgun and the other a .45-caliber handgun: They both fire projectiles, but the ammunition is not interchangeable.

There are several types of memory cards, including SD (secure digital), memory sticks, compact flash, xD-Picture Card, the RS-MMC (reduced size multimedia card), mini-SD card, and many more.

Forensic Digital Imaging

Forensic can be defined by the term "as pertains to a court of law." The word *forensic* merely adds "legal" to a phrase. *Forensic digital imaging* is another way of saying "digital imaging—as pertains to a court of law." The word *forensic* can be added to a number of words, for example, forensic entomology (insects as pertains to a court of law), forensic physical anthropology (the study of human remains as pertains to a court of law), forensic engineering (engineering as pertains to a court of law), and many more.

Figure 1.1 Various types of memory cards available. These are the recording media in most digital single-lens reflex (SLR) cameras.

The addition of *forensic* to digital imaging adds a number of layers to the correct practice of this discipline. Good digital imaging requires knowledge of the technical aspects of recording objects and locations. Forensic digital imaging not only requires knowledge of the technical aspects of recording objects and locations but also requires the use of method, a set policy, and procedures all approved and accepted by law, the courts, and judicial decision. SWGIT, the Scientific Working Group on Imaging Technology, created a document that recommends standard operating procedures as relates to photo imaging and the courts.

Evidence or lack of evidence must be documented at a crime scene. To understand what happened at a crime scene, it is necessary to reconstruct the scene and the scenario that accompanies it to investigate the crime and, if necessary, prosecute the perpetrator successfully.

We cannot just take several snapshots of a scene and expect those few images to be acceptable. We must tell the story. The St. Valentine's Day massacre of 1929 was a poorly documented scene. There were only approximately five images taken. The camera used was a Speed graphic 4 × 5 inch sheet film camera (Figures 1.2 and 1.3). The images were taken by a news photographer. In fact, as the story goes, the photographer thought the image would look better with a hat on one of the victim's chest, so the photographer placed it there (Figures 1.4 and 1.5). So much for the integrity of that crime scene.

Do the five or so images taken tell the story? Do they show the wounds? Do they show the correct positions of objects? Are the images distorted? What about livor mortis? Were scales used to size objects in the scene? What did the other sides of the room look like? Where was the door or doors? Were there windows, and if so, how many were there? What were the victims looking at before they were killed? These may have been

Figure 1.2 This is a Speed Graphic camera from the "old days." It was the workhorse for newspaper and crime scene photography from the 1930s to the early 1960s. The camera took a 4 × 5 inch sheet negative.

Figure 1.3 This is a film holder. It was loaded with two sheets of film, one on each side. To take pictures, you would have to place the holder in the camera, pull out the film cover, then take the picture. Then, you had to put the slide cover back in the holder, remove the holder, turn it over, place it back into the camera, and pull out the slide cover; then, you were ready to take the next picture.

sensational newspaper photographs, but they certainly did not tell the story; they were not good technical images.

You must identify the case and location. Your must record the overall area of the scene. You must image evidence and items of interest and their perspective to each other. You must capture each piece of evidence, record it correctly, and scale it (show relative size), and you must do so without appearing to hide exculpatory evidence—evidence that could be used by the opposition in the case.

St. Valentine's Massacre- Feb. 14, 1929 2122 No. Clark, Chicago, Illinois.

Figure 1.4 This is one of only two images taken at the St. Valentine's Day massacre. They were taken by a news photographer.

The use of a narrative to explain the condition, the exact location of items, and the existence of artifacts, of course, is also important and a necessary part of the overall documentation of a scene.

Digital imaging allows us to visually re-create the scene for investigators, prosecutors, and jurors deciding the fate of individuals charged with a crime.

The old adage that "a picture is worth a thousand words" may not be true. I believe that the picture is worth many thousands of words. If the narrative of a report states "The handgun was located on the table next to the phone," we can summon a visual picture in our mind. But as we look at the picture, we see that the image that we conjured may be quite different from what was actually described. Look at Figure 1.6. Is this the image that came to mind when you read the verbal description of the image? The image shows the location of the handgun, which is a semiautomatic pistol with the slide open and locked to the rear position, indicating that the handgun is not loaded. The phone is a cell phone, which may or may not belong at this scene. Since it is a cell phone, it may belong to anyone—the victim, a witness, or even the perpetrator.

Documentation of a scene or of evidence requires us to document the documentation. This sounds redundant, but it is something that has to be done. The images must be documented, and I strongly recommend that they be listed on the report (Figure 1.7).

The first thing that must be done is to identify the images. We want to identify them as unique or individual. As an example, when an object is analyzed in a laboratory, we can sometimes identify it as belonging to a class. We can identify a handgun as a .38 caliber. But, to make it unique, the handgun is further examined and found to have a serial number. Now, the handgun is unique, one of a kind. It is the same with digital images. Images

Figure 1.5 The second picture of the St. Valentine's Day massacre. It was said that the news photographer placed the hat on the victim's chest because it looked more dramatic—talk about scene contamination.

belong to the class of "images of a scene." We must make them unique by specifically identifying them. We do this by making our first image on the memory card, a color balance/ID card, sometimes called a *gray card* (Figure 1.8). On this card, we place the case number, the image taker's name, the date, and the agency. This is done so that if the CD, magnetic media, or memory card is misfiled, it can be discovered and identified as belonging to a specific case. It also identifies the case and images at trial. The ID/color balance card can be laminated. A dry marker can be used to print the appropriate information. It can then be reused by CSI again and again.

The second image on the roll of film or the second digital image should be an image of the letter *N* (for "north"; Figure 1.9). This *N* can be held by an assistant or propped against the wall or an object. The important thing is that the north card is on the north side of the room or location. The image should include a good portion of the north wall or north side of the crime scene. This allows the crime scene investigator (CSI) to document the north direction so that there is no confusion at trial. When cases go to trial, too often there is a span of time between the time the images were taken and the actual trial. Sometimes,

Figure 1.6 This is an image of a gun and phone on a table. The picture tells more than the simple description.

years pass. This is compounded by the fact that since the CSI works many cases, the odds of remembering which direction is north at a particular scene are rather slim.

Images taken at a crime scene should be listed on the report form used by the CSI. If the amount of images exceeds the number of spaces on the report, an image continuation sheet should be used. The use of the log is a matter for each individual agency to set as its policy and procedure. The FBI (Federal Bureau of Investigation), for example, advocates the use of the image log. There are advantages and disadvantages to the use of an image log. It is helpful for the prosecutor to have an inventory of the images available to prepare a solid case. It also eliminates any question regarding whether all images taken were delivered to the defense during the discovery phase of the trial. It also identifies any images that may have been lost or misplaced.

The type of description placed on the log should be short but descriptive, such as "gray card/image ID," "north shot," "handgun on end table," "overall living room s/n." (Note that s/n is an abbreviation meaning from the south to the north).

A disclaimer should be added to the report form indicating that directions, such as s/n (south to north) are approximate and are used as such to identify each image. The disclaimer eliminates the potential for a defense attorney to nitpick the description, such as, "Isn't it true, detective, that the image log states that this image was taken south to north, and the image taken was actually southeast to northwest?" If the defense can call into question one image, the defense can then attempt to call all the images into question and move to have all images thrown out.

Documenting with digital images also records items of evidence out of place. Items out of place are called *artifacts* (Figure 1.10). An *artifact*, in forensic science, can be defined as "an object that does not belong." Artifacts can be a bullet hole in a mirror or glass window. An artifact could be a letter clutched in the hand of a victim. It could even be a VCR in the middle of the living room floor. An item out of place could be a fireplace poker in a bathroom. Imaging these items tells a paragraph or chapter in the story that is the crime scene.

Crime Scene Investigator's Report

| Print Form |

Report Classification | Case Number |

Date/Time | Type of Location | Agency | Investigator |

Victim's Name | Victim's Address |

Injuries | Taken for Treatment | Victim Rape Kit | Suspect In Custody |

Suspect Rape Kit | Weapon | Gunshot Residue | Gun Sheet |

Weather | Inside Temperature | Outside Temperature | Crime Scene Drawing |

Alcohol | Drugs | Lighting Conditions |

Vehicle | Make | Model | Year | Color |

Vehicle Sheet | License Plate | License Plate State |

Other Distinguishing Characteristics |

Inventory Control Number | Images Taken |

Evidence Collected			Photo Images	
1		23	1		23
2		24	2		24
3		25	3		25
4		26	4		26
5		27	5		27
6		28	6		28
7		29	7		29
8		30	8		30
9		31	9		31
10		32	10		32
11		33	11		33
12		34	12		34
13		35	13		35
14		36	14		36
15		37	15		37
16		38	16		38
17		39	17		39
18		40	18		40
19		41	19		41
20		42	20		42
21		43	21		43
22		44	22		44

© 2003, 2005 Patrick Jones - All Rights Reserved

Note: Start listing photo images on this report - if additional space is needed use Photo Listing Sheet

Signature | Page |

Figure 1.7 A crime scene report. Reports similar to this are used by law enforcement agencies throughout the country. Each agency develops its reports based on its needs.

We must also document items that are not there. For example, a table with one bottle of wine, one wine glass, and *two* wine glass rings on a glass table should prompt the questions: Where is the second glass? Was it taken by the perpetrator?

Then, what is missing? Have the napkins been removed? Has an ashtray been emptied? It is important to record negatives as well as positives.

An area on a table, dresser, or counter free from dust with an area of dust around it indicates that something was there and is now gone (Figure 1.11). Photo image it.

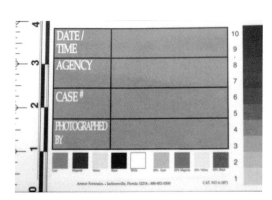

Figure 1.8 This is a photo ID card. When laminated and used with a dry erase marker, it can be used again and again. It is always the first image shot at a crime scene. It identifies the images that follow (successive numbered images) taken at a scene.

Figure 1.9 This is the "north" card. It can be laminated on the back of the photo ID card for convenience. It is used as the second shot at the crime scene. It is shot with a significant area of scene in the background so that all of the images taken can be directionally oriented.

Figure 1.10 An artifact. An artifact, at a crime scene, is something that does not belong. The artifact is the zebra.

Items of interest must be documented. An item of interest is something that by its position, location, or condition, may help in further understanding the story of the crime scene. An image of a toilet seat in the up position in a home with only women in residence, a kitchen knife in the bedroom, and a tire iron in a living room all are items of interest (Figure 1.12).

Remember, tell the story with your images. You can never take too many images. Document, document, document.

Figure 1.11 A shelf top with a clear area in the midst of dust indicates that something was here and was removed.

Figure 1.12 A raised toilet seat. In a home with only women in residence, this is an artifact.

The Transition from 35-mm Film to Digital Imaging 2

Introduction

Digital imaging did not just appear on the horizon one day; it had its roots in film photography (Figure 2.1). The 35-mm camera has been around for a long time. In time, the standard developed (no pun intended) to the 35-mm SLR (single-lens reflex) camera, which will continue to be important in forensic imaging for a long time. However, the photographic industry is in a state of migration from film to digital imaging. For example, Eastman Kodak, the world's largest photography company, announced in June 14, 2004, that it would stop making 35-mm film cameras because of the rise of digital technology. And on June 16, 2005, Kodak announced that it would stop producing black-and-white photo paper. If this giant of industry makes such a decision, you can be sure that the others will eventually follow suit.

The writing is on the wall concerning film photography and digital imaging. Agencies, crime scene investigators (CSIs), and forensic scientists are migrating not only to a more modern state-of-the-art technology but also are looking to reduce operating expenses and storage issues for their respective departments. The capital investment will be substantial; however, when we look at the savings to be had due to the storage, distribution, and printing of images, there will be a cost savings in the overall picture. Over time, the capital investment will be far overshadowed by the savings on the distribution of images alone. Cost of printing a set of images from a crime scene taken on film and printed on photo paper could be considerable.

In a capital case, sets of images are made for officers involved in the case, for the detective on the case, for the prosecutor's office, and then for the defense, and perhaps still another set is enlarged for court presentation. Court pictures are often requested by the prosecutor in sizes of 8 × 10, 11 × 14, and sometimes in 16 × 20 inch format. The prosecutor wants large images that will make an impact on the jury, and 8 × 10 inch images can cost several dollars each. If there are 100 pictures in the case, that could add up to $300 per set. These multiple copies can be costly.

With digital images, a CD can be made of all the images in the case file for under $1 per CD, so six sets would equal a cost of $6.

Storage and filing are also easier. Negatives stored using archival methods and materials can be quite costly. Negatives stored and preserved must be kept in inert negative sleeves. They should further be kept in an area controlled for temperature and humidity. They must be kept in an environment that will not change or affect the chemical makeup of the film. In many jurisdictions, evidence is kept for 99 years. The film should then also be kept for that period.

Digital images can be stored on CDs or DVDs. The cost for these media is minimal. In addition, exact digital copies can be stored on hard drives. These hard drives in turn can be backed up, providing an additional level of safe storage.

Figure 2.1 This is an early 35-mm film camera. It is a range-finder camera (no TTL [through the lens] viewing) with the shutter built into the lens.

4 × 5 Sheet Film Cameras

The 4 × 5 inch sheet film cameras are categorized as large-format cameras. Other large-format cameras use 5 × 7 and 8 × 10 inch sheet film. The large format produces a print with very high resolution; however, the high resolution is offset by cumbersomeness and inefficiency (Figure 2.2).

The 4 × 5 sheet film cameras are unwieldy and, because of the sheet film used, are difficult and time consuming to use. The sheet film is loaded into a film carrier, each of which holds two sheets of film or two photo images. The film carrier is then inserted into the camera, the film cover is removed, and the image is taken. The film cover is then replaced, and the film carrier removed from the camera. The film carrier is turned over and reinserted

Figure 2.2 A speed graphic 4 × 5 inch sheet film camera. Notice the sighting (picture composition) device on the top of the camera. It consists of a small metal rectangle with sights through a larger metal rectangle.

Figure 2.3 These are 4 × 5 inch film holders.

into the camera. The film cover is removed, and the second image is taken. After all this, only two images are taken (Figure 2.3).

Processing of the sheet film must be done in your own photo lab or in a special processing lab with the necessary equipment to develop and print large-format negatives.

The 120 Roll Film Cameras

The 120 roll film cameras fall into the category of medium-format cameras. Their negatives are of higher resolution than 35-mm negatives. The film is on a roll, which is either loaded directly into the camera or preloaded on film cassettes. The actual size of the negative varies with the camera used, but all in this category take the 120 roll film (or 220, the same size except twice as long). Some of the negative sizes are 2¼ × 2¼ inches, 1⅝ × 2½ inches, 6 × 4.5 cm, and 6 × 7 cm (Figure 2.4).

The 35-mm SLR

The 35-mm film camera has a versatile format, utilizing a wide variety of film types and film speeds. It can take many photographs in a short amount of time. Its lenses may be changed as needed. It is relatively small and light (Figure 2.5).

There are three basic types of 35-mm SLR cameras: automatic, manual, and automatic/manual. With the automatic mode, the camera makes all the decisions concerning exposure. The photographer composes the picture and takes the image. With the manual camera, the photographer estimates the light intensity and adjusts the aperture and shutter speed, then takes the image. With the automatic/manual, the photographer sets the film speed, then uses the internal meter of the camera and sets the aperture (aperture priority) or sets the shutter speed (shutter priority). The camera will then automatically adjust the opposite (shutter or aperture) for an acceptable exposure.

The viewing system of an SLR camera is built around a mirror. Light from a subject comes through the lens (Figure 2.6). It is reflected upward by a mirror (thus the name reflex), then reflected again to the back of the camera by a prism. This system allows the

Figure 2.4 Rolleiflex twin-lens reflex cameras. The camera views through one lens (top) and uses the bottom lens to expose the film. The camera takes 120 and 220 roll film.

Figure 2.5 A Nikon EM 35-mm film camera.

photographer to see what the camera lens sees through a viewfinder in the back of the camera. Since the photographer sees what the lens "sees," there is no parallax error.

Parallax error, also sometimes called "viewfinder error," is the difference between what is seen in the viewfinder of a camera and what actually appears in the image recorded. The picture could be larger than the viewfinder image. There is no parallax error in an SLR camera.

The SLR camera also features interchangeable lenses. Lenses for the 35-mm camera are available in a wide range: fish-eye, wide-angle, normal, and telephoto lenses. The "zoom" lens can be adjusted from wide angle to a telephoto. Macro lenses are also available that allow for extreme close-up photography (Figure 2.7).

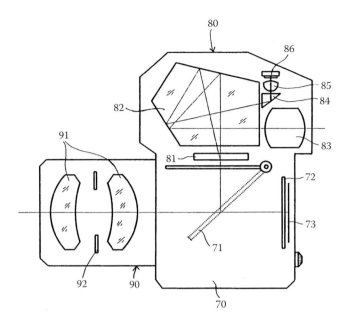

Figure 2.6 This image shows how the SLR camera sees exactly what the lens sees. It demonstrates the path of light as it travels from the subject to the photographer's eye. When the shutter is depressed, the mirror drops down, and the film is exposed.

Figure 2.7 Just some of the many Nikon lenses available for Nikon film and digital SLR cameras.

Other Camera Types

The Snapshot Camera

The snapshot camera also uses film to record images. It is relatively inexpensive. It has a fixed-focus lens and a built-in flash. As with the disposable camera, the flash is only effective for approximately 15 feet. The camera does not come preloaded with film. The 35-mm film, which must be purchased separately, is loaded by the user. This allows the use of different types of film with different film speeds. A viewfinder, located on the top of the camera, is used to aim the camera. As with all range-finder-type cameras, there is a

Figure 2.8 An early Nikon "snapshot" camera. It uses digital media to record images instead of film.

Figure 2.9 A Nikon snapshot camera. As technology developed, the cameras became smaller; there are more features available, and the quality of images has increased.

parallax error due to the inability to compose the picture directly through the lens (TTL) (Figure 2.8). The camera is not adjustable for either aperture or shutter speed. It is limited in its abilities; therefore, it is not designed to take technical photographs or images of evidence or crime scenes, but rather snapshots of family and friends.

Because of the advances in technology, Nikon and others have developed the snapshot camera into a high-quality imaging device. While this type of camera will not replace a digital SLR camera, it does produce excellent-quality images (Figure 2.9).

The Polaroid Camera

The Polaroid camera uses a special film that produces a photograph (a positive) within 60 seconds of taking the image (Figure 2.10). While the camera does produce a viewable photo image within 60 seconds, it does not produce a negative. This is not desirable, especially when a case is going to trial. In the discovery phase of the trial, the defense will request all reports and images concerning the case in question. To produce an

Figure 2.10 A Polaroid camera. It creates a small color photograph with no negative. The picture would self-develop in 1 minute and was somewhat costly at about a dollar a shot. With the introduction of digital cameras, we now have instant images available that can be reprinted as exact duplicates of the original. The digital age has basically relegated the Polaroid to dinosaur status.

additional image or positive of the Polaroid image, you will have to scan or photograph the Polaroid image. When this is done, like with all copies, a generation of quality is lost.

Polaroid images tend to fade with time. This can also be a problem at trial. The defense can raise the issue of the color in the images: "Detective, do these Polaroid images truly and accurately represent the scene as you saw it on the date and time in question?" The answer would be, "No, sir, the color has faded." The attorney could then reply "Then if the color has faded, what else could be wrong or is different in the images as a result of time's effect on the images?" Remember, the defense only needs to raise "reasonable doubt" to impeach the images.

There are some high-end (expensive) Polaroid cameras that have adjustable focus, aperture, and shutter speed, but these cameras are normally used in studio imaging and product and model photography.

There is still a place for a Polaroid camera in forensic work but not in documenting crime scenes and evidence. Polaroid imaging in forensic work has basically been replaced by digital imaging. The digital image retains the original color and shading in digital format and can be then be printed as required in hard-copy form with the same reliability as printing a photograph from a 35-mm negative.

The Disposable or Single-Use Camera

The camera body, lens, film, and flash are all in one manufactured unit in a disposable or single-use camera (Figure 2.11). The camera uses film to record images. It is usually inexpensive and can be purchased anywhere. Using 35-mm format, the camera comes preloaded with film and has a built-in flash. The flash has an effective range of from 3 to 15 feet.

The flash is relatively ineffective. Think of a football stadium: When a TV camera pans the crowd, you see many flashes of light coming from the stands. Those flashes are people in the stands taking pictures using a flash that is only effective for a maximum of 15 feet. The flash at that distance is useless; however, it does make a pretty picture for the TV camera.

Figure 2.11 The 35-mm disposable camera. It comes preloaded with film and has a battery that supplies the flash. When the last shot is taken, it is taken to the processor, and camera and film are processed. The camera is not returned. In the "film" days, it was always a good idea to carry a few of these cameras in case your 35-mm camera failed.

The lens is made of plastic and is fixed focus. The minimum focus is approximately 3 feet. Aiming the camera is accomplished by using a viewfinder located on the top of the camera. This is similar to the sight on a gun and is relatively accurate. It does, however, have a parallax error. The camera is not adjustable. It is designed to take snapshots, not technical photographs of evidence at a crime scene. When the images are taken, the camera and film are both taken to the photo processor. When developed, the film and images are received from the processor. The camera is destroyed.

Even with all of its drawbacks, this camera does have a place in forensic photo imaging. It makes a usable backup camera. I would recommend that one or two of these cameras be part of your equipment. A not-so-perfect image is better than none at all if for some reason your digital camera fails.

Film

There are many different types of film for the 35-mm film camera. This is just one more reason that the 35-mm camera is so versatile. Kodak, a leader in film development and manufacture, has a wide variety of films available (Figure 2.12).

- Kodachrome: color slide film using unique proprietary technology.
- Ektachrome: color slide film suitable for normal processing.
- Ektar: semiprofessional color negative film.
- Portra: professional color negative film with controlled color balance; available at 160 and 400 ASA in "natural" and "vivid" color varieties and 100 ASA as a tungsten-compensated variety. Kodak also offers an 800-ASA Portra film. Portra films are available in 35-mm and 120 formats.
- Ultra Color: color negative film in 100 and 400 ASA.
- Elite Color: color negative film in 35-mm format but based on improved emulsions developed for the APS format; various speeds, including high speed.

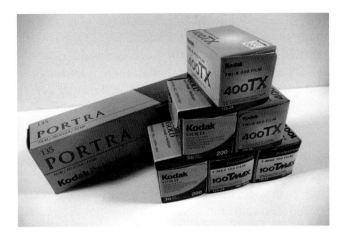

Figure 2.12 A small sampling of film available for the 35-mm camera.

- T-MAX: professional black-and-white (B&W) negative film; uses a technology called "tabular grain" or T-grain; available in a wide range of speeds, including 3,200 ASA intended for photojournalism.
- Tri-X: older, relatively fast (320- to 400-ASA) B&W negative film with different grain characteristics; based on classic "cubical" grain. The premier photojournalism film for many decades, it is still widely available.
- Plus-X: B&W slow (125-ASA) negative film with finer grain.
- HIE: a professional, infrared-sensitive B&W film used for taking pictures through a dark (infrared-pass) filter. It is coated onto a thin Estar base and lacks an antihalo layer. It was discontinued as of May 2007.
- Technical Pan: a very slow (not rated by Kodak, but generally established as 16–25 ASA), very-fine-grain, professional B&W film particularly aimed at architectural and engineering photography. As of 2004, this has been discontinued.
- BW400CN: B&W negative film that can be processed using the normal process.
- E100 and E200: professional color slide film; several varieties exist for each; ASA 100 and 200, respectively.
- Kodacolor-branded color negative films and their non-Kodacolor-branded successors: Kodak Gold (formerly Kodacolor Gold) and Kodak Gold MAX, which are consumer color negative film—the "MAX" indicating the coarser-grained, general-purpose variety. The remaining consumer films are marketed by use rather than trade names (e.g., "Bright Sun&Flash," "High Definition").
- Ortho: B&W negative film; ASA 3. There are no gray tones, only black and white. Used for lithography and for fingerprint photo imaging.

Proper Evidentiary Handling and Storage of Film

Negatives must be stored as carefully and with the same integrity as a gun or fingerprints recovered at a scene. For this to be accomplished, the following, at a minimum, should be established as policy and procedure:

No more than one case should be shot on a single roll of film. If a 36-exposure roll is in the camera and only three pictures are taken, the rest of the roll should be left blank. When the film is returned from the processor, the unexposed film *must* be filed and maintained with the three exposed pictures even though there is nothing there. *Do not destroy the blank negatives.* The blank negatives are retained so the other side in court cannot say that you are hiding something that would prove the opposite of what you are showing with the three images you have taken. This is called "exculpatory evidence," evidence that could help prove the opposition's case. Do not mix cases on a single roll of film. If you use your own camera at a crime scene, do not mix your personal images with those of the crime scene.

Each cut negative strip must be marked (using an indelible marking pen such as a Sharpie) with, at a minimum, your initials and case number. When marking them, spread the strips out until they dry. Nothing is more embarrassing that having your negatives ruined by a wet marker.

It is important that if for some reason the negatives are misfiled, they can be easily identified. Also, and most important, when asked in a court of law, "Detective, are these the photo images that you took on the date and time in question?" You answer, "Yes." You are then asked, "How do you know that they are?" You can answer, "Because each negative strip bears my initials and the case number."

Digital Camera Hardware

3

Goal: Understand the nomenclature of the camera, its components, and peripherals and the basics of how it works.

The Digital Point-and-Shoot Camera

The digital point-and-shoot camera is a good basic, inexpensive camera. It is able to record digital images on an internal memory, with most having the ability to record to a memory card of varying sizes (Figure 3.1). The camera has either a range-finder-type aiming device or a video display screen. Most cameras in the category have built-in flashes and are for the most part fully automatic. They produce an adequate image but lack the versatility of the digital single-lens reflex (SLR) camera.

These digital point-and-shoot cameras do not have the ability to use interchangeable lenses. The lens that comes with the camera is what you have. The ability to zoom in and out to your subject is limited. In some cases, the zoom feature is not optical but rather software driven.

The Digital Camera Body

The digital camera body is similar to that of the film camera. Most of the controls are located on the body. There is usually a screen on which the menu can be displayed. There are many options that can be set from the menu. Some will be specific to your particular brand of camera, and some are generic to most or all (Figures 3.2 and 3.3).

The Menu

In film cameras, there are knobs and buttons to adjust the settings. Digital cameras use a menu to adjust the settings on the camera (Figures 3.4 and 3.5).

Image Numbering

The image-numbering setting can be set to reset or continuous. You want to set it to continuous for several reasons. You want the photo image identifier to be unique. If set to continuous, it will assign a number in successive order and will not repeat any number previously used. If the reset setting is used, the camera will reset the photo image identifier each time the memory card is removed and reinserted or after each time the pictures are

Figure 3.1 Nikon digital point-and-shoot camera.

uploaded to the computer and deleted from the camera. If you wished to upload additional images taken to the same folder, the computer might advise you that there are already images with those numbers and ask whether you want to overwrite (and destroy) the original images. You could change the image file name/number, but this would not adhere to the rule that we do not change a photo image. For both of these reasons, set the image-numbering setting to "continuous."

The Lenses

One of the greatest advantages of the digital SLR camera is the ability to change lenses. Whereas point-and-shoot cameras rely on zooming (either optical or software), the digital SLR camera lens can be changed to fit the job or assignment (Figure 3.6).

Wide-angle lenses allow us to see more area of an image; however, we have to consider distortion. One can use a fish-eye lens to image 180 degrees of an image. It is a good idea to be able to get so much in a single image; however, the wider the lens angle is, the more distortion you will see in the image (Figure 3.7). Obviously, we do not use a fish-eye lens when we are taking crime scene images due to the distortion factor. For example, you may be asked, "Officer, do these images truly and accurately depict the crime scene on the date and time in question?" If you used a fish-eye lens, then you would probably answer, "No. The walls do not bend; they are straight." We want to be able to answer, "Yes, it does."

Telephoto lenses allow us to see objects at distances as much closer. Again, this is a good feature; however, there is some distortion with this as well (Figure 3.8).

So, what do we do? We use a normal lens. What is a normal lens? Just like people, there is not a true normal lens. Because each of the camera makers has its own proprietary design, normal may be slightly different for each. The "normal" lens as we speak of it, on a 35-mm film camera, is often referred to as a range. This range is approximately 47- to 57-mm focal length.

The digital SLR camera, while based on the 35-mm film camera, differs based on its particular design and the CCD (charge coupled device) used. The digital SLR cameras

Figure 3.2 Nikon D-80, digital SLR camera.

are usually sold with a body and lens combination. In most cases, they are bundled with a moderate zoom lens, f/3.5, 18–55 mm (Figure 3.9). The 18–55 mm is the focal length of the lens. This means it zooms from a moderately wide angle to a moderately telephoto lens. The "f/3.5" is the widest the aperture will open. This is also referred to as how fast the lens is. The smaller the f-stop number, the more light that is let in through the lens (or the faster is the lens).

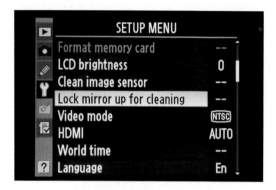

Figure 3.3 Nikon D-80. The menu is activated by a button on the back side of the camera.

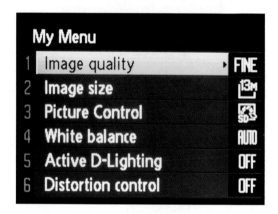

Figure 3.4 Nikon setup menu.

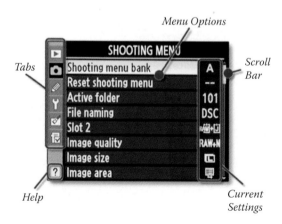

Figure 3.5 Nikon shooting menu.

Figure 3.6 Nikon lenses.

Figure 3.7 Nikon "fish-eye" lens. This is an ultra-wide-angle lens that creates extreme distortion. It is used for special effects.

Figure 3.8 This is a Nikon 200-mm telephoto lens. It brings distant objects closer; however, there is some distortion.

Figure 3.9 The Nikon D-80.

Aperture

The aperture of the camera is how large the hole is that lets the image through to the CCD (sensor) in the camera. They are identified as f-stops and are usually designated as follows:

- 1.2   This is a very large opening and is considered a "fast lens" (least depth of field).
- 2.8
- 3.5
- 4.0
- 5.6
- 8.0
- 11
- 16
- 22
- 32
- 64   This is a very small opening (most depth of field) (Figure 3.10).

Focusing the SLR Camera

When you focus the digital SLR camera in the manual mode, the camera automatically allows you to "see the image" at the largest opening available on the lens. If the aperture is set to f/22, there is a small amount of light passing through the lens. This would make it difficult to focus the camera, so the camera opens the lens to the widest opening to focus, and when the image is taken, the lens is automatically set back to the aperture that you set to take the image.

Aperture Preview

On many cameras, there is an aperture preview button. This button allows the imager to see the composition of the picture as it will look with the actual f-stop setting. The button

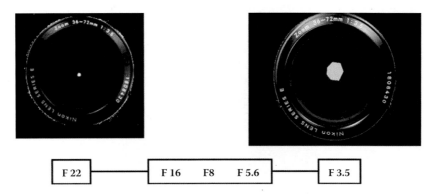

Figure 3.10 This image shows how the aperture opens to allow more light to pass through to the CCD, the light sensor in the digital camera. The larger the number (f/22), the smaller the opening and the less light that passes through to the light sensor, the CCD. The smaller the number (f/3.5), the more light that passes through to the sensor, the CCD.

overrides the automatic setting of the lens to open to the widest setting (as you compose your image). This is a useful tool to check your depth of field. When the aperture preview button is pressed, the lens reverts to the actual f-stop set, allowing you to see what will be in focus and what will be in acceptable focus.

Shutter

The shutter is the "door" that, in a film camera, would open and shut (this is where the term *shutter* was derived), allowing a specific amount of light through the lens to the film. With film cameras, there were two basic types of shutters: focal plain and leaf.

The focal plane shutter opens from side to side, similar to a pocket or sliding door. This shutter is located in the body of the camera. It makes a "cachunk"-type sound (Figure 3.11). The leaf shutter is similar to the iris of the eye and opens from the center out. This type of shutter is located in the lens, not the camera (Figure 3.12).

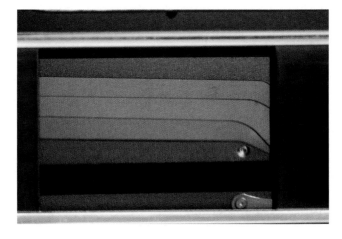

Figure 3.11 This is a focal plane shutter. This shutter opens side to side.

Figure 3.12 This is a leaf shutter. It opens from the center out.

The shutter stays open for a specific time. The most common times are as follows:

- 1/2,000 second　Very fast; good to stop action.
- 1/1,000 second　Fast.
- 1/500 second
- 1/250 second
- 1/125 second　Usual sync speed. At this speed and slower, the shutter syncs with the flash or strobe. When the shutter (especially a focal plain shutter) is not synced with the flash or strobe, a phenomenon called "curtaining" occurs. If the shutter is too fast, a part of the image will not receive light from the strobe or flash. Only a portion of the image will be lit (Figure 3.13).
- 1/60 second
- 1/30 second　Slow. At this point, you will need to use a tripod.
- 1/15 second
- 1 second
- B　B stands for bulb or flashbulb. This goes back to the "olden days" when photographers used flashbulbs and flash powder. On the B setting, when the shutter button was pressed, the shutter would open. It would stay open until the shutter button was released. The B is still a setting so that we can open the shutter for long periods to take extended time images.

The shutter in the Nikon D-80 is an electronically controlled, vertical-travel focal plane shutter.

Exposure

Exposure is simply the amount of light that the sensor sees and records. The equation is ISO + Shutter speed + Aperture = Exposure. ISO is the sensitivity of the sensor to light (or film in a film camera). Just like an algebraic equation, you can increase one of the parts if you reduce another part by the same number.

ISO = 100　　　　　　Shutter = 1/60　　　　　　Aperture = f/8　　　　= Correct exposure

Figure 3.13 This is an example of "curtaining." It is produced in a camera with a focal plane shutter when the shutter speed is not synced with the flash or strobe. In most film cameras, the sync speed is 1/60 of a second or less. For some of the better cameras, such as Nikons, syncs are 1/125 of a second.

If we make the shutter speed faster 1/125 and we open the aperture by one setting, f/5.6, then we still have a correct exposure (Figure 3.14):

| ISO = 100 | Shutter = 1/125 | Aperture = f/5.6 | = Correct exposure |
| Same | Faster by 1 | Slower by 1 | |

If we make the shutter speed slower 1/30 and we close the aperture by one setting, f/11, then we still have a correct exposure (Figure 3.15):

| ISO = 100 | Shutter = 1/30 | Aperture = F 11 | = Correct exposure |
| Same | Slower by 1 | Faster by 1 | |

Figure 3.14 This image was taken with the settings ISO-100, shutter 1/125, and aperture f/5.6.

Figure 3.15 This image was taken with the settings ISO-100, shutter 1/30, and aperture f/11. Even though this image was shot with different settings than Figure 3.14, both images look the same—they have the same exposure. This is because we decreased the shutter speed by two increments and increased the aperture by two increments. This made the end exposure the same.

Remote Shutter Release

The remote shutter release is merely an accessory that allows you to activate the shutter without manually pressing the shutter release button on the camera. It is useful when you are working with slow shutter times and extended time photography for which you are using the B setting and extending the exposure to multiple seconds. This assists in keeping the camera from moving when the shutter release button on the camera is pressed. It reduces "camera shake."

There are several types of remote shutter release. One is cable-connected. This type is connected to a wire that plugs directly into the remote shutter release jack on the camera (Figure 3.16). The second type is an infrared wireless. The camera must have a setting accessible in the menu that must be activated. The good news is that it is wireless. The bad news is that it must be "line of sight" with the camera (Figure 3.17). The third is a generic radio-wave-type remote shutter release. This type will work with most SLR cameras that have a pc jack on the camera. It is an RF (radio-frequency) wireless and does not need line

Figure 3.16 This is an electronic, hardwired remote shutter release for the D-80 Nikon camera.

Figure 3.17 This is an IR (infrared; line of sight only) remote shutter release for the Nikon D-50.

Figure 3.18 A generic radio-controlled remote shutter release. This will work on many film and digital SLR cameras.

of sight. It can be programmed to a number of frequencies so that RI (radio interference) does not affect your photography (Figure 3.18).

Resolution

The term *resolution* applies to digital images, film images, and other types of images. Higher resolution means more image detail. The term *resolution* is often used as a pixel count in digital imaging; the more pixels there are, the higher the resolution will be (Figure 3.19). The 1951 U.S. Army resolution test target is a classic test target used to determine spatial resolution of imaging sensors and imaging systems (Figure 3.20).

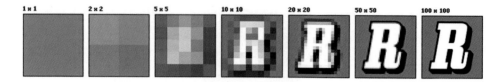

Figure 3.19 This is an illustration of resolution. The resolution starts out at 1 × 1 pixels on the left and increases to 100 × 100 pixels on the right.

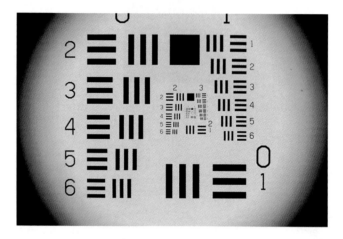

Figure 3.20 This is a U.S. Army test target developed in 1951. It is still used today to determine spatial resolution.

ASA, DIN, and ISO

ASA, DIN, and ISO are all scales used to identify the sensitivity to light of films or, in the case of a digital camera, the sensor (CCD). ASA stands for the former American Standards Association, DIN is the German Institute for Standardization, and ISO stands for the International Organization for Standardization. It is used as a method of identifying the sensitivity of film to light. With a digital camera, the ISO is set in the menu and is a virtual setting. It tells the CCD, the sensor, that its sensitivity should be slower or faster.

Hyperfocal Distance

In optics and photography, hyperfocal distance is a distance beyond which all objects can be brought into an "acceptable" focus. The hyperfocal distance is the closest distance at which a lens can be focused while keeping objects at infinity acceptably sharp, that is, the focus distance with the maximum depth of field. When the lens is focused at this distance, all objects at distances from half of the hyperfocal distance to infinity will be acceptably sharp.

Disposable and inexpensive cameras use hyperfocal distance in their lenses. It is inexpensive to produce, and the camera user does not have to focus the camera.

Digital Imaging

4

Introduction

When we speak of *digital imaging*, we are referring to taking photographs or images with a digital camera. The digital camera records the image on a sensor, a CCD (a charged coupled device), rather than film. The images are processed in the digital camera and recorded on some type of magnetic or chip set media (a memory card) instead of on film. In the digital format, the image may be viewed immediately after it is recorded. In a film format, the film must first be developed, then printed on photo paper, which also must be developed.

The fact that you can see your results immediately is a great benefit. While photo imaging an alleged suicide, which turned into a homicide after full investigation of the scene, I took two rolls of 36-exposure color photographs. On that day, something made me take black-and-white film backups. As often happens with 35-mm film cameras, when I loaded the film in the camera, it did not catch on the film take-up reel (Figure 4.1). When I snapped a picture and advanced it for the next shot, the film did not advance, and I had zero color images. The black-and-white backups were a lifesaver (mine). If I would have had a digital camera, there would have been no problem with the take-up reel not functioning, and I immediately could have seen the images that I had shot.

There is a great deal of time saved using the digital format. Images can be viewed by the criminalists to ensure that the images tell the story of the scene and are in proper focus. Remember, you may not delete an image that is out of focus. You must keep such images as a part of the scene images. If removed, it could be misconstrued as exculpatory evidence in court. Exculpatory evidence is evidence that can be used for the other side. If an image is out of focus, retake the image so that it is in focus, but *do not delete* the out-of-focus image.

This is just one of the advantages when using digital imagery. With film photography, if an image is out of focus, you would not be aware of it until after the film was developed and image printed. Time has elapsed, and you may not have the opportunity to return and rephotograph the out-of-focus picture.

Money

Money is always an issue. A crime scene unit still must operate based on a budget. The good news is that digital SLR cameras are affordable and are equivalent in cost to the 35-mm film cameras previously used as the workhorses of the crime scene photographers. The best news is the savings in distributing the images to those who need them.

In the days of film, if there were 100 images as a part of a case, most agencies used the 5 × 7 inch format for a usable photograph (unless, of course, on a TV show, then you get 8 × 10 inch or wall murals). At approximately $1.00 per print, that comes to $100 per set. I know you could have brought the film to a "1-hour photo lab" or the like, but these places are not

Figure 4.1 The film take-up reel inside a 35-mm film camera.

professional labs. Photos are processed on the premises, often by part-time workers with little photo lab experience. I also have a problem with the security of the film in this type of lab.

Who receives a set of photos? The detective in charge of the case, the prosecutor, the defense (at the point in the trial when discovery is filed), crime scene investigator (CSI) case file, and sometimes the chief of police will receive sets of the case photographs—a total of five sets for $500.

With digital images, a set of images can be burned to a CD or DVD disk. The images are exact copies of the original because they are digital. The cost for a CD (if bought in bulk) is about $0.19. We have saved $499.05 for the five sets. The money saved should cause a migration to digital photo imaging from film.

Protection

You, your department, or your agency have invested a good amount of money in your camera, lens, and various accessories. You need to protect them. Use a camera and accessory case. There are several kinds. It is your choice; just use one. It should be large enough to carry what you need (remember, you do not need a camera studio in your case).

Cases

The hard case is good (Figure 4.2). It takes a lot of punishment and protects the equipment well. These are expensive if you get a good one. Remember, you will be carrying this case (as well as other equipment) to remote sites on occasion, so think about the weight as well.

The soft case is much lighter (Figure 4.3). The case still offers an acceptable amount of protection for the camera and accessories. Usually, this case has a strap to aid in carrying.

The other option is the soft backpack case (Figure 4.4). This type offers good protection, more than adequate space, and the ability to carry it like a bag or use it like a backpack. There are many sizes and shapes; again, pick one that fills your needs.

Figure 4.2 A hard-sided camera case.

Figure 4.3 A soft-sided camera case.

Camera Strap

Use a camera strap. It sounds silly to bring this up; however, it may save you time, head-aches, and the ridicule of your associates (Figure 4.5). I was working the investigation of a rather seriously decomposed dead individual in one of the forest preserves. My partner was using a 35-mm camera without a strap. He was leaning over the body, attempting to get a good shot of what appeared to be a knife still lodged in the torso. One of the firemen, who was standing to the right and slightly to the rear, decided to "lose his lunch." He did so, striking my partner. This in turn caused my partner to drop his camera into the "remains of the remains." It was like dropping a rock into a mud puddle. After I got myself under

Figure 4.4 A soft backpack type of camera case.

Figure 4.5 A camera strap.

control, we assisted the fireman and got him some water. We then retrieved the dropped camera. It was eventually cleaned up. Fortunately, I had my Nikon (with strap I might add), and we continued to process the scene. There are a number of morals to this story; however, the most important is: Use a camera strap.

The Ultraviolet Filter

The lens is an expensive part of your camera. In many cases, it can be worth more than the camera body. There is an easy way to protect it. Every time you purchase a new lens or camera body with lens, purchase an ultraviolet (UV) filter for the lens (Figure 4.6). Your

Figure 4.6 An ultraviolet (UV) filter. It filters out UV light. It also acts as protection for the lens.

lens may cost $300. The filter costs $15. If your lens gets scratched, you have to buy a new lens at $300. If the filter gets scratched, you can buy a new filter at $15.

Forensic photographers, professional photographers, and advanced amateurs are much harder on their cameras and lenses than the snapshot shooter. We have to protect our equipment.

If you are going to be doing UV photo imaging, you will want to remove the UV filter, although in most of the newer lenses, there is UV protection built in. All digital cameras have what is called a "hot" filter inside the camera in front of the CCD (the sensor). This filters out unwanted UV light (unless you want the UV light). For further discussion, see Chapter 23 on UV and infrared (IR) photo imaging.

The Camera

One of the nice things about most digital SLR cameras is that you can pick one up and began using it right away without a lot of training. This is good; however, as a forensic photo imager, you need to know your equipment, how it works, and how to use it to the full extent of its capabilities.

As you have probably have guessed, my camera of choice is the Nikon. There are many other excellent brands, but I have been using Nikons for over 40 years, and I like them. I used a Nikon FM to shoot one of the more famous cases I worked on, that of John Wayne Gacy (Figures 4.7 and 4.8). Through cold and damp, it never failed.

Flash or Strobe

Most digital SLR cameras have built-in flashes (Figure 4.9). The flash is a part of the body. This is an adequate flash for most situations, most small scenes, and evidence. There are many other flashes available for the digital SLR camera that can be attached to the camera on the hot shoe. Some of these flashes are "dedicated" flashes. They are made by the same manufacturer as the camera and electronically "sync" with the camera (Figure 4.10). They are excellent but somewhat pricey.

Figure 4.7 Patrick Jones at John Wayne Gacy's house with a Nikon camera.

Figure 4.8 Nikon FM 35-mm film camera. This is the camera that shot 95% of all slides at the Gacy crime scene.

I use a Vivitar 283. It is a strong flash and mounts to the hot shoe on digital and film cameras (Figure 4.11). It "meters" the light based on the settings. I would consider it an automatic flash. One sets the 283 based on ISO (International Organization for Standardization setting) and aperture. This is the flash that I used in photographing the Gacy case. It is versatile and runs around $90. Vivitar has made a number of improvements in the 283, and it is the same workhorse today that it was years ago. I still have mine from 30 years ago.

One of the features of the 283 is the ability to move the flash off camera and still read the flash on the camera (you want to read the light exposed to the sensor on the camera, not at the distance that the light source is from the subject) (Figure 4.12). The 283 allows you to do this by removing the sensor from the front of the flash and attaching a cord (purchased

Figure 4.9 Nikon D-80 internal flash.

Figure 4.10 Nikon dedicated flashes. Speedlight SB 600.

Figure 4.11 Nikon D-80 hot shoe.

Figure 4.12 Nikon D-80 with Vivitar 283 flash off camera and flash sensor mounted on a hot shoe.

separately). You then put one end of the cord on the camera with the sensor and the other end of the cord into the plug on the flash. You can then move the flash to any position, and the light will be read on the camera for a correct exposure.

To use indirect flash with the 283, one can rotate the flash head upward. There are about four "stops," including 90 degrees, at which the strobe is pointed directly up. With a small, inexpensive attachment, with the 283 pointed straight up, you can bounce your flash, diffuse the flash, or add a warmer tone to the image (Figure 4.13). The bounce card affixes to the 283 by Velcro. On one side of the card is a white surface; the other side is gold.

Automatic versus Manual

Most digital SLRs have automatic capabilities. Automatic is good. Automatic transmission in a car is good. You do not have to shift so much. Automatic focusing in a camera is also good. But, remember that you need to know and understand the manual use of the camera. And, automatic focusing is not always desirable. Even in a car with automatic cruise control, you still have to oversee the operation of the car and have the final say over its control. Obviously, if you were driving in a motor home and you placed the vehicle on automatic cruise control, you would not leave the driver's seat and go back to the kitchen to have a cup of coffee. You have to oversee the vehicle and have the final say regarding the operation of the vehicle.

There are a number of automatic functions on the camera. The focus is an excellent example. This works well when there is available light for the camera to "see." Some cameras use IR light to focus in the dark. It sends out an invisible beam and uses it as a range finder, automatically moving the lens to the proper focus. However, you must set the areas that will be looked at during this operation. You can set the camera to focus on the center

Figure 4.13 Nikon D-80 with Vivitar 283 mounted on the hot shoe, set up for bounce flash.

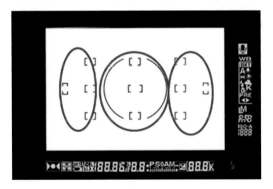

Figure 4.14 Nikon D-80 viewfinder. Circled are areas that can be set in "menu" to autofocus. The area of concentration can be set in the menu.

area, to the left of center, to the right of center, or anywhere in between. You can also use the "spot" focus. The camera will focus only on a single spot in the viewfinder (Figure 4.14). The camera is a computer, so in computer terms, "Garbage in—garbage out."

The closer you get to your subject, the harder it is to use an automatic focus. A better way to focus with a digital SLR camera is to set the lens or focus to *manual*. Then, rotate the focus ring on the lens to the closest setting possible. If you are holding the camera in your hand, move your body in and out, closer and farther away, until the object is sharp in the viewing screen.

Figure 4.15 Nikon D-80 mode-setting knob.

Settings

There is a mode settings knob on the top of most digital SLR cameras (Figure 4.15). There are a number of settings.

M	**Manual.** The user controls both the shutter speed and aperture. The shutter speed can be set to B for long exposures.
A	**Aperture Priority Auto.** The user chooses the aperture, and the camera selects the shutter speed for best results.
S	**Shutter Priority Auto.** The user chooses the shutter speed, and the camera selects the aperture for the best results.
P	**Programmed Auto.** The camera selects both shutter speed and aperture for optimal exposure.

Shutter

The shutter release is the button on the camera that takes the picture. It is operated by depressing the button all the way (Figure 4.16). The button may be pressed halfway, and this does not take the picture. It does "lock the focus," which is helpful at times. When in automatic focus mode, if the camera is having a hard time focusing on an object in your scene, focus on an object that may not be your prime subject but is on the same plane as the prime subject. You should hear a small beep. When you do, press the shutter release halfway down. This will lock the focus. Now, while keeping the button half pressed, return to the image composition with your prime subject in the center. Depress the shutter release button all the way down to take the picture.

Figure 4.16 Nikon D-80 with the shutter circled in red.

Slave

A slave is a handy object used when more than a single strobe light source is desired (Figure 4.17). This device is mounted on a tripod, clamp, or light stand. It is a small cube-shaped device with a sensor on the front and a hot shoe on the top. The flash unit, such as a Vivitar 283, is then attached to the slave via the hot shoe. There can be one slave and flash or any number of slaves with flash units. The camera has a built-in flash that is activated. When the shutter release button of the camera is depressed, the camera and internal flash fire. The light from the internal flash strikes the sensor on the slave, firing the flash unit attached to the slave. This happens to all slaves in the area that receive light from the initial

Figure 4.17 A "slave" for a flash. This unit senses the flash from the main flash and triggers the remote flash to which it is attached.

Figure 4.18 Image taken with a "normal" lens (55 mm).

flash from the camera. With this inexpensive accessory, a photo imager can use multiple flashes without the use of wires.

The "Normal" Lens

There really is not anything called a "normal" lens. A good definition is an image that, when viewed, has the least amount of distortion possible. This is based, in a film camera, on the size of the format or negative. The normal lens for a 35-mm film camera is about 47 to 52 mm. If a different format or film size, such as 4 × 5 inch sheet film, is used, then the normal lens would be 135 mm. In digital imaging, we have much the same problem. The size of the sensors in the digital SLR cameras vary. We have full frame, ⅔ frame, ½ frame, and others (Figure 4.18).

The Telephoto Lens

The telephoto lens is a bit easier to define. A telephoto lens makes the image bigger in the viewfinder and subsequently in the image stored (Figure 4.19). It is as if we were using a telescope to view an object at a long distance. Because of this, there is some distortion in the image. This is why we use a normal lens or a moderate telephoto to a moderate wide-angle zoom. We do not use a telephoto lens in crime scene photography often, but there are cases. I had a case in which a small plane had clipped a tower, which damaged the plane, which had to make an emergency landing. It was helpful to have a telephoto lens to photo image the top of the 200-foot tower.

Figure 4.19 Image taken with a telephoto lens (135 mm).

The Wide-Angle Lens

The wide-angle lens allows a wider view than the normal lens (Figure 4.20). While there is distortion when a wide-angle lens is used, there is definitely a place in crime scene photography for this lens. Often, a scene is in a very small room. It is difficult to get the "whole picture."

The definitions in this book may sound somewhat simple. Most will probably have a basic understanding of normal, telephoto, and wide angle. You may, however, have to testify in this regard on the witness stand to jurors who believe that DNA can be analyzed in 15 minutes, and that someone can do a complete reconstruction of a body working with only a femur.

The Macro Lens

The macro lens is a close-up lens. Unlike the macro setting on point-and-shoot cameras, to photo image true "macro" with a SLR camera, one changes the lens to a macro lens. A true macro lens allows you to shoot 1:1, size wise. The lenses are usually marked as a macro lens (not just a macro setting). Many are also marked with ratios like 1:1, 1:5 (see Figure 4.21). Macro lenses sometimes have what is called a limit switch. This switch limits the focus to no closer than a 1:3 ratio. It is used when you are not shooting macro so that the lens does not extend to the 1:1 ratio setting.

The macro lens gives a sharp image at a close distance. Compare Figures 4.22 through 4.26. Figures 4.22 and 4.24 show examples of the closest that a normal lens can shoot.

Figure 4.20 Image taken with wide-angle lens (28 mm).

Figure 4.21 Macro lens extended to 1:1 ratio.

Figures 4.23 and 4.25 show examples of the closest that a macro lens (at 1:1 ratio) can shoot. There is quite a difference.

Lighting with the Macro Lens

Because you are so close to the subject, it is difficult to light the subject properly when using a macro lens. Basically, sometimes when you are holding the camera in your hands it blocks some of the light; sometimes, the camera itself will block part of the light (Figure 4.26). When shooting this close (1:1 ratio), you may have to use an off-camera flash. You can also used fixed lighting (incandescent or halogen) to light your subject.

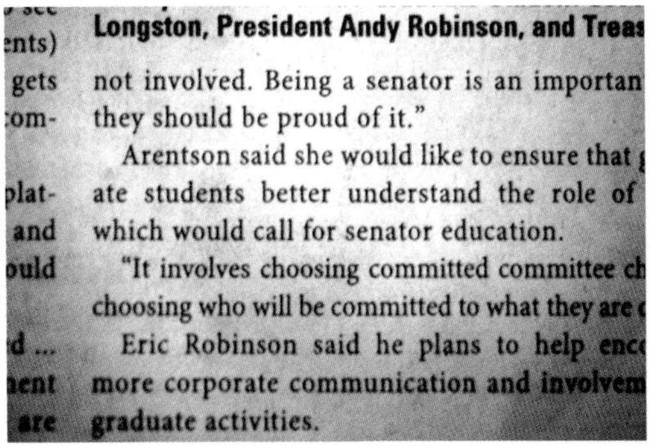

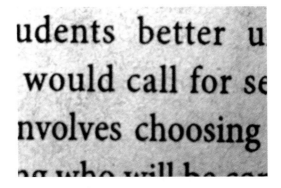

Figure 4.22 Image of the printed word shot with a normal lens.

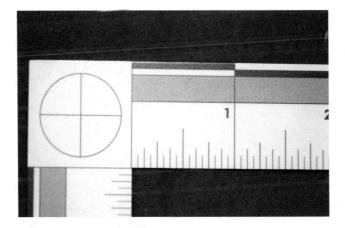

Figure 4.23 Image of the printed word shot with a macro lens.

Figure 4.24 Image of the scale shot with a normal lens.

Another technique is to use a copy stand. The stand acts similar to a tripod, using a tube or rail to increase or decrease the distance from the camera to the subject. When imaging at the minimum distance, extend the lens to the 1:1 ratio and turn off autofocus. Move the camera on the camera stand up and down until the subject is in focus. Lock in the camera stand and take the image (Figure 4.27).

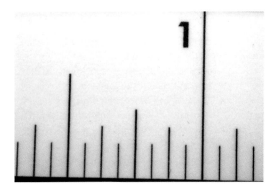

Figure 4.25 Image of the scale shot with a normal lens.

Figure 4.26 The shadow in this image is from the camera blocking the light from the flash.

Figure 4.27 The camera is equipped with a macro lens with an off-camera fixed light.

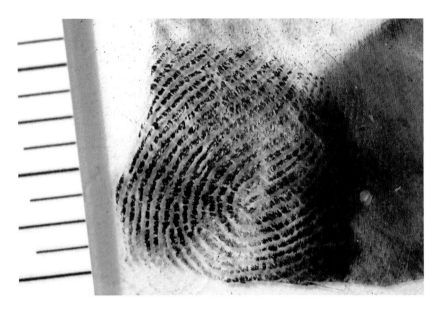

Figure 4.28 This latent lift was shot with a Nikon camera equipped with a Nikkor macro lens at a 1:1 ratio.

The definition or resolution of the image is excellent when the macro lens is used. Figure 4.28 displays a fingerprint lift imaged with a macro lens (1:1 ratio). Because of the resolution, the image can be made larger (in software) to assist the fingerprint examiner. Many times, the pores in the fingerprint ridges can be identified. When an examiner is working with only a partial latent lift, the ability to see and possibly match the pores can be a great help (Figure 4.29).

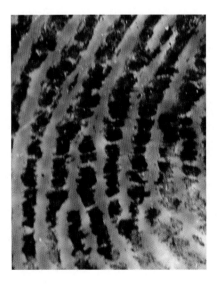

Figure 4.29 This is the same latent image as in Figure 4.28. It has been enlarged using ACDSee version 10. Notice the pores in the ridges.

Using the Flash on Your Camera

The On-and-Off Switch

Know how to turn the flash on and off as simply stated in the manual that came with your camera. This is important because there will be a time when you wish to turn it off, for example, when you are getting a "flashback" from a reflective surface. You will want to know how to turn it on and "force" the flash even though there is plenty of light to take your image. There will be times that there is plenty of light but not in the places you want or need. You need this forced flash as "fill" light. *Fill light* is defined as highlighting the shadowed area. You have a photo image of a box (Figure 4.30). It is a great picture of a box, but that is not what is important. It is the gun in the box that should be seen. You "force" the flash—make the strobe flash even though there is enough light to take a good picture of the box. Use a flash off camera at a 45-degree angle to the box. Now, we see the gun (Figure 4.31).

Turn the Camera Upside Down

There are times that the flash is attached to the wrong part of the camera. When you get close to your subject, a portion of the light may be cut off by other obstacles around the area in which you are shooting. Do not be afraid to turn the camera upside down or even sideways, placing the flash on the bottom or on the side. The image, when viewed in printed form, can be turned any direction (Figures 4.32–4.34).

Figure 4.30 This box was shot with available light. It seems that the important image is the box.

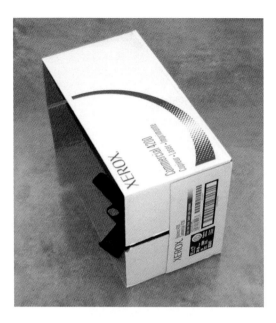

Figure 4.31 This box was shot with available light and a fill light. Notice the important item is actually the gun in the box.

Figure 4.32 Nikon is equipped with a hot shoe-mounted Nikon flash unit on top.

Figure 4.33 Nikon is equipped with a hot shoe-mounted Nikon flash unit on top. It has been turned upside down. This is so the light from the flash is directed under the camera instead of over it. This is useful when photographing items under beds, couches, and furniture.

Figure 4.34 Nikon is equipped with a hot shoe-mounted Nikon flash unit on top. The camera and flash are turned to the side. The light will be directed to the side.

List Photo Images

I suggest that you list your images in your report either on a separate sheet or as a part of your main report. The Federal Bureau of Investigation (FBI) also recommends this. You, of course, must follow the policy of your department or agency. There are several advantages to this:

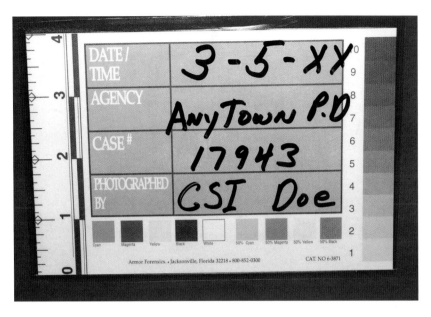

Figure 4.35 Photo ID card.

- The first image taken should be a photo ID card (Figure 4.35). This image (close-up of the card) is shot to identify the images that follow. If for some reason file names become corrupt or another type disaster occurs, you can ID the images in the file by case number, date, and photo imager.
- A listing is helpful to the detective. The detective can check to see if a particular image was taken.
- It is helpful to the prosecutor, who will know exactly what was taken and if any images are missing.
- While it is also helpful to the defense, it protects you. When individuals for the defense sign a receipt for the images, the receipt should say "all images listed on the report and contained on the CD, item number 12345." There can be no question that images were not included in the set.
- The second shot that should be taken is an *N* or north card. This card is not a close-up but includes some of the background. This is so that, at a later date, the images can be oriented even if a great deal of time has passed between the taking of the images and the trial (Figure 4.36).
- It is also helpful to the CSI who took them. It allows the CSI to see if additional imaging is needed, such as rephotographing a gun originally pictured under a tree.
- It further assists in identifying the evidence in the image (Figure 4.37).

The 90-Degree Rule

The 90-degree rule is easy to follow, but of critical importance. It applies to evidence images or images taken for record. These images must truly and accurately represent the object in question.

Figure 4.36 North card.

Figure 4.37 What is the evidence? Is it the stones? Is it the pail? Is it the cone? You do not really know unless it is listed somewhere. It is the cone.

It is all a matter of distortion. If a circle is photo imaged at 90 degrees (the lens of the camera is perfectly parallel to the plane where the circle resides), the image taken will look like a circle when it is viewed on a monitor or as a printed image (Figure 4.38).

If the same circle is photo imaged at 45 degrees (the lens of the camera is 45 degrees to the plane where the circle resides), then the circle will look like an oval when it is viewed on a monitor or as a printed image (Figure 4.39).

Take a quarter out of your pocket and look at it straight on, 90 degrees. Now, take the same quarter and look at it at an angle. Not so round? This phenomenon happens to all images that are not imaged at 90 degrees.

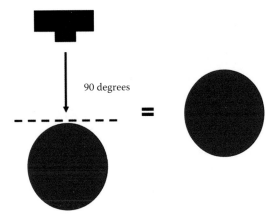

Figure 4.38 Diagram of a circle shot at 90 degrees to the subject (a circle). The image when printed is a circle.

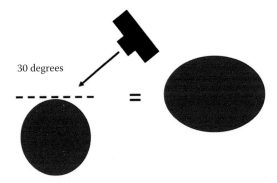

Figure 4.39 Diagram of a circle shot at 45 degrees to the subject (a circle). The image when printed is an oval. There is distortion unless you image at 90 degrees to the subject.

Perspective Images

Not all of the images we take at crime scenes are at 90 degrees. You are thinking, "But you just said … ." Yes, but those images were for the record or objects of evidence that must truly and accurately represent the objects in question. We also need to know and be able to explain the location of one object in relation to another object. It may be the relative distance and position of the gun in relation to the victim's left hand (Figure 4.40).

We need 90-degree evidence shots of the victim's left hand and the gun, but we need the third shot of both together to tell the story of the scene in images. We need the perspective shots so that we can testify that these images (all) truly and accurately represent the scene on the day and time in question (Figures 4.41 and 4.42).

The Scale

The scale is nothing more than a small ruler, usually about 6 inches in length. It is a most necessary piece of equipment for every forensic photo imager. The scale allows us to give

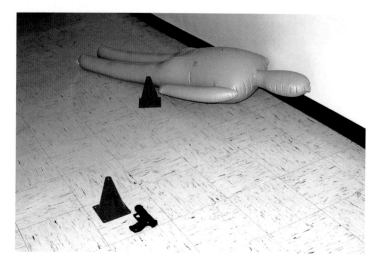

Figure 4.40 A perspective shot: One object is shown to the relative position of a second object or a group of objects, in this case the relative position of the body to the gun.

Figure 4.41 Close-up of gun in Figure 4.40.

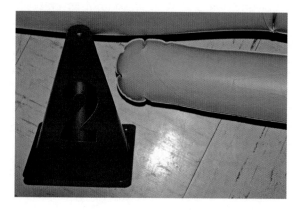

Figure 4.42 Close-up of subject's hand in Figure 4.40.

accurate dimensions in our images of an object. It allows us to be able to size and compare two different images. If each image was shot at different magnifications, and each image had a scale in it, then the objects could be compared (Figures 4.43 and 4.44). Also see the discussion of exculpatory evidence, next.

Figure 4.43 Gun with scale.

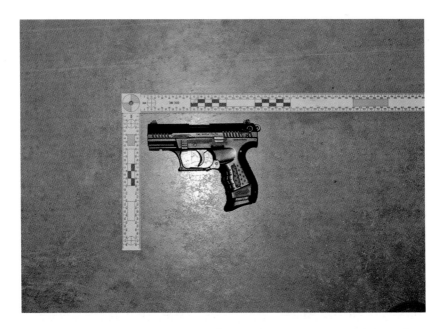

Figure 4.44 Same gun with scale shot at a different distance. Because of the scale in each, the images can be compared.

Figure 4.45 Note with scale.

Exculpatory Evidence

Exculpatory evidence could be used by the other side, the defendant. It is the duty and requirement of the prosecutor to disclose any exculpatory evidence to the defense at a stage in the trial called *discovery* (*Brady v. Maryland*, 373 U.S. 83 (1963)). In this case, the prosecutor did not disclose a note that may have affected the outcome of the trial.

In photo imaging of the scene, we of course do not want to violate this ruling. This is a point for listing all photo images taken. We may not delete any images, even if they are out of focus or improperly lit. They must be maintained with the file, and if you do list the images, the image can be identified as "out of focus" or "flash did not fire—bad lighting." When you document this type of mistake, you cannot be criticized for failure to document or report exculpatory evidence.

When photo imaging evidence at a crime scene, we use a scale to identify its dimensions and relative size. We duplicate each of these images "evidence—with scale" with the exact same shot "evidence without scale." Why? This is because the scale could be hiding exculpatory evidence. To prevent any possibility of this type of hidden evidence, we take images of evidence both with and without the scale.

It sounds rather "nitpicky." It is, but it is also a valid argument by the defense. Here is an example: We photo image a note with scale (see Figure 4.45). This will assist the handwriting examiner in knowing the length and depth of each stroke of the pen as it was written. The information in the note clearly identifies Jack as a prime suspect in the victim's death.

As we examine the note shot without scale, we see that this changes everything, and the note—instead of an accusation—becomes a suicide note (see Figure 4.46).

Extreme Conditions

There are three extreme conditions: snow, sand, and the aftermath of a fire (Figure 4.47). Each of these requires us to take action to modify settings on our camera. The setting is "exposure compensation." Exposure compensation is used to change the exposure value

Figure 4.46 Note without scale and exculpatory evidence.

Figure 4.47 Examples of extreme conditions.

suggested by the camera. Exposure compensation can be set in most cameras in the manual, shutter priority, aperture priority, and program modes.

What we are in effect doing is telling the camera to over- or underexpose the picture by a specific number of "f-stops." The camera uses its internal meter; then we tell it to overexpose the image two f-stops. Why do we lie to our camera? It is a very sophisticated piece of equipment. This is because the camera is set for average conditions. Our extreme conditions are not average.

Snow. Snow is about 90% white. This means that it reflects 90% of the light shown on it. If the meter in our camera is basing its computations on 18% reflectance and reflectance is actually 90%, you can see why the images come out "flat" and "muddy." A rule of thumb is to "stop down" the camera by three stops. This means to make the aperture smaller by a factor of 3. If the aperture is at f/5.6, we change it to f/16. Some distal SLRs have an EI (exposure index) setting. In that case, set it to −3.

Sand. Sand reflects about 50% of the light. This means that it reflects 50% of the light shown on it. If the meter in our camera is basing its computations on 18% reflectance and reflectance is actually 50%, you can again see why the images come out flat and muddy. A rule of thumb is to stop down the camera by 1.5 stops. This means to make the aperture smaller by a factor of 1½. If the aperture is at f/5.6, we change it to between f/11 and f/8. If there is an EI setting, set it to −1.5.

Aftermath of Fire. Fires turn buildings and things black. Black does not reflect; rather, it absorbs light. This is the exact opposite of snow and sand. If the meter in the camera is basing its computations on 18% reflectance and reflectance is actually 5%, you can see why the images come out extremely underexposed. A rule of thumb is to "stop up" the camera by three stops. This means to make the aperture larger by a factor of 3. If the aperture is at f/5.6, we change it to 2.8. If there is an EI setting, set it to +3.

18% Gray Card

A gray card is a flat object of a neutral gray color that derives from a flat reflectance spectrum. A typical example is the Kodak R-27 set, which contains two 8 × 10 inch cards and one 4 × 5 inch card, which have 18% reflectance across the visible spectrum, and a white reverse side, which has 90% reflectance (Figure 4.48).

A gray card is placed in a scene to be imaged. A reading is taken either with the internal exposure meter in the camera or with an external exposure meter. This reading allows the photographer to get constant-quality exposures.

The internal meter in most cameras, D-SLRs, film SLR cameras, and point-and-shoot cameras use the 18% reflective gray card as a basis for their exposure meters.

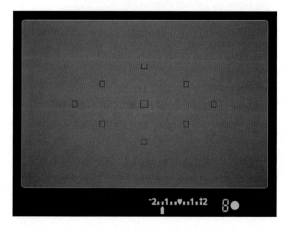

Figure 4.48 Gray card as seen through the viewfinder of an SLR camera. This card reflects 18% of light.

Light

5

Introduction

With the exception of the camera, light is probably the most important factor in imaging. Without light, there would not be an image. The camera, with only a few exceptions, records the reflection of light rather than the light itself. Only when the object that is being imaged produces the light, such as a candle, a lightbulb, or fire, does the camera record the light itself.

We actually see a very small part of the electromagnetic spectrum. We see from about 385 to 780 nm (Figure 5.1). This covers the blues through the reds and slightly into the ultraviolet and infrared regions.

When colored light is projected red, green, and blue, you will notice (in Figure 5.2) that the colors combine to make white light. Red and green make yellow. Red and blue make magenta. Blue and green make cyan.

Ambient Light

Ambient light is another way of saying "the light that exists" or "existing light." This is the level of light that will primarily affect your image. Many photographers shoot with ambient light only. They use it to convey a mood or an idea. As forensic photographers, we wish to record, document, and convey facts. If the existing or ambient light can do this, then we use it. If the ambient light will not do this, then we must use other light sources to augment the ambient light.

There are many methods that can accomplish this goal. We can use a stronger flash unit on the camera. We can use an additional flash unit with the camera connected by a pc cord. Note that a pc cord has nothing to do with a computer; it is a cord or wire connecting the camera to the flash. We can also use single or multiple flash units connected by a "slave." A slave is a device that responds to an external trigger. Many slave flashes are triggered by light (called optical slaves). When the primary flash fires due to depression of the shutter button, the optical sensor "sees" the primary flash and triggers the slave flash. This occurs so fast that the camera sees both flashes as simultaneous.

Ambient light can fall into many categories: incandescent (common lightbulbs), fluorescent, halogen, sodium vapor, daylight, dawn, and dusk, to name a few. It is a good idea to indicate in your report form the type or types of ambient light present.

Combinations that make up ambient light can also exist. An example is a scene in which daylight is streaming through a window, but there are fluorescent lights on in the room. In this case, there is a combination of light sources that make up ambient light. The ambient light is daylight and fluorescent light.

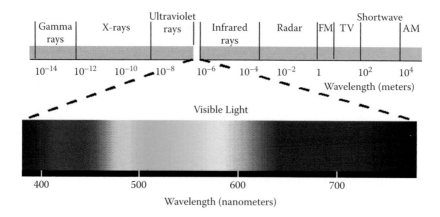

Figure 5.1 The electromagnetic spectrum.

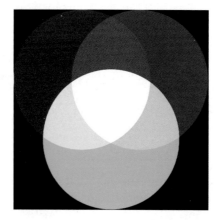

Figure 5.2 The projected colors.

Color Temperature

A measure of the distribution of power in the spectrum of white, or colorless, light, is stated in terms of the kelvin temperature scale. The human eye is incredibly adept at quickly correcting for changes in the color temperature of light. Many different kinds of light all seem white to us. Photographic film is not so forgiving; daylight film is made to be exposed at 5,500 K light, while indoor film requires light with a color temperature of 3,400 K (or 3,200 K for professional film) (Table 5.1). Photographs taken indoors under incandescent light on ordinary daylight film will come out orange; photographs on indoor film taken in sunlight will be blue, as will photographs taken outdoors in shade illuminated by blue sky.

While a digital camera is not as adept as the human eye at quickly correcting for changes in the color temperature of light, it does a much better job than film cameras. In digital photography, calibration of the white point is accomplished with either an automatic or a manual setting. The assumed white point can vary depending on the light conditions; the concept of "white" is not an absolute thing. Most digital cameras let you specify whatever

Table 5.1 Color Temperature in Kelvin

Source	Color Temperature (K)
Skylight (blue sky)	12,000–20,000
Average summer shade	8,000
Light summer shade	7,100
Typical summer light (sun + sky)	6,500
Daylight fluorescent	6,300
Xenon short arc	6,400
Overcast sky	6,000
Clear mercury lamp	5,900
Sunlight (noon, summer, midlatitudes)	5,400
Design white fluorescent	5,200
Special fluorescents used for color evaluation	5,000
Daylight photoflood	5,500
Sunlight (early morning and late afternoon)	4,300
Bright white deluxe mercury lamp	4,000
Sunlight (1 hour after dawn)	3,500
Cool white fluorescent	3,400
Photoflood	3,400
Professional tungsten photographic lights	3,200
100-watt tungsten halogen	3,000
Deluxe warm white fluorescent	2,950
100-watt incandescent	2,870
75-watt incandescent	2,820
40-watt incandescent	2,500
500-watt incandescent tungsten lamp	2,960
200-watt incandescent tungsten lamp	2,980
1000-watt incandescent tungsten lamp	2,990
High-pressure sodium light	2,100
Sunlight (sunrise or sunset)	2,000
Candle flame	1,850–1,900
Match flame	1,700

white point you want, usually by pointing the camera at a white object illuminated by the current light used by the imager. Some cameras also can detect the ambient light and determine the white point from that, called automatic white balance.

Color Rendering Index

The color rendering index (CRI) is a scale from 0 to 100, used by manufacturers of fluorescent, metal halide, and other nonincandescent lighting equipment to describe the visual effect of the light on colored surfaces. Natural daylight and any light source approximating a blackbody source is assigned a CRI of 100.

To determine a CRI value, observers view eight standard pastel colors under the light source being rated and under light from a blackbody source (such as an incandescent lamp)

Table 5.2   Typical Color Rendering Index (CRI) Values for Light Sources

Light Source	CRI
Clear mercury	17
White deluxe mercury	45
Warm white fluorescent tube	55
Cool white fluorescent tube	65
Deluxe warm white fluorescent	73
Daylight fluorescent	79
Metal halide 4,200 K	85
Deluxe cool white fluorescent	86
Metal halide 5,400 K	93
Low-pressure sodium	0–18
High-pressure sodium	25
100-watt incandescent	100

having the same color temperature. The CRI is calculated, roughly speaking, by averaging the observers' estimation of the extent of the differences in the appearance of the colors under the two lights.

The CRI can only be used to compare two light sources that have the same color temperature. A 5,000-K, 80-CRI light source is not necessarily superior to a 4,000-K, 70-CRI light source (Table 5.2).

Flash/Strobe

The strength of the flash is measured and documented as the guide number. As you get farther away from any light source, the intensity of the flash drops off. It drops off using the inverse square law (Figure 5.3).

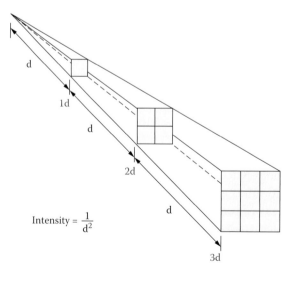

$$\text{Intensity} = \frac{1}{d^2}$$

Figure 5.3 Diagram showing the inverse square law.

Table 5.3 Film Speed Guide Number

Film Speed	Guide Number
25	40
50	56
100	80
200	110
400	160

As you change the f-stop of a lens, the intensity of the light at the film plane also changes. They change at the same rate, so this statement is always true: Distance × f-stop = Fixed number (called the guide number). Every combination of flash and film speed has one guide number. Faster films and more powerful flashguns have higher guide numbers. Often, manufacturers use the guide number as part of the model name of a flashgun. You can figure out what f-stop to use by dividing the guide number by the distance from the flash to the subject. If a flashgun has a guide number of 80, at 10 feet use f/8 (80 ÷ 10 = 8), at 5 feet use f/16 (80 ÷ 5 = 16), and at 20 feet use f/4 (80 ÷ 20 = 4).

When the film speed is increased by a factor of 4, the guide number is doubled. If the guide number for ISO (International Organization for Standardization speed of the film) 100 is 80, the guide number for ISO 400 is 160. The increase as film speeds double is just like the 1.4 times increase in the f-stop numbers on your lens: f/4, f/5.6, f/8, f/11, f/16 (Table 5.3).

Direct Flash

Direct flash is a flash that originates on the camera. This would be the internal flash of the camera or an external one attached to the hot shoe on the camera body. This flash lights the subject well but does create shadows. In forensic and technical photo imaging, shadows are not necessarily bad; however, at times they are undesirable (Figure 5.4).

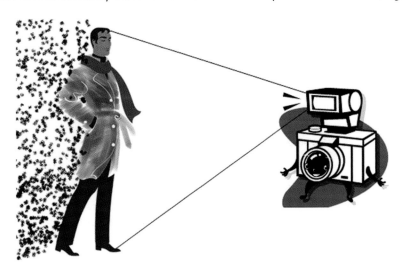

Figure 5.4 Diagram demonstration of direct flash; harsh shadows but sharply lit subject.

In forensic photo imaging, our main job is to document, record, and identify. A directly lit shot will do this well. However, if the image would be more clear in "telling the story" of the scene, then there are other options available.

Indirect Flash

We can use indirect lighting. Indirect lighting is sometimes called "bounce lighting." To use indirect or bounce lighting, we do not aim the light source at the subject. The flash is pointed toward the ceiling or a side wall. This diffuses the light, reducing shadows (Figure 5.5).

There are other methods of using indirect flash. The flash is pointed into an umbrella, and the flash is bounced off the umbrella and onto the subject. This provides a soft, homogeneous light with little or no shadows (Figure 5.6).

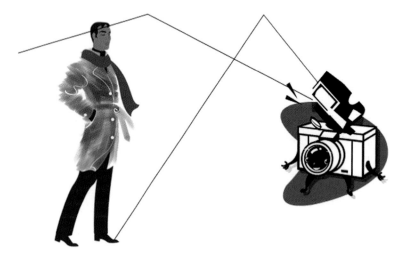

Figure 5.5 Indirect or bounce light; soft (if any) shadows, subject lit with soft or diffused light.

Figure 5.6 Umbrella-diffused flash, which creates soft, even lighting.

A whiteboard can also be used to reflect light onto the subject. This board can be obtained from any office supply store and comes in a number of sizes.

Fill Light

Fill light uses an auxiliary light source to light the shadowed area of an image. There are times when direct light or a camera-mounted flash does not light the area of interest in a photo. For example, in the photo of a box, what we are trying to show is not the box but rather what is in the box (Figure 5.7). To do this, we need fill light. We need to light not only the box but also the interior of the box. The second image of the box is light from both an on-camera flash and a second slave flash. In the second image, we can see the gun, which is what we are trying to show (Figure 5.8).

Subtractive Light

Subtractive light is exactly as is sounds. We are subtracting, or blocking, a light source. If the main light source is the sun, we can use a blackboard to block the direct light from the sun and allow the subject to be lit only by the diffused light. We use this technique when there is a reflection or "shine" from the subject. An example would be a round glass ball. Place the board (or, if necessary, several boards) to block the light source that is causing the reflection.

Additive Light

Additive light is actually the exact opposite as subtractive. Light is provided in some method, whether a flash or strobe or a fixed light source like tungsten or halogen.

Figure 5.7 Box with available light.

Figure 5.8 Box with available light and fill light. Notice gun.

Ambient or Available Light

Simply, ambient light is the light that is on the subject of the image. The light that is around you is ambient. Ambient light can come from a single source, such as sunlight. It can also come from a number of sources, such as when standing next to a window and the tungsten light from a lamp is mixed with the daylight streaming through the window. Please remember that you should never write in your report that lighting was "ambient" or "available" light. Ambient light on a given subject in a given place can and does change throughout the day.

Painting with Light

Painting with light is not often done; however, the few times that it is necessary makes knowing the technique most valuable. There is a large scene that you must photo image. The scene is several acres in size. While you can photo image the scene in smaller areas, the ability to have an image of the entire area, at night, closest to the time of occurrence, is most helpful.

This requires two persons. We start out with our digital camera on a tripod. The ISO of the camera should be set to 100 or less. The aperture should be adjusted to the widest setting. The shutter should be set to B. This setting on most digital single-lens reflex (SLR) cameras allows the shutter to remain open as long as the shutter button is depressed. Note that it is best to use a shutter cable release rather than just pressing the shutter button on the camera.

Have your partner take the flash unit and proceed to one end of the scene. With a baseball cap (real low tech here), place the cap over the lens and press the shutter button down and hold it down. This opens the shutter and keeps it open. Remove the baseball cap from the lens and give your partner the signal to fire the flash. After the partner fires the

Figure 5.9 Painting with light. Example of 2- to 3-acre crime scene.

Figure 5.10 Painting with light. Arrows indicate locations that strobe flashed.

flash, immediately cover the camera with the baseball cap—keeping the shutter open. Your partner should then move to a new position and the procedure is repeated. The procedure is repeated as many times as is necessary to light the entire scene (Figures 5.9 and 5.10). In the second image of the scene, arrows are drawn to show where the flash was fired. In the third image (Figure 5.11), you will note that a "ghost" is circled. This is not a real ghost, but the partner who is firing the flash. You should note in your report that the painting-with-light technique was used, and that there may be ghost images seen in the picture. Stating this in your report removes the potential for the opposition in court to bring this up to impeach your testimony.

Figure 5.11 Painting with light. "Ghost" of individual flashing the strobe. If you use this technique and you are explaining the technique, note the fact that there will be ghosting. You want to bring this up under direct testimony (questions from the prosecutor). You do not want it brought up under cross (defense) examination as it may appear that you were trying to "hide" something.

Ring Light

A ring light is similar in effect to using a tent in that it produces an even and homogeneous light with little if any shadows (Figure 5.12). It differs in that it is attached to the lens of the camera. The advantage to that is that when the lens is close to the object, if the light source is an on-camera flash, the flash will light above the focused area of the lens. The ring light attached to the lens projects an even light directly onto the object (Figure 5.13).

Diffusing Your On-Camera Flash with Tissue

There are times you will need diffused light (soft light), light with a minimal amount of harsh shadows. An easy method is to use a facial tissue and rubber band. Take a sheet of facial tissue and fold it over so that there are about four layers. This can be increased or decreased as you wish. You will need to experiment to find the best thickness (Figure 5.14). Next, place the tissue around the flash. This technique works well with both on-camera and auxiliary flashes. Use the camera as you would normally. You will see a more diffused light with fewer harsh shadows (Figures 5.15 and 5.16).

Other Lighting Equipment

While some of the following lighting accessories are not normally used in forensic photo imaging, one should at least be familiar with their names.

Figure 5.12 This is a ring light. It provides an even, almost shadowless light when imaging with a macro lens.

Figure 5.13 Camera utilizing a ring light.

Figure 5.14 Camera with tissue affixed to internal flash with a rubber band.

Figure 5.15 Image of a lamp using direct flash from the internal flash.

Figure 5.16 Image of a lamp using direct flash from the internal flash with a tissue over the flash to diffuse the light.

Figure 5.17 This is a "snoot." It is used to direct a small cone of light to a subject.

Snoot

The snoot is an object that is placed on a light source to concentrate the light on a small area within the composed image. A snoot is often used as a hair light to highlight an individual's hair in a portrait (Figure 5.17).

Barn Doors

Barn doors are another device used to direct specific patterns of light on a subject. The flaps or "doors" can be manipulated separately to highlight a specific area while holding back light from others (Figure 5.18).

Figure 5.18 These are "barn doors." They are used to direct odd configurations of light on a subject.

Figure 5.19 This is an umbrella used to diffuse the light. The flash is pointed into the umbrella, and the light is reflected onto the subject.

Umbrella

The umbrella is used for soft lighting effects as in portraiture. The light source is aimed into the umbrella, and the light is reflected onto the subject. We sometimes use this lighting technique if we are attempting to image an object with many shadowed areas in it. The reflected light from the umbrella will not create shadows as would direct lighting (Figure 5.19).

Filters

6

Introduction

A filter is simply a piece of glass or other transparent material used over the lens that alters the nature, color, or quality of the light passing through it (Figure 6.1). In forensic photo imaging, we do not wish to change or alter the image in any way. This would not be recording or documenting the image as it appeared at the original crime scene. What we wish to do is to enhance the quality of the image to make it a better image, a clearer image, and one in which we can see and understand the object or objects of interest. When using filters, we must understand what they can and cannot do.

We use various color filters to enhance the image, to increase contrast, or when using a forensic or alternate light source, to enhance the image by narrowing the bandwidth of light that the camera sees.

There are many filters that are used in photo imaging but not in technical or forensic imaging. Examples of these nontechnical filters would be a soft-focus filter, which blurs the image, making it pleasing to the eye. A bride or model may be photo imaged with this type of filter. It makes a pretty picture, but it changes the essence of the photo image. Another filter that forensic photo imagers do not use is the star filter. This is a filter that makes bright light points in the image to appear to radiate beams outward (Figures 6.2 and 6.3).

Polarizing Filter

The polarizing filter is used in technical photo imaging. It is a filter that can block light polarized in a single plane. A polarizing filter can reduce nonmetallic reflections and enhance contrast in photo images under specific conditions.

A polarizing filter is made from a thin sheet of polarizing material laminated between two circular pieces of glass and mounted in a frame (the filter ring). The filter can be rotated while it is fastened to the lens, affecting the angle of polarization of the filter, changing the amount of polarized light in the area imaged that can pass through the lens and to the CCD (the charged coupled device or camera sensor).

Polarizing filters are useful for reducing reflections from water and glass surfaces. They are commonly used for reducing reflective glare from windows or for imaging a lake *without* a reflection on the surface of the lake. They can also be used to increase color saturation of blue sky and of specific types of vegetation. Note that the effect of a polarizer on the sky varies depending on the angle to the sun.

There are two basic kinds of polarizing filters, linear and circular. Linear polarizing filters work well with manual focus cameras, but they interfere with autofocus cameras. Circular polarizing filters contain another element, a "quarter-wave" plate, which ensures compatibility of the filter with autofocus systems. As most digital cameras, including

Figure 6.1 A variety of filters.

Figure 6.2 This is an image taken with a star filter. Any bright light in the image will have this star effect. The filter can be chosen to have a specific number of "rays" (e.g., 5,6,7, etc.).

Figure 6.3 This image was taken with a soft-focus filter. The filter is a diffuser of sorts and makes the subject slightly out of focus. Another similar filter is a center sharp. The center of the filter is clear optical glass, while the rest of the area is diffused.

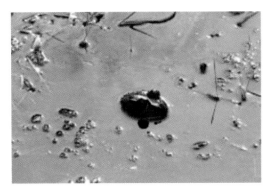

Without Polarizer   With Polarizer

Figure 6.4 These two images are examples of what a polarizing filter can do. In the image without polarizer, the frog is sitting in the water, but the ambient light is reflected off the water. The polarizing filter, which is adjustable, eliminates the glare, and one can see the entire frog and its surrounding area. This works equally well when photo imaging something behind glass.

digital single-lens reflex (SLR) cameras are autofocus cameras, the circular polarizing filter is the type that should be used.

There are many instances when you will use a polarizing filter in the documentation of scenes and evidence, such as when photo imaging through glass, such as a jewelry display case, through a window, or through a fish tank. On one occasion, it was necessary to take photo images of a gun that had been placed in a fish tank. Perhaps the perpetrator thought he could hide the gun "in plain sight."

Another situation in which a polarizing lens is helpful is when the object of interest is in shallow water. If a weapon, knife, gun, pipe, or other object is under several inches of water, by using a polarizing filter the object can be effectively imaged (Figure 6.4).

Band-Pass and Band-Block Filters

A band-pass filter is one that will allow a specific range of wavelengths to pass through the filter. A band-block filter blocks a specific range of wavelengths from going through the filter.

Filter Factors

Each time a filter factor is doubled, the exposure needs to be increased by one stop. As an example, a filter factor of two requires a one-stop exposure increase. A filter factor of four requires a two-stop exposure increase (Table 6.1). Use this example for filter factors not listed in Table 6.1.

Color-Compensating Filters

Color-compensating filters control light by attenuating principally the red, green, or blue part of the spectrum. While controlling one color, the filter transmits one or both

Table 6.1   Filter Factors

Filter Factor	+ Stops	Filter Factor	+ Stops	Filter Factor	+ Stops
1.25	½	4	2	12	3⅔
1.5	⅔	5	2⅓	40	5⅓
2	1	6	2⅔	100	6⅔
2.5	1½	8	3	1000	10
3	1⅔	10	3⅓	—	—

of the other two colors. Thus, color-compensating filters can make changes to the color balance of pictures recorded on color films or compensate for deficiencies in the spectral quality of a light source. For optimum results, use the single recommended color-compensating filter rather than combining filters (e.g., CC20Y + CC20M = 20R, so using 20R only is preferable). Kodak Wratten gelatin filters/color-compensating filters have excellent optical quality and are suitable for image-forming optical systems over-the-camera lens, for example. There are also a number of special-purpose Wratten filters. These and others are listed in Table 6.2.

Kodak Light-Balancing Filters

Light-balancing filters enable the photographer to make minor adjustments in the color quality of illumination to obtain cooler (bluer) or warmer (more yellow) color rendering. One of the principle uses for Kodak light-balancing filters is when light sources frequently exhibit color temperatures different from that for which a color film is balanced. When using a color temperature meter to determine the color temperature of prevailing light, you can use Table 6.3, which converts the prevailing temperature to either 3,200 K or 3,400 K.

Conversion Filters for Color Films

Conversion filters for color films filters are used with film cameras. They are intended for use whenever significant changes in the color temperature of the illumination are required (e.g., daylight to artificial light). The filter may be positioned between the light source and other elements of the system or over the camera lens in conventional photographic recording.

Stacking Filters

Filters may be "stacked." This is a technique used to place more than one filter on the lens. Care must be taken so that unwanted results do not occur that would change the essence of the image, making it unusable in court.

Neutral-Density Filters

The neutral-density filter is most helpful when the light source is too bright. These filters effectively darken the image by allowing less light to reach the CCD in a digital camera

Table 6.2   Kodak Filters

Filter Number	
	Yellow Kodak Wratten Gelatin Filters
2B	Pale yellow. Absorbs UV radiation below 390 nm. Slightly more effective when an excess of ultraviolet radiation is present. Attenuates UV radiation for fluorescence photography and for the optical system of color printers when printing certain color materials.
2E	Pale yellow. Absorbs UV radiation below 415 nm. similar to No. 2B but absorbs more violet.
3	Light yellow. Provides partial correction for excess blue in black-and-white aerial photography and motion picture photography.
8	Yellow. Alters rendition of sky, clouds, and foliage in black-and-white photography with panchromatic materials.
9	Deep yellow. Similar to No. 8, but tends to exaggerate sky rendition for more dramatic effect.
11	Yellow greenish. Alters color response of panchromatic emulsions to match color brightness response of the eye to objects exposed to tungsten illumination. Reproduces greens slightly lighter in daylight.
12	Deep yellow. Minus-blue filter (see No. 32 for minus green and No. 44A for minus red). Provides haze penetration in aerial photography. Cancels blue light when exposing infrared-sensitive films.
15	Deep yellow. Darkens sky in landscape photography more dramatically than No. 8 or 9. Useful for copying documents on yellowed paper. Greater blue attenuation for infrared photography and for fluorescence photography.
	Orange and Red Kodak Wratten Gelatin Filters
16	Yellow-orange. Permits greater overcorrection of sky than No. 15. Absorbs small amount of green.
21	Orange. Contrast filter used for blue and blue-green absorption.
22	Deep orange. Contrast filter with greater green absorption than No. 21. In photomicrography, increases contrast of blue preparations. Transmits only yellow radiation from mercury vapor illumination.
25	Red tricolor. For color separation work and tricolor printing, used with Nos. 58 (green) and No. 47B (blue). Contrast effects in commercial and outdoor black-and-white photography. Haze penetration aerial work. Removes blue in infrared photography.
26	Red. For anaglyph viewing for a three-dimensional effect with No. 58 (green).
29	Deep red tricolor. Used for color separation and tricolor printing work. Tricolor projection (tungsten) with No. 47 (blue) and No. 61 (green).
92	Red. Used for densitometric measurement of color films and papers.
	Magenta and Violet Kodak Wratten Gelatin Filters
32	Magenta. Minus green (see No. 12 for minus blue and No. 44A for minus red).
34A	Violet. For minus-green and plus-blue separation.
	Blues and Blue-Green Kodak Wratten Gelatin Filters
38A	Blue. Contrast filter for some UV and green absorption and much red absorption. In photomicrography, for increasing contrast in records of faintly yellow or orange preparations.
44	Light blue-green. Minus-red filter with much UV absorption.
44A	Light blue-green. Minus-red (see No. 12 for minus blue and No. 32 for minus green).
47	Blue tricolor. For color separation work. For contrast effects in commercial and outdoor black-and-white photography. Tricolor projection (tungsten) with Nos. 29 and 61.

(continued on next page)

Table 6.2 (continued)   Kodak Filters

Filter Number	
47A	Light blue. For exciting fluorescein in medical applications of fluorescence photography.
47B	Deep blue tricolor. For color separation work and tricolor printing, with No. 25 (red) and No. 58 (green).
98	Blue. Equivalent to No. 47B plus No. 2B filter. For making separation positives from color negative films. Also for three-color printing on color papers.

Green Kodak Wratten Gelatin Filters

58	Green tricolor. For color separation work and tricolor printing, with No. 25 (red) and No. 47B (blue). For contrast effects in commercial photography and micrography.
61	Deep green tricolor. For color separation and tricolor printing work. For tricolor projection (tungsten) with No. 29 and No. 47.
99	Green. Equivalent to No. 61 plus No. 16 filter. For making separation positives from color negative films. Also for three-color printing on color paper.

Conversion Filters

80A, 80B, 80C, 80D	Blue series of conversion filters for color films. Used to provide significant changes in color temperature of various light sources.
85, 85N3, 85N6, 85N9, 85B, 85C	Amber series of conversion filters for color films. Used to provide significant changes in color temperature of various light sources.

Light-Balancing Filters

8EF, 81, 81A, 81B, 81C, 81D,	Yellowish series of light-balancing filters. Used over the camera lens to produce subtle changes in color balance (to warmer appearance) with color films.
82, 82A, 82B, 82C	Bluish series of light-balancing filters. Used over the camera lens to produce subtle changes in color balance (to cooler appearance) with color films.

Miscellaneous Filters

18A	Visibly opaque glass filter. Transmits only UV radiation between about 300 and 400 nm (e.g., 365 nm line of mercury spectrum) and infrared radiation. Isolates UV radiation for ultraviolet reflection photography.
39	Blue. Glass contrast filter.
87, 87C	Visibly opaque filters absorb unwanted visible light in infrared photography.
89B	Visibly opaque. For infrared photography, especially aerial.
90	Dark grayish-amber. Monochrome viewing filter. Visually approximates the relative tones of gray produced in black-and-white prints by different colors under daylight illumination.
96	Neutral. In color and black-and-white photography, reduces intensity of visible light. Uniform attenuation throughout the visible spectrum. Greater transmission in IR. Available in 13 densities, covering the transmittance range from 80 to 0.01.
102	Yellow-green. Converts the response characteristics of a barrier-layer photocell (as in a densitometer) to the luminosity response of the eye.
106	Amber. Converts the response characteristics of an S-4 type photocell (as in a densitometer) to the luminosity response of the eye.

Color-Compensating (CC) Filters (Gelatin)

In image-forming systems, singly or in combinations, change overall color balance for viewing or printing. Compensate for deficiencies in lighting in photographic recording.

Table 6.2 (continued)   Kodak Filters

Filter Number

Color-Printing (CP) Filters (Acetate)

Singly or in combination, provide for color correction of enlarger light sources in color printing. Not suitable for image-forming systems.

Polycontrast/Polymax Filters

Provide contrast control for Kodak variable-contrast printing papers.

Note: Kodak, Polycontrast, Polymax, and Wratten are trademarks of Kodak.

Table 6.3   Light-Balancing Filters

Filter Color	Filter Number	Exposure Increase in Stops[a]	To Obtain 3,200 K from (K)[a]	To Obtain 3,400 K from (K)[a]
Bluish	82C + 82C	1⅓	2,490	2,610
	82C + 82B	1⅓	2,570	2,700
	82C + 82A	1	2,650	2,780
	82C + 82	1	2,720	2,870
	82C	⅔	2,800	2,950
	82B	⅔	2,900	3,060
	82A	⅓	3,000	3,180
	82	⅓	3,100	3,290
Yellowish	81	⅓	3,300	3,510
	81A	⅓	3,400	3,630
	81B	⅓	3,500	3,740
	81C	⅓	3,600	3,850
	81D	⅔	3,700	3,970
	81EF	⅔	3,850	4,140

[a] Light color in kelvins needed to change to balance color with standard daylight color.

and the film in a film camera. The neutral-density filter can therefore adjust the exposure without any change to the shutter speed, aperture opening, or light source. They are available in 1X, 2X, 3X, 4X, and 5X. The 1X equals one f-stop or one shutter speed increment (Figure 6.5).

In black-and-white and color photography, filters such as Kodak Wratten Neutral Density Filters No. 96 reduce the intensity of light reaching the film without affecting the tonal rendition in the original scene. In motion picture work or other photography, neutral-density filters allow use of a large aperture to obtain differential focusing. You can use them when filming in bright sunlight or with very fast films. These filters control exposure when the smallest aperture is still too large. Also available are Kodak Wratten gelatin filters with combinations of neutral density and color conversion filters (e.g., No. 85N3). These filters combine the light conversion characteristics of Kodak Wratten Gelatin Filter No. 85 with neutral densities (Table 6.4).

Infrared and Ultraviolet Filters

Filters used in infrared (IR) and ultraviolet (UV) photo imaging are covered in Chapter 23.

Figure 6.5 These are neutral-density filters. They are pure optical glass that filters the reflected light from the object as it passes through the lens to the image sensor (CCD). The density is measured in f-stops. If a correct exposure is {ISO 100, shutter 1/125 second, and aperture f/8}, if we put a neutral-density filter with a factor of one on the lens, we would have to change the settings to {ISO 100, shutter 1/60 second, and aperture f/8}. This is sometimes used when the subject of the picture is so bright that you cannot obtain a good exposure unless the neutral-density filters are used, such as for the flame of a carbon arc.

Table 6.4   Neutral Density Filters

Neutral Density	Transmittance (%)	Filter Factor	Exposure Increase in Stops
0.1	80	1¼	⅓
0.2	63	1½	⅔
0.3	50	2	1
0.4	40	2½	1⅓
0.5	32	3	1⅔
0.6	25	4	2
0.7	20	5	2⅔
0.8	16	6	2⅔
0.9	13	8	3
1.0	10	10	3⅓
2.0	1	100	6⅔
3.0	0.1	1,000	10
4.0	0.01	10,000	13⅔

Macro/Micro Imaging

7

Introduction

Macro photography is close-up photography that does not involve the use of microscopes. True *macro* photography is generally considered to have a ratio of 1:1 or greater, and the lens used will be able to focus on an object less than 8 inches away. Nikon uses the term *micro* instead of *macro* in describing its lens. The meaning, however, is basically interchangeable. Many digital cameras identify the macro setting on the camera with a flower icon (Figure 7.1).

Photo Image Evidence at 90 Degrees to the Object

This is important. When photo imaging evidence or objects of interest, the image *must* be taken at 90 degrees to the subject of the image. If a photo image of a circle is taken at 90 degrees to the circle, the circle will appear as a circle in the image when viewed or printed (Figures 7.2 and 7.3). If that same circle is photo imaged at 45 degrees or anything other than 90 degrees, the circle will appear as an oval when observed or printed. If the image is not taken at 90 degrees, then the image is *distorted*.

On the stand, in court, if you have imaged a circle at 45 degrees, you could be asked the following:

Attorney: Investigator, does the photo image I have here in front of me, marked by you as your photo image, truly and accurately represent the circle at the crime scene on the date and time in question?

You: Yes sir.

Attorney: Then, why does the circle you photo imaged look like an oval in this photo image?

You: Uh, …, uh.

Attorney: Your honor, if this image does not truly and accurately represent the scene on the date and time in question, what about the other 123 photo images that have been entered into evidence in this case? Your honor, I move that all 124 photo images be ruled as bad evidence, and all testimony and these photos be removed from the record.

Figure 7.1 The icon of the flower on the setting knob is for close-up imaging. It is a "macro" setting but is not a macro lens.

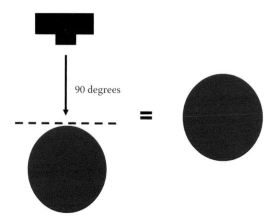

Figure 7.2 The drawing demonstrates a circle being photographed at 90 degrees. The image will print as a circle without distortion.

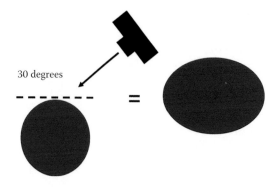

Figure 7.3 The drawing demonstrates a circle being photographed at 45 degrees. The image will print as an oval (i.e., with distortion).

Bench Imaging

Bench imaging is defined as either macro or close-up imaging. This is usually done in the laboratory or at the crime scene investigator's (CSI's) office. Even though the evidence was photographed at the scene, additional imaging is sometimes desired. It is done in the lab on a photo bench, hence the term *bench*.

The lab setting allows the imager much more control over the lighting, temperature, conditions, and posing of the object of evidence. One example would be that of a handgun at the scene of a shooting. The scene was dark with relatively no ambient light. The gun was found at the base of a bush. Only a single image was taken of the gun at the scene for perspective for scene context. Due to the bush, additional images were impossible to obtain. Only one side of the gun was recorded.

Backgrounds

Objects are photo imaged for the record, imaging an object so that it can be viewed by investigators, prosecutors, defense, jury, and the court. An example would be a knife. In court, the judge may not want the knife passed around. The photo image can be shown to all without requiring the actual knife to be removed from its sealed packaging (Figure 7.4).

Using a bright background allows the object of interest to stand out. A background frame can easily be made from PVC (polyvinyl chloride) piping available at any home improvement store. Design it, then shop for the parts. It can be as large or as small as you desire. I suggest obtaining a PVC cutter; it will save a lot of time, and it makes cleaner cuts than a saw (Figure 7.5). When assembling the frame, you can use PVC glue if you wish the frame to be permanent. The other option is not to use the glue, which allows the frame to be folded for convenient storage.

Now that you have the frame, you should obtain some clamps, again available at any home improvement store. The clamps will be used to hold and secure the colored background (Figure 7.6). You can attach the clamps permanently to the frame or just use the individual clamps as needed.

Next, you will need the backgrounds. I suggest that you obtain them from a fabric store. Felt makes an excellent background, is inexpensive, and comes in many bright colors.

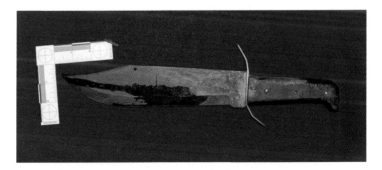

Figure 7.4 Image of a knife with scale. This is a rephotographed piece of evidence. It has already been photographed at the scene. It was rephotographed in the lab for the record. Notice that it is with scale only. This is because it has been imaged at the scene, and the scale is not covering any of the subject matter (the knife).

Figure 7.5 A background frame that can be built from PVC pipe available at any home or hardware store.

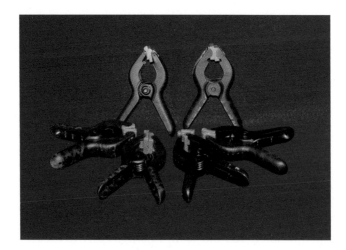

Figure 7.6 Clamps, available at any home or hardware store.

I would suggest red, dark blue, and white. About 2 yards of each will do nicely unless you have built your frame extremely large (Figure 7.7).

Clamp the felt onto the frame as shown in Figure 7.8. The base should curve out and lay on the counter. This is what is called a "zero horizon." When the image is taken, there are no creases or corners. The image of the background frame (in red) was shot on a much larger frame with a blue background.

Handguns

Back at the lab, the handgun can be "posed" under controlled conditions. Light can be manipulated to provide a perfect recording of the gun. Both sides of the gun can be imaged. A macro lens can be employed to take images of scratches, marks, blood, the serial number, and other artifacts at a 1:1 ratio. Remember to photo image negative aspects (missing parts), the absence of blood, or the area from which a serial number was removed.

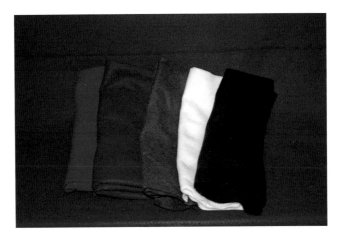

Figure 7.7 Felt fabric in different colors available at any fabric store, usually by the yard. Several yards of each color are desirable.

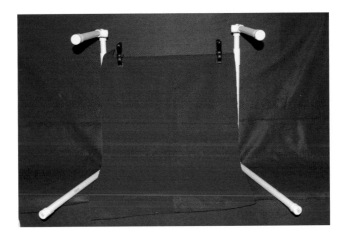

Figure 7.8 Fabric clamped to background frame to make a zero-horizon background. The bottom of the background curves out toward the camera. Images photographed on this type of background do not have a distracting crease.

There will be occasions when you will wish to photo image the inside of the barrel. This could be important if the wound was a contact wound or was made at a close range. In these instances, there is "blowback." This a phenomenon occurring in contact and close-range wounds made with a gun. Blood and tissue are "blown back" into the barrel of the gun. This can be documented by photo imaging (Figure 7.9).

The gun should be secured in a vise or with a clamp. If the gun is a semiautomatic, the slide should be opened and locked to the rear. If the gun is a revolver, the gun should be photo imaged with the cylinder opened. Using an additional clamp, secure a light source and aim it into the chamber of the gun so that the light shines through and out the end of the barrel. A battery-powered flashlight with a "gooseneck"-type adjustable shaft works well (Figure 7.10). In Figure 7.11, we are using a fiber-optic light (dual source) with adjustable light intensity.

Disable the flash on the camera when working with movable light sources. If you cannot disable the flash on the camera, temporarily cover it with black electrician's tape. If the

Figure 7.9 Blood or tissue as a result of "blowback" in the barrel of a gun. The gun was secured in a vise. A fiber-optic multihalogen light source was used to image the interior of the barrel. The light source is available from laboratory supply companies for about $450.

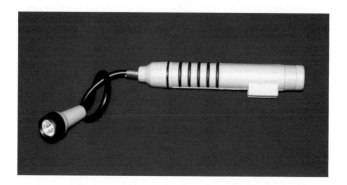

Figure 7.10 A gooseneck portable light available at many home or hardware stores for under $15.

flash is not disabled, the flash will overlight the area of interest, the barrel, and the blood or tissue will not be photo imaged clearly; you will observe that your image is a bright white blob (Figure 7.12).

Use a tripod to steady the camera. Aim the camera at 90 degrees to the barrel so that the center of the lens is centered on the barrel. Switch your focus to manual. Set your camera to aperture priority and choose an opening of f/16 or f/32. This will give you more depth of field. This is important because it allows more of the length of the barrel to be in acceptable focus.

The Scale

The scale is nothing more than a 6-inch ruler. We use the scale to size the object in the photo image. This is exceedingly important when photo imaging an object to compare to an original. When photo imaging a latent fingerprint, the scale allows the examiner to

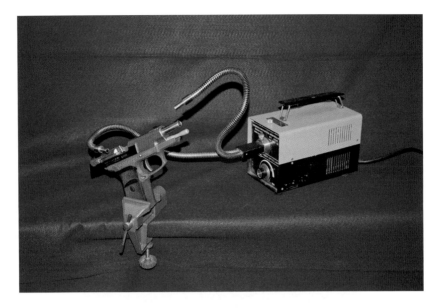

Figure 7.11 Gun with fiber-optic multihalogen light source.

Figure 7.12 Gun with portable gooseneck light source.

compare "apples to apples" sizewise. It is important in footwear impressions, tire impressions, and tool marks. We use it for all types of evidence. This is one of the most important forensic photo imagers' tools (Figure 7.13).

An important thing to remember for scene photo imaging is to photograph the item both with and without scale. This is so that there can be no doubt that you are not hiding something behind the scale. We do this to show that there is no exculpatory evidence covered by the scale. Exculpatory evidence is evidence that could prove an individual innocent of a crime.

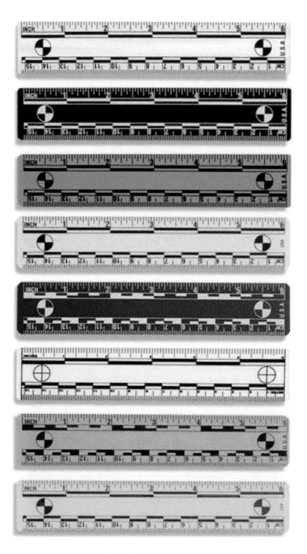

Figure 7.13 Scales come in a variety of colors.

In the lab, when photo imaging an object for the record, it is not necessary to photo image with and without a scale. Images should be taken with a scale only. At this point, the object is no longer part of a scene. It stands alone, and nothing else, exculpatory or otherwise, is in the image.

Studio in a Box

Studio in a box is a generic term for a kit of equipment sold for photo imaging small objects using a lighting technique known as *tenting* (Figures 7.14 and 7.15). The object is placed in the tent, and lights are placed on both sides. The sides soften the light and eliminate harsh shadows. Lights can be adjusted simply by moving them closer or farther away from the sides of the tent. The result is a perfectly lit photo image (Figures 7.16 and 7.17). The sides and the lights are included in the kits, which are available for under $70.

Figure 7.14 This is a "studio in a box." It is available online and from photographic supply companies. It facilitates taking professional images of objects. It works on the "tent lighting" principle.

Figure 7.15 An example of studio-in-a-box setup for lighting a cup.

Figure 7.16 The cup shot with studio in a box with the included light setup.

Figure 7.17 This cup was shot with blue fabric clamped to background frame with zero-horizon background as shown in Figure 7.8. Lighting was from the on-camera flash. Notice the harsh shadow.

Figure 7.18 Common gallon plastic milk jug.

A less-expensive method for using the tenting technique is to use a plastic milk jug (Figure 7.18). Cut the top and bottom from the jug (Figure 7.19). Place the object in the center under the jug and position lights (lights can be standard gooseneck desk lamps) on either side of the milk jug. Results using this method are good. Photo imaging jewelry, diamonds, and other small objects can be accomplished when images for the record are needed (Figures 7.20 and 7.21).

The Light Box

The light box is useful in photo imaging many types of objects, but it works exceedingly well with fingerprints developed using black powder (Figure 7.22). The light box is nothing

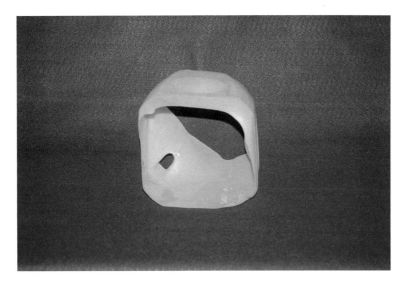

Figure 7.19 Milk jug with the top and bottom removed.

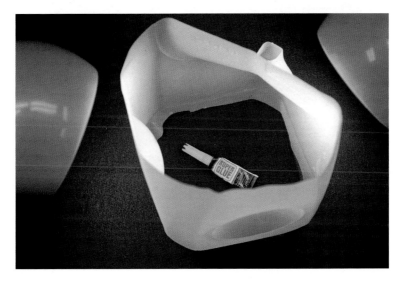

Figure 7.20 Milk jug with two fixed incandescent light sources acting as a light tent with a tube of superglue as a subject.

more than a box with lights in it covered by a piece of frosted glass or Plexiglas. The frosted requirement assists in the diffusion of the light. We use the light box to provide light from underneath the object of interest.

Light boxes can be purchased commercially; however, if you are slightly handy, you can make one. Build a box approximately 6 × 18 × 18 inches (open at the top). Groove the top so that glass will fit inside the groove (Figure 7.23). Attach four porcelain lightbulb bases to the inside of the box. Connect them in parallel. (You may add a switch or just attach a cord set to the bulb base.) Have a piece of frosted glass cut at a hardware store, and you are in business (Figure 7.24).

Figure 7.21 An image of the tube of superglue photo imaged with the lighting setup in Figure 7.20.

Figure 7.22 A light box.

Turn it on and place the object to be imaged on top. Do not use flash. If additional lighting is needed, use fixed-bulb illumination (a gooseneck lamp with 60-watt bulb) (Figure 7.25).

Rope Caulk

Rope caulk is a handy tool in the bench photo imagers' bag of tricks. It allows us to "pose" objects that do not want to be placed as we want them to be. Rope caulk is available at any hardware store. It is like clay except that it can be easily removed from objects (Figure 7.26).

When attempting to image the engraving on the inside of a ring, the rope caulk is most helpful. Tear off a small piece from the roll and press it onto your work area. Move the object around until you can obtain the composition that you want (Figure 7.27).

Figure 7.23 Interior of the light box. Note that if you build one and use incandescent bulbs, make sure you drill some airholes in the sides. The bulbs get hot. A better method of lighting your box is to use the new fluorescent screw-in bulbs. They produce much less heat.

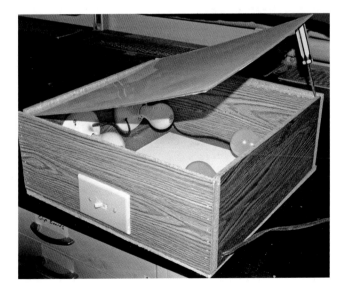

Figure 7.24 The light box with frosted glass top. The glass is available at any home or hardware store. Ace Hardware will cut it to size for you.

Helping Hands

Helping hands is a tool that can be obtained at many hardware stores. The helping hands consist of a base with one or two alligator clips attached to movable arms. This tool gives you a "third hand" that can hold a scale or help pose an object too large for the rope caulk (Figure 7.28).

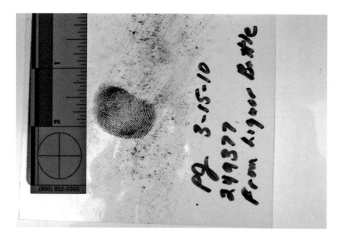

Figure 7.25 A latent lift photographed using the light box as the light source (no flash). The box lights from the bottom rather than the top. The light box is good for documents as well because it lights the ink on the paper from the bottom and shows different levels of ink. Ultraviolet (UV) bulbs can be used also (remember to add the vent holes). If you want to use UV bulbs, make sure that the bulbs are UV and not "black light" bulbs. Black light bulbs are merely regular tungsten light bulbs with dark blue glass.

Figure 7.26 Rope caulk. This is a great tool for assistance in rephotographing objects. It is used to "pose" objects.

The Tripod

The tripod is a piece of equipment used in the lab for bench photo imaging and in scene work as well. It is used to steady the camera, especially when shutter speeds are 1/30 second and slower.

There are many types of tripods. Each has its particular niche in photo imaging (Figure 7.29). There are flexible tripods, which can be set on objects and can be wrapped around a pole or post (Figure 7.30). There are tabletop tripods, which are helpful if there is a table available (Figure 7.31). A monopod is also available. While this device has only

Figure 7.27 Gold-colored ring "posed" with rope caulk.

Figure 7.28 Helping hands. These are most helpful when you need a third, fourth, or even a fifth hand. They are available at any hobby or hardware store.

one leg, when held by the photo imager, it provides acceptable control of the camera (Figure 7.32).

There are times that you will be caught without a tripod when one is needed. In this case, you must make yourself into a tripod, a human tripod (Figure 7.33). Lean against a wall, pole, or post. Hold the camera in both hands and place your upper arms so they touch your torso. Presto! You are now a tripod. I have used this technique on a number of occasions. I would have rather had a tripod, but this technique works. Note that it will not work with the painting-with-light technique.

Figure 7.29 Standard tripod.

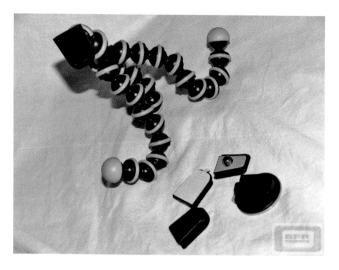

Figure 7.30 Flexible tripod. Can also be secured to a post or pipe.

Figure 7.31 Tabletop tripod.

Figure 7.32 A monopod.

Figure 7.33 A human tripod. (Courtesy of Marissa McDonough, Purdue University.)

Law

8

The Lay Witness

A *witness* can be defined as "one who has personal knowledge of something" (Merriam-Webster, 2010). This is an individual who has seen something and can testify to it in a court. This person has no special legal or forensic training and as a reasonable person can relate his or her experience to the court. Because of a lack of specific training, this person may not recognize or be able to relate technical information. This is Joe or Joan Citizen. He or she can give testimony about anything.

The Professional Witness

The professional witness has had specific training in forensics or in a specific discipline and can relate those technical observations to a court. This person uses proper nomenclature when describing objects in a court of law. He or she can give testimony about anything, but testimony in this person's specific area of training will be more accepted. This is Joe/Joan Police Officer, Joe/Joan Detective, or Joe/Joan CSI (crime scene investigator).

The Expert Witness

The expert witness has had a great amount of training in his or her specific area of expertise. This would consist of formal education, experience, publications, and lectures pertaining to this discipline. This person can testify about anything, but in his or her specific area of expertise, he or she can give an opinion in court based on this level of training and expertise. This is Dr. Joe/Joan Forensic Scientist.

The Nature of Law

We call ourselves forensic scientists, forensic imagers, and forensic practitioners. The definition of *forensic* means "as pertaining to a court of law" (Merriam-Webster, 2010). Therefore, forensic science means science as pertains to a court of law. Forensic, when used with another word, adds the phrase "as pertains to a court of law." Forensic engineering means engineering as pertains to a court of law. Forensic psychology means psychology as pertains to a court of law.

Do we have a justice system? That would be a system that seeks justice above all else. It would punish the guilty and free the innocent. Our symbol for justice in the United States is a blindfolded woman holding a sword in one hand and a balance beam in the other. The sword symbolizes punishment. The balance beam symbolizes balance and equality.

Figure 8.1 Lady Justice. A symbol of justice in the United States. The sword is for punishment, the balance means that the law is applied equally to all, and the blindfold means that she does not see race, religion, sexual preference, or financial standing.

The fact that she is blindfolded indicates that she looks only to the law and does not see race, creed, or national origin (Figure 8.1).

If our system were based on law only, the guilty would indeed be punished, and the innocent freed. If a person were to commit X and the law states persons will not commit X, then the person who committed X would be guilty and be punished. If the person did not commit X, then he or she would be free.

We *do not* have a justice system; rather, we have an adversary system (Figure 8.2). It is as if two knights "joust" to win the decision for their side. Many things are taken into

Figure 8.2 Knight jousting, just as attorneys joust in the courtroom.

Figure 8.3 O. J. Simpson on trial. (Photo courtesy *The Times, U.K. News and Opinions*, 2008.)

account concerning the decision of guilt or innocence. The first is precedent. What has been done before in cases similar to this case? Second are decisions by higher courts. Have judges in appellate or supreme courts reversed decisions handed down in lower courts? The third consideration is who has the most money and resources. If a party has access to considerable funds, that party can hire a string of lawyers and expert witnesses to argue and influence the thinking of the judge or jury.

A method that is sometimes used is to concentrate the mind of the court on an issue that does not affect the guilt or innocence of the person accused of a crime. A perfect example of this is the O. J. Simpson murder trial (Figure 8.3). Specifically, if the defense attorney cannot attack the evidence, then he or she can attack the individual collecting the evidence. Mark Furman was a detective on the case. He documented evidence in this case as well as conducted part of the investigation. Furman had been overheard using the "N" word. He was accused of being a bigot. We all learned a new word as it was added to our vocabulary: *racial epithet*. My personal philosophy is that I judge a man or a woman on what he or she does, not the color of skin, what religion is practiced, or what his or her favorite baseball team is (Figure 8.4).

Figure 8.4 Mark Fuhrman (the O. J. Simpson trial). (Photo from *ID: Investigation Discovery: Hollywood Crimes, Forensics, Murders, 2010.*)

That fact that Furman may or may not be a bigot is irrelevant. However, the racial epithet usage was brought up in court, and a great deal of time was spent on this issue. The media, of course, picked it up and, by doing so, made it a major issue of the case. The fact that Furman used the "N" word does not change what was documented, collected, or investigated. If attorneys cannot attack the evidence, they will attack the witness.

Miranda Warnings

If a person who is arrested and questioned and is not Mirandized, that is, given his or her rights under the Miranda decision [*Miranda v. Arizona*, 384 U.S. 436 (1966)], even if the person has admitted to the crime, that admission may not be used in court. That means that even though the person is guilty and has admitted to the guilt, he or she may go free (Figure 8.5).

While attending a coroner's conference, I had an opportunity to listen to some war stories from Dr. Henry Lee, a renowned forensic scientist. I very much respect Dr. Lee and his work. When he speaks, not only does he teach, but he also entertains. I cannot quote Dr. Lee's exact words, but what follows is an accurate approximation. I hope I do it justice.

He told of a time when he was on the stand during the Simpson trial. Dr. Lee always carries a forensic scale (a 6-inch ruler) with him. And, as a forensic scientist, chief deputy coroner, and former CSI, I would strongly recommend that we all do so. He had a number of these forensic scales made and imprinted with his name. A commercial company had manufactured and produced these scales for him (Figure 8.6). During the discovery portion of the trial (when all information is exchanged by the prosecution and defense, including evidence, reports, images, and witness lists), the defense had obtained one of Dr. Lee's scales and had sent it to a national institute for weights and measures for testing. After examination, it was found to be 1/100 inch off.

While on the stand, Dr. Lee was asked about a specific measurement that he had made while examining evidence that had been collected during the investigation. Dr. Lee gave the measurement. The defense attorney smiled and said that they had had Dr. Lee's scale checked with the national institute for weights and measures and that the scale was in fact 1/100 inch off. Dr. Lee, who is not a newcomer to testifying in court, calmly stated

MIRANDA WARNING
1. YOU HAVE THE RIGHT TO REMAIN SILENT.
2. ANYTHING YOU SAY CAN AND WILL BE USED AGAINST YOU IN A COURT OF LAW.
3. YOU HAVE THE RIGHT TO TALK TO A LAWYER AND HAVE HIM PRESENT WITH YOU WHILE YOU ARE BEING QUESTIONED.
4. IF YOU CANNOT AFFORD TO HIRE A LAWYER, ONE WILL BE APPOINTED TO REPRESENT YOU BEFORE ANY QUESTIONING IF YOU WISH.
5. YOU CAN DECIDE AT ANY TIME TO EXERCISE THESE RIGHTS AND NOT ANSWER ANY QUESTIONS OR MAKE ANY STATEMENTS.

WAIVER
DO YOU UNDERSTAND EACH OF THESE RIGHTS I HAVE EXPLAINED TO YOU?
HAVING THESE RIGHTS IN MIND, DO YOU WISH TO TALK TO US NOW?

Figure 8.5 The *Miranda* rights card. (*Miranda v. Arizona*, 384 U.S. 436 (1966).)

Figure 8.6 Dr. Henry Lee, forensic scientist. (Photo courtesy *The Mason Gazette*, 2006.)

that if the attorney would check his report, he would find that Dr. Lee had stated approximately the measurement in question. The smile disappeared from the attorney's face.

When the attorney could not attack the evidence itself, and he could not attack the individual, in this case, Dr. Lee, he attacked whatever he could—the accuracy of the scale. Would the inaccuracy of the scale (1/100 inch) make a difference in a calculation? Perhaps, but it is doubtful. The object here is to discredit the witness, not necessarily the measurement or calculation. If the attorney can create doubt in the minds of the jury on the insignificant measurement issue, then the attorney can create doubt in the minds of the jury regarding other points of testimony. The defendant must be convicted *beyond a reasonable doubt*. If this doubt is created in the minds of the jury, then regardless of whether the charged person is guilty, he or she will be declared "not guilty" and go free.

Types of Witnesses[*]

There are several types of witnesses used by both the prosecutor and the defense. These are: the lay witness, the professional witness, and the expert witness.

The Lay Witness

The lay witness is usually a person who is at the wrong place at the right time. He or she just happened to walk into the bank while it was being robbed or stopped off to purchase a carton of milk while the store was being robbed. This person has no training to assist in remembering descriptions or actions that may or may not have been observed. While "eyewitnesses" are touted as providing the best evidence, often from the untrained person it can be unintentionally misleading. This person, when placed on the stand, will be instructed to answer the questions asked, often with a yes or no answer. These witnesses are frustrated because they want to "tell" their whole story. Opposition attorneys want

---

[*] Criteria governing witness testimony as found in Rule 701 Federal Rules of Evidence (LII 1975 ed.); Rule 702 Federal Rules of Evidence (LII 2000 ed.); and Rule 703 Federal Rules of Evidence (LII 2009 ed.) are reprinted in this and subsequent sections. With permission of the Legal Informaton Institute of Cornell University Law School.

these witnesses to answer with a yes or no so that they can tell the story, resulting with the best effects for their side.

Some questions cannot be answered with a yes or no and require qualification, and a witness with little or no experience testifying can easily be manipulated. For example, if an attorney asks, "Do you still beat your wife?" if no is answered, then it is implied that you used to beat your wife. If you answer yes, obviously you beat your wife. The correct answer is to look to the judge and state that this question cannot be answered with a yes or no answer, and qualification is required. The professional witness will answer in this manner, but a witness without training may not. Witnesses are necessary and good, but they lack training. They can be helpful in court proceedings, and they can be a problem as well.

The Professional Witness

The professional witness is usually a police officer, detective, CSI, fireman or firewoman, first responder, or other person who has received training in observation, procedure, and sometimes proper methods for testifying in court. The police officer, detective, and CSI will usually testify as a professional witness and not an expert witness.

The professional witness has had a modest amount of training and experience. In most cases, this person has prepared reports and drawings and has taken images. This person is an excellent witness. He or she does, however, lack the credentials necessary to be declared an expert witness by a judge in a competent jurisdiction.

As a professional witness, proper nomenclature should be used when testifying. For example, while testifying concerning a firearm case, the term *cartridge* is used to describe a live round of ammunition, which includes the bullet, shell casing, primer, and powder. It should not be referred to as a "bullet" as that is the correct term for the part of the cartridge that is expelled through the barrel. While the bullet is in flight, it is referred to as a "projectile."

A rifle should not be called a gun, and a shotgun should not be referred to as a rifle. Each has its own proper *nomenclature*, and the correct name should be used. Improper nomenclature can be used to *impeach the witness*, thereby eliminating or discrediting his or her testimony.

The professional witness and the lay witness are both governed by Rule 701 of the Federal Rules of Evidence.

Rule 701. Opinion Testimony by Lay Witnesses

If the witness is not testifying as an expert, the witness' testimony in the form of opinions or inferences is limited to those opinions or inferences which are (a) rationally based on the perception of the witness, and (b) helpful to a clear understanding of the witness' testimony or the determination of a fact in issue, and (c) not based on scientific, technical, or other specialized knowledge within the scope of Rule 702. (Pub. L. 93-595, § 1, Jan. 2, 1975, 88 Stat. 1937; Mar. 2, 1987, eff. Oct. 1, 1987; Apr. 17, 2000, eff. Dec. 1, 2000)

For example, the lay witness can testify to the odor of alcohol on a suspect's breath. He or she has no scientific base and has not performed any scientific tests. As a reasonable person who has smelled alcohol on the breath of family, friends, or associates, the lay witness has built within him- or herself a reasonable standard or developed a common everyday knowledge with which to compare to the suspect in question. The keys here are "reasonable" and "common everyday knowledge."

The Expert Witness

The expert witness is governed by Rule 702 of the Federal Rules of Evidence.

Rule 702. Testimony by Experts

If scientific, technical, or other specialized knowledge will assist the trier of fact to under-stand the evidence or to determine a fact in issue, a witness qualified as an expert by knowl-edge, skill, experience, training, or education, may testify thereto in the form of an opinion or otherwise, if (1) the testimony is based upon sufficient facts or data, (2) the testimony is the product of reliable principles and methods, and (3) the witness has applied the principles and methods reliably to the facts of the case. (Pub. L. 93-595, § 1, Jan. 2, 1975, 88 Stat. 1937; Apr. 17, 2000, eff. Dec. 1, 2000)

Notes of the Advisory Committee

An intelligent evaluation of facts is often difficult or impossible without the application of some scientific, technical, or other specialized knowledge. The most common source of this knowledge is the expert witness, although there are other techniques for supplying it. Most of the literature assumes that experts testify only in the form of opinions. The assumption is logically unfounded. The rule accordingly recognizes that an expert on the stand may give a dissertation or exposition of scientific or other principles relevant to the case, leaving the trier of fact to apply them to the facts. Since much of the criticism of expert testimony has centered upon the hypothetical question, it seems wise to recognize that opinions are not indispens-able and to encourage the use of expert testimony in non-opinion form when counsel believes the trier can itself draw the requisite inference. The use of opinions is not abolished by the rule, however. It will continue to be permissible for the experts to take the further step of suggesting the inference which should be drawn from applying the specialized knowledge to the facts. See Rules 703 to 705. Whether the situation is a proper one for the use of expert testimony is to be determined on the basis of assisting the trier. "There is no more certain test for determining when experts may be used than the common sense inquiry whether the untrained layman would be qualified to determine intelligently and to the best possible degree the particular issue without enlightenment from those having a specialized understanding of the subject involved in the dispute." Ladd, Expert Testimony, 5 Vand.L.Rev. 414, 418 (1952). When opinions are excluded, it is because they are unhelpful and therefore superfluous and a waste of time. 7 Wigmore § 1918. The rule is broadly phrased. The fields of knowledge which may be drawn upon are not limited merely to the "scientific" and "technical" but extend to all "specialized" knowledge. Similarly, the expert is viewed, not in a narrow sense, but as a person qualified by "knowledge, skill, experience, training or education." Thus within the scope of the rule are not only experts in the strictest sense of the word, e.g., physicians, physicists, and architects, but also the large group sometimes called "skilled" witnesses, such as bankers or landowners testifying to land values.

Committee Notes on Rules, 2000 Amendment

Rule 702 has been amended in response to *Daubert v. Merrell Dow Pharmaceuticals, Inc.*, 509 U.S. 579 (1993), and to the many cases applying *Daubert*, including *Kumho Tire Co. v. Carmichael*, 119 S.Ct. 1167 (1999). In *Daubert* the Court charged trial judges with the responsibility of acting as gatekeepers to exclude unreliable expert testimony, and the Court in *Kumho* clarified that this gatekeeper function applies to all expert testimony, not just tes-timony based in science. See also *Kumho*, 119 S.Ct. at 1178 (citing the Committee Note to the proposed amendment to Rule 702, which had been released for public comment before the date of the *Kumho* decision). The amendment affirms the trial court's role as gatekeeper and provides some general standards that the trial court must use to assess the reliability and helpfulness of proffered expert testimony. Consistently with *Kumho*, the Rule as amended provides that all types of expert testimony present questions of admissibility for the trial court in deciding whether the evidence is reliable and helpful. Consequently, the admissibility of all expert testimony is governed by the principles of Rule 104(a). Under that Rule, the proponent has the burden of establishing that the pertinent admissibility requirements are met by a preponderance of the evidence. See *Bourjaily v. United States*, 483 U.S. 171 (1987).

Daubert set forth a nonexclusive checklist for trial courts to use in assessing the reliability of scientific expert testimony. The specific factors explicated by the *Daubert* Court are (1) whether the expert's technique or theory can be or has been tested—that is, whether the expert's theory can be challenged in some objective sense, or whether it is instead simply a subjective, conclusory approach that cannot reasonably be assessed for reliability; (2) whether the technique or theory has been subject to peer review and publication; (3) the known or potential rate of error of the technique or theory when applied; (4) the existence and maintenance of standards and controls; and (5) whether the technique or theory has been generally accepted in the scientific community. The Court in *Kumho* held that these factors might also be applicable in assessing the reliability of nonscientific expert testimony, depending upon "the particular circumstances of the particular case at issue." 119 S.Ct. at 1175.

No attempt has been made to "codify" these specific factors. *Daubert* itself emphasized that the factors were neither exclusive nor dispositive. Other cases have recognized that not all of the specific *Daubert* factors can apply to every type of expert testimony. In addition to *Kumho*, 119 S.Ct. at 1175, see *Tyus v. Urban Search Management*, 102 F.3d 256 (7th Cir. 1996) (noting that the factors mentioned by the Court in *Daubert* do not neatly apply to expert testimony from a sociologist). See also *Kannankeril v. Terminix Int'l, Inc.*, 128 F.3d 802, 809 (3d Cir. 1997) (holding that lack of peer review or publication was not dispositive where the expert's opinion was supported by "widely accepted scientific knowledge"). The standards set forth in the amendment are broad enough to require consideration of any or all of the specific *Daubert* factors where appropriate. Courts both before and after *Daubert* have found other factors relevant in determining whether expert testimony is sufficiently reliable to be considered by the trier of fact. These factors include:

(1) Whether experts are "proposing to testify about matters growing naturally and directly out of research they have conducted independent of the litigation, or whether they have developed their opinions expressly for purposes of testifying." *Daubert v. Merrell Dow Pharmaceuticals, Inc.*, 43 F.3d 1311, 1317 (9th Cir. 1995).

(2) Whether the expert has unjustifiably extrapolated from an accepted premise to an unfounded conclusion. See *General Elec. Co. v. Joiner*, 522 U.S. 136, 146 (1997) (noting that in some cases a trial court "may conclude that there is simply too great an analytical gap between the data and the opinion proffered").

(3) Whether the expert has adequately accounted for obvious alternative explanations. See *Claar v. Burlington N.R.R.*, 29 F.3d 499 (9th Cir. 1994) (testimony excluded where the expert failed to consider other obvious causes for the plaintiff's condition). Compare *Ambrosini v. Labarraque*, 101 F.3d 129 (D.C.Cir. 1996) (the possibility of some unelimined causes presents a question of weight, so long as the most obvious causes have been considered and reasonably ruled out by the expert).

(4) Whether the expert "is being as careful as he would be in his regular professional work outside his paid litigation consulting." *Sheehan v. Daily Racing Form, Inc.*, 104 F.3d 940, 942 (7th Cir. 1997). See *Kumho Tire Co. v. Carmichael*, 119 S.Ct. 1167, 1176 (1999) (*Daubert* requires the trial court to assure itself that the expert "employs in the courtroom the same level of intellectual rigor that characterizes the practice of an expert in the relevant field").

(5) Whether the field of expertise claimed by the expert is known to reach reliable results for the type of opinion the expert would give. See *Kumho Tire Co. v. Carmichael*, 119 S.Ct. 1167, 1175 (1999) (*Daubert's* general acceptance factor does not "help show that an expert's testimony is reliable where the discipline itself lacks reliability, as, for example, do theories grounded in any so-called generally accepted principles of astrology or necromancy."); *Moore v. Ashland Chemical, Inc.*, 151 F.3d 269 (5th Cir. 1998) (en banc) (clinical doctor was properly precluded from testifying to the toxicological cause of the plaintiff's respiratory problem, where the opinion was not sufficiently grounded in scientific methodology); *Sterling v. Velsicol Chem. Corp.*, 855 F.2d 1188 (6th Cir. 1988) (rejecting testimony based on "clinical ecology" as unfounded and unreliable).

All of these factors remain relevant to the determination of the reliability of expert testimony under the Rule as amended. Other factors may also be relevant. See *Kumho*, 119 S.Ct. 1167, 1176 ("[W]e conclude that the trial judge must have considerable leeway in deciding in a particular case how to go about determining whether particular expert testimony is reliable."). Yet no single factor is necessarily dispositive of the reliability of a particular expert's testimony. See, e.g., *Heller v. Shaw Industries, Inc.*, 167 F.3d 146, 155 (3d Cir. 1999) ("not only must each stage of the expert's testimony be reliable, but each stage must be evaluated practically and flexibly without bright-line exclusionary (or inclusionary) rules."); *Daubert v. Merrell Dow Pharmaceuticals, Inc.*, 43 F.3d 1311, 1317, n.5 (9th Cir. 1995) (noting that some expert disciplines "have the courtroom as a principal theatre of operations" and as to these disciplines "the fact that the expert has developed an expertise principally for purposes of litigation will obviously not be a substantial consideration."). A review of the case law after *Daubert* shows that the rejection of expert testimony is the exception rather than the rule. *Daubert* did not work a "seachange over federal evidence law," and "the trial court's role as gatekeeper is not intended to serve as a replacement for the adversary system." *United States v. 14.38 Acres of Land Situated in Leflore County, Mississippi*, 80 F.3d 1074, 1078 (5th Cir. 1996). As the Court in *Daubert* stated: "Vigorous cross-examination, presentation of contrary evidence, and careful instruction on the burden of proof are the traditional and appropriate means of attacking shaky but admissible evidence." 509 U.S. at 595. Likewise, this amendment is not intended to provide an excuse for an automatic challenge to the testimony of every expert. See *Kumho Tire Co. v. Carmichael*, 119 S.Ct. 1167, 1176 (1999) (noting that the trial judge has the discretion "both to avoid unnecessary 'reliability' proceedings in ordinary cases where the reliability of an expert's methods is properly taken for granted, and to require appropriate proceedings in the less usual or more complex cases where cause for questioning the expert's reliability arises").

When a trial court, applying this amendment, rules that an expert's testimony is reliable, this does not necessarily mean that contradictory expert testimony is unreliable. The amendment is broad enough to permit testimony that is the product of competing principles or methods in the same field of expertise. See, e.g., *Heller v. Shaw Industries, Inc.*, 167 F.3d 146, 160 (3d Cir. 1999) (expert testimony cannot be excluded simply because the expert uses one test rather than another, when both tests are accepted in the field and both reach reliable results). As the court stated in *In re Paoli R.R. Yard PCB Litigation*, 35 F.3d 717, 744 (3d Cir. 1994), proponents "do not have to demonstrate to the judge by a preponderance of the evidence that the assessments of their experts are correct, they only have to demonstrate by a preponderance of evidence that their opinions are reliable. . . . The evidentiary requirement of reliability is lower than the merits standard of correctness." See also *Daubert v. Merrell Dow Pharmaceuticals, Inc.*, 43 F.3d 1311, 1318 (9th Cir. 1995) (scientific experts might be permitted to testify if they could show that the methods they used were also employed by "a recognized minority of scientists in their field."); *Ruiz-Troche v. Pepsi Cola*, 161 F.3d 77, 85 (1st Cir. 1998) ("*Daubert* neither requires nor empowers trial courts to determine which of several competing scientific theories has the best provenance.").

The Court in *Daubert* declared that the "focus, of course, must be solely on principles and methodology, not on the conclusions they generate." 509 U.S. at 595. Yet as the Court later recognized, "conclusions and methodology are not entirely distinct from one another." *General Elec. Co. v. Joiner*, 522 U.S. 136, 146 (1997). Under the amendment, as under *Daubert*, when an expert purports to apply principles and methods in accordance with professional standards, and yet reaches a conclusion that other experts in the field would not reach, the trial court may fairly suspect that the principles and methods have not been faithfully applied. See *Lust v. Merrell Dow Pharmaceuticals, Inc.*, 89 F.3d 594, 598 (9th Cir. 1996). The amendment specifically provides that the trial court must scrutinize not only the principles and methods used by the expert, but also whether those principles and methods have been properly applied to the facts of the case. As the court noted in *In re Paoli R.R. Yard PCB Litig.*, 35 F.3d 717, 745 (3d Cir. 1994), "*any* step that renders the analysis unreliable . . . renders the expert's testimony inadmissible. *This is true whether the step completely changes a reliable methodology or merely misapplies that methodology.*"

If the expert purports to apply principles and methods to the facts of the case, it is important that this application be conducted reliably. Yet it might also be important in some cases for an expert to educate the fact finder about general principles, without ever attempting to apply these principles to the specific facts of the case. For example, experts might instruct the fact finder on the principles of thermodynamics, or blood clotting, or on how financial markets respond to corporate reports, without ever knowing about or trying to tie their testimony into the facts of the case. The amendment does not alter the venerable practice of using expert testimony to educate the fact finder on general principles. For this kind of generalized testimony, Rule 702 simply requires that: (1) the expert be qualified; (2) the testimony address a subject matter on which the fact finder can be assisted by an expert; (3) the testimony be reliable; and (4) the testimony "fit" the facts of the case.

As stated earlier, the amendment does not distinguish between scientific and other forms of expert testimony. The trial court's gatekeeping function applies to testimony by any expert. See *Kumho Tire Co. v. Carmichael*, 119 S.Ct. 1167, 1171 (1999) ("We conclude that *Daubert's* general holding—setting forth the trial judge's general 'gatekeeping' obligation—applies not only to testimony based on 'scientific' knowledge, but also to testimony based on 'technical' and 'other specialized' knowledge."). While the relevant factors for determining reliability will vary from expertise to expertise, the amendment rejects the premise that an expert's testimony should be treated more permissively simply because it is outside the realm of science. An opinion from an expert who is not a scientist should receive the same degree of scrutiny for reliability as an opinion from an expert who purports to be a scientist. See *Watkins v. Telsmith, Inc.*, 121 F.3d 984, 991 (5th Cir. 1997) ("[I]t seems exactly backwards that experts who purport to rely on general engineering principles and practical experience might escape screening by the district court simply by stating that their conclusions were not reached by any particular method or technique."). Some types of expert testimony will be more objectively verifiable, and subject to the expectations of falsifiability, peer review, and publication, than others. Some types of expert testimony will not rely on anything like a scientific method, and so will have to be evaluated by reference to other standard principles attendant to the particular area of expertise. The trial judge in all cases of proffered expert testimony must find that it is properly grounded, well-reasoned, and not speculative before it can be admitted. The expert's testimony must be grounded in an accepted body of learning or experience in the expert's field, and the expert must explain how the conclusion is so grounded. See, e.g., American College of Trial Lawyers, *Standards and Procedures for Determining the Admissibility of Expert Testimony after Daubert*, 157 F.R.D. 571, 579 (1994) ("[W]hether the testimony concerns economic principles, accounting standards, property valuation or other non-scientific subjects, it should be evaluated by reference to the 'knowledge and experience' of that particular field.").

The amendment requires that the testimony must be the product of reliable principles and methods that are reliably applied to the facts of the case. While the terms "principles" and "methods" may convey a certain impression when applied to scientific knowledge, they remain relevant when applied to testimony based on technical or other specialized knowledge. For example, when a law enforcement agent testifies regarding the use of code words in a drug transaction, the principle used by the agent is that participants in such transactions regularly use code words to conceal the nature of their activities. The method used by the agent is the application of extensive experience to analyze the meaning of the conversations. So long as the principles and methods are reliable and applied reliably to the facts of the case, this type of testimony should be admitted.

Nothing in this amendment is intended to suggest that experience alone—or experience in conjunction with other knowledge, skill, training, or education—may not provide a sufficient foundation for expert testimony. To the contrary, the text of Rule 702 expressly contemplates that an expert may be qualified on the basis of experience. In certain fields, experience is the predominant, if not sole, basis for a great deal of reliable expert testimony. See, e.g., *United States v. Jones*, 107 F.3d 1147 (6th Cir. 1997) (no abuse of discretion in admitting the testimony of a handwriting examiner who had years of practical experience and extensive training, and who explained his methodology in detail); *Tassin v. Sears Roebuck*, 946 F.Supp. 1241, 1248 (M.D.La. 1996) (design engineer's testimony can be admissible when the expert's opinions "are based on facts, a reasonable investigation, and traditional technical/mechanical expertise, and he provides a reasonable link between the information and procedures he uses and the conclusions he reaches"). See also *Kumho Tire Co. v. Carmichael*, 119 S.Ct. 1167, 1178 (1999) (stating that "no one denies that an expert might draw a conclusion from a set of observations based on extensive and specialized experience.").

If the witness is relying solely or primarily on experience, then the witness must explain how that experience leads to the conclusion reached, why that experience is a sufficient basis for the opinion, and how that experience is reliably applied to the facts. The trial court's gatekeeping function requires more than simply "taking the expert's word for it." See *Daubert v. Merrell Dow Pharmaceuticals, Inc.*, 43 F.3d 1311, 1319 (9th Cir. 1995) ("We've been presented with only the experts' qualifications, their conclusions and their assurances of reliability. Under *Daubert*, that's not enough."). The more subjective and controversial the expert's inquiry, the more likely the testimony should be excluded as unreliable. See *O'Conner v. Commonwealth Edison Co.*, 13 F.3d 1090 (7th Cir. 1994) (expert testimony based on a completely subjective methodology held properly excluded). See also *Kumho Tire Co. v. Carmichael*, 119 S.Ct. 1167, 1176 (1999) ("[I]t will at times be useful to ask even of a witness whose expertise is based purely on experience, say, a perfume tester able to distinguish among 140 odors at a sniff, whether his preparation is of a kind that others in the field would recognize as acceptable.").

Subpart (1) of Rule 702 calls for a quantitative rather than qualitative analysis. The amendment requires that expert testimony be based on sufficient underlying "facts or data." The term "data" is intended to encompass the reliable opinions of other experts. See the original Advisory Committee Note to Rule 703. The language "facts or data" is broad enough to allow an expert to rely on hypothetical facts that are supported by the evidence. *Id.*

When facts are in dispute, experts sometimes reach different conclusions based on competing versions of the facts. The emphasis in the amendment on "sufficient facts or data" is not intended to authorize a trial court to exclude an expert's testimony on the ground that the court believes one version of the facts and not the other.

There has been some confusion over the relationship between Rules 702 and 703. The amendment makes clear that the sufficiency of the basis of an expert's testimony is to be decided under Rule 702. Rule 702 sets forth the overarching requirement of reliability, and an analysis of the sufficiency of the expert's basis cannot be divorced from the ultimate reliability of the expert's opinion. In contrast, the "reasonable reliance" requirement of Rule 703 is a relatively narrow inquiry. When an expert relies on inadmissible information, Rule 703 requires the trial court to determine whether that information is of a type reasonably relied on by other experts in the field. If so, the expert can rely on the information in reaching an opinion. However, the question whether the expert is relying on a *sufficient* basis of information—whether admissible information or not—is governed by the requirements of Rule 702.

The amendment makes no attempt to set forth procedural requirements for exercising the trial court's gatekeeping function over expert testimony. See Daniel J. Capra, *The Daubert Puzzle*, 38 Ga.L.Rev. 699, 766 (1998) ("Trial courts should be allowed substantial discretion in dealing with *Daubert* questions; any attempt to codify procedures will likely give rise to unnecessary changes in practice and create difficult questions for appellate review."). Courts have shown considerable ingenuity and flexibility in considering challenges to expert testimony under *Daubert*, and it is contemplated that this will continue under the amended Rule. See, e.g., *Cortes-Irizarry v. Corporacion Insular*, 111 F.3d 184 (1st Cir. 1997) (discussing the application of *Daubert* in ruling on a motion for summary judgment); *In re Paoli R.R. Yard PCB Litig.*, 35 F.3d 717, 736, 739 (3d Cir. 1994) (discussing the use of *in limine* hearings); *Claar v. Burlington N.R.R.*, 29 F.3d 499, 502–05 (9th Cir. 1994) (discussing the trial court's technique of ordering experts to submit serial affidavits explaining the reasoning and methods underlying their conclusions).

The amendment continues the practice of the original Rule in referring to a qualified witness as an "expert." This was done to provide continuity and to minimize change. The use of the term "expert" in the Rule does not, however, mean that a jury should actually be informed that a qualified witness is testifying as an "expert." Indeed, there is much to be said for a practice that prohibits the use of the term "expert" by both the parties and the court at trial. Such a practice "ensures that trial courts do not inadvertently put their stamp of authority" on a witness's opinion, and protects against the jury's being "overwhelmed by the so-called 'experts'." Hon. Charles Richey, *Proposals to Eliminate the Prejudicial Effect of the Use of the Word "Expert" Under the Federal Rules of Evidence in Criminal and Civil Jury Trials*, 154 F.R.D. 537, 559 (1994) (setting forth limiting instructions and a standing order employed to prohibit the use of the term "expert" in jury trials).

GAP Report—Proposed Amendment to Rule 702

The Committee made the following changes to the published draft of the proposed amendment to Evidence Rule 702:

1. The word "reliable" was deleted from Subpart (1) of the proposed amendment, in order to avoid an overlap with Evidence Rule 703, and to clarify that an expert opinion need not be excluded simply because it is based on hypothetical facts. The Committee Note was amended to accord with this textual change.

2. The Committee Note was amended throughout to include pertinent references to the Supreme Court's decision in *Kumho Tire Co. v. Carmichael*, which was rendered after the proposed amendment was released for public comment. Other citations were updated as well.

3. The Committee Note was revised to emphasize that the amendment is not intended to limit the right to jury trial, nor to permit a challenge to the testimony of every expert, nor to preclude the testimony of experience-based experts, nor to prohibit testimony based on competing methodologies within a field of expertise.

4. Language was added to the Committee Note to clarify that no single factor is necessarily dispositive of the reliability inquiry mandated by Evidence Rule 702.

Rule 703. Bases of Opinion Testimony by Experts

The facts or data in the particular case upon which an expert bases an opinion or inference may be those perceived by or made known to the expert at or before the hearing. If of a type reasonably relied upon by experts in the particular field in forming opinions or inferences upon the subject, the facts or data need not be admissible in evidence in order for the opinion or inference to be admitted. Facts or data that are otherwise inadmissible shall not be disclosed to the jury by the proponent of the opinion or inference unless the court determines that their probative value in assisting the jury to evaluate the expert's opinion substantially outweighs their prejudicial effect. (Pub. L. 93–595, § 1, Jan. 2, 1975, 88 Stat. 1937; Mar. 2, 1987, eff. Oct. 1, 1987; Apr. 17, 2000, eff. Dec. 1, 2000.)

Notes of Committee on Rules

Facts or data upon which expert opinions are based may, under the rule, be derived from three possible sources. The first is the firsthand observation of the witness, with opinions based thereon traditionally allowed. A treating physician affords an example. Rheingold, The Basis of Medical Testimony, 15 Vand.L.Rev. 473, 489 (1962). Whether he must first relate his observations is treated in Rule 705. The second source, presentation at the trial, also reflects existing practice. The technique may be the familiar hypothetical question or having the expert attend the trial and hear the testimony establishing the facts. Problems of determining what testimony the expert relied upon, when the latter technique is employed and the testimony is in conflict, may be resolved by resort to Rule 705. The third source contemplated by the rule consists of presentation of data to the expert outside of court and other than by his own perception. In this respect the rule is designed to broaden the basis for expert opinions beyond that current in many jurisdictions and to bring the judicial practice into line with the practice of the experts themselves when not in court. Thus a physician in his own practice bases his diagnosis on information from numerous sources and of considerable variety, including statements by patients and relatives, reports and opinions from nurses, technicians and other doctors, hospital records, and X rays. Most of them are admissible in evidence, but only with the expenditure of substantial time in producing and examining various authenticating witnesses. The physician makes life-and-death decisions in reliance upon them. His validation, expertly performed and subject to cross-examination, ought to suffice for judicial purposes. Rheingold, *supra*, at 531; McCormick § 15. A similar provision is California Evidence Code § 801(b).

The rule also offers a more satisfactory basis for ruling upon the admissibility of public opinion poll evidence. Attention is directed to the validity of the techniques employed rather than to relatively fruitless inquiries whether hearsay is involved. See Judge Feinberg's careful analysis in *Zippo Mfg. Co. v. Rogers Imports, Inc.*, 216 F.Supp. 670 (S.D.N.Y. 1963). See also Blum et al, The Art of Opinion Research: A Lawyer's Appraisal of an Emerging Service, 24 U.Chi.L.Rev. 1 (1956); Bonynge, Trademark Surveys and Techniques and Their Use in Litigation, 48 A.B.A.J. 329 (1962); Zeisel, The Uniqueness of Survey Evidence, 45 Cornell L.Q. 322 (1960); Annot., 76 A.L.R.2d 919.

If it be feared that enlargement of permissible data may tend to break down the rules of exclusion unduly, notice should be taken that the rule requires that the facts or data "be of a type reasonably relied upon by experts in the particular field." The language would not warrant admitting in evidence the opinion of an "accidentologist" as to the point of impact in an automobile collision based on statements of bystanders, since this requirement is not satisfied. See Comment, Cal.Law Rev.Comm'n, Recommendation Proposing an Evidence Code 148.150 (1965).

Qualifying an Expert Witness

An expert witness is a specialist in a subject who may present his or her expert opinion *without being a witness* to the occurrence related to the lawsuit or criminal case. If the expert is qualified by evidence of his or her expertise, training, or special knowledge, the witness is an exception to the rule against providing an opinion as testimony. The attorney for the party calling the expert must show the expert's qualifications if they are challenged, and the *trial judge* has the discretion to rule if he or she is qualified as an expert or is limited on the subjects on which he or she is qualified as an expert.

The expert witness, unlike the eyewitness or the lay witness, *can render an opinion* on a specific matter for which he or she has been qualified. The expert witness *may be* limited or restricted by the court to testify regarding a specific matter within his or her field of expertise.

Before testifying, the expert witness must be qualified. The lawyer who has hired the expert will attempt to establish that his or her expert is sufficiently qualified during direct examination on voir dire. The opposing lawyer may cross-examine the expert to show that the person's qualifications or competence is inadequate. The court will then rule on whether the expert will be accepted as an expert witness. The following questions are designed to assist attorneys in qualifying an expert in forensic dentistry and in particular on bite mark evidence. The questions are designed to focus on a candidate's background, knowledge, training, education, skill, and experience. The quality of the expert (and usually the expertise) will most certainly be affected by the answers provided to the following sample questions that may be used in qualifying the expert witness.

General

What is your name?
What is your current occupation?
What other positions have you held?
What are your degrees?
What specialized training have you had?
How long have you been engaged in the practice of forensic imaging?

Practice

How long have you been engaged in the practice of forensic imaging?
By whom have you been employed as a forensic expert?
Have you been employed in an official capacity by a government agency as a forensic expert?
What agencies?
What are your duties with the agency?
How many forensic cases have you done for the agency?
How many forensic cases have you done for other agencies?

Certification

Do you hold any certifications?
How many years have you been certified?

Membership in Forensic Organizations

Of which professional forensic-related organizations are you a member?
What is your current status with these organizations?
Have you held any post within any of these organizations?
How long have you been a member of the American Academy of Forensic Sciences?

Studies and Continuing Education

What, when, and where have you undertaken any studies in forensic science and in particular in forensic imaging?
What, when, and where have you followed continuing education courses?

Teaching of Forensic Science

Have you in the past or do you currently teach forensic science at an educational institution?
Where and when?

Lectures

Have you ever lectured on forensic science or evidence to a scientific or learned society (other than the university that employs you)?

Publications

Have you written any articles on forensic science or evidence for peer-reviewed scientific journals?
What are the titles, and when and where have they been published?

Research

Have you ever conducted any research in forensic science?
Have you given lectures on the results of this research?
When and where?
Have you published these results?
Where?

Court Experience

In how many cases involving forensic science or evidence have you testified as an expert witness in a court of law?
Name the cases, please.
Name the jurisdictions, please.

Reports

Under the amended Rule 26 of the Federal Rules of Civil Procedure in the United States expert witness reports must follow the following guidelines:

- The report must be prepared by the witness.
- The witness must sign the report.
- The report must include a complete statement of all opinions to be expressed.
- The bases and reasoning must be included.
- The data or other significant information considered by the expert in forming the opinion must be included.
- Exhibits to be used as a summary or as support must be included.
- All publications authored by the witness within the last ten years, regardless of relevance, must be listed.
- The compensation to be paid for this testimony and study must be included.
- A list of other cases in which this expert gave depositions or trial testimony within the last four years must be submitted with the report, without regard to relevance or relationship to the subject matter and issue.

Changes

As of December 1, 1993, the following changes to the Federal Rules of Civil Procedure in the United States became law:

Rule 16: Pretrial Conferences

- [(c)(4)]Imposes restrictions and/or limitations on the use of expert testimony under Rule 702 of the Federal Rules of Evidence (addresses scientific, technical or other specialized knowledge) and allows such restrictions to be entered at pretrial conference.
- [(c)(15)] Allows orders limiting the time to present evidence during pretrial conference.

Rule 26: Discovery

- [(a)(l)(A,B,C)] All witnesses must be voluntarily identified and the subject matter of their testimony must be voluntarily presented to opposing counsel; all relevant documents must be identified; and damage calculations must be presented.
- [(a)(2)]Disclosure of expert testimony is required.
- [(3)(a)]Disclosure of all impeachment of evidence and witnesses must take place during the pretrial conference.
- [(a)(5)]All former discovery devices, such as depositions and interrogatories, are preserved by the new Rules.
- [(b)(4)]Allows expert depositions only after experts file reports. Also allows for discovery of non-testifying expert's opinion only under exceptional circumstances.
- [(b)(5)]Maintains privilege for consulting and non-testifying experts.
- [(c)]Allows for protective orders if discovery is embarrassing, oppressive or unduly burdensome.
- [(e)]Discovery must be supplemented or corrected as new information is learned.

Rule 30: Oral Depositions

- [(b)(1)]Reasonable notice is required for all depositions. Video depositions may be noticed without court order.
- [(2)]The court may limit how many times a deposition may be taken and may sanction parties for undo delay.

- [(b)(7)] Allows for phone depositions.
- [(e)]Experts have the right to read and sign their depositions.

Daubert

The following is a synopsis of the *Daubert* case:

Supreme Court of the United States

DAUBERT et ux., individually and as guardians and litem for DAUBERT, et al. v. MERRELL DOW PHARMACEUTICALS, INC.
certiorari to the United States Court of Appeals for the ninth circuit
No. 92-102. Argued March 30, 1993—Decided June 28, 1993

Petitioners, two minor children and their parents, alleged in their suit against respondent that the children's serious birth defects had been caused by the mothers' prenatal ingestion of Bendectin, a prescription drug marketed by respondent. The District Court granted respondent summary judgment based on a well credentialed expert's affidavit concluding, upon reviewing the extensive published scientific literature on the subject, that maternal use of Bendectin has not been shown to be a risk factor for human birth defects. Although petitioners had responded with the testimony of eight other well credentialed experts, who based their conclusion that Bendectin can cause birth defects on animal studies, chemical structure analyses, and the unpublished "reanalysis" of previously published human statistical studies, the court determined that this evidence did not meet the applicable "general acceptance" standard for the admission of expert testimony. The Court of Appeals agreed and affirmed, citing *Frye v. United States*, 54 App. D. C. 46, 47, 293 F. 1013, 1014, for the rule that expert opinion based on a scientific technique is inadmissible unless the technique is "generally accepted" as reliable in the relevant scientific community.

Held: The Federal Rules of Evidence, not Frye, provide the standard for admitting expert scientific testimony in a federal trial. pp. 4–17.

(a) Frye's "general acceptance" test was superseded by the Rules' adoption. The Rules occupy the field, *United States v. Abel*, 469 U.S. 45, 49, and, although the common law of evidence may serve as an aid to their application, id., at 51–52, respondent's assertion that they somehow assimilated Frye is unconvincing. Nothing in the Rules as a whole or in the text and drafting history of Rule 702, which specifically governs expert testimony, gives any indication that "general acceptance" is a necessary precondition to the admissibility of scientific evidence. Moreover, such a rigid standard would be at odds with the Rules' liberal thrust and their general approach of relaxing the traditional barriers to "opinion" testimony. pp. 4–8.

(b) The Rules—especially Rule 702—place appropriate limits on the admissibility of purportedly scientific evidence by assigning to the trial judge the task of ensuring that an expert's testimony both rests on a reliable foundation and is relevant to the task at hand. The reliability standard is established by Rule 702's requirement that an expert's testimony pertain to "scientific . . . knowledge," since the adjective "scientific" implies a grounding in science's methods and procedures, while the word "knowledge" connotes a body of known facts or of ideas inferred from such facts or accepted as true on good grounds. The Rule's requirement that the testimony "assist the trier of fact to understand the evidence or to determine a fact in issue" goes primarily to relevance by demanding a valid scientific connection to the pertinent inquiry as a precondition to admissibility. pp. 9–12.

(c) Faced with a proffer of expert scientific testimony under Rule 702, the trial judge, pursuant to Rule 104(a), must make a preliminary assessment of whether the testimony's underlying reasoning or methodology is scientifically valid and properly can be applied to the facts at issue. Many considerations will bear on the inquiry, including whether the theory or technique in question can be (and has been) tested, whether it has been subjected to peer review and publication, its known or potential error rate, and the existence and maintenance of standards controlling its operation, and whether it has attracted widespread acceptance within a relevant scientific community. The inquiry is a flexible one, and its focus must be solely on principles and methodology, not on the conclusions that they generate. Throughout, the judge should also be mindful of other applicable Rules. pp. 12–15.

(d) Cross-examination, presentation of contrary evidence, and careful instruction on the burden of proof, rather than wholesale exclusion under an uncompromising "general acceptance" standard, is the appropriate means by which evidence based on valid principles may be challenged. That even limited screening by the trial judge, on occasion, will prevent the jury from hearing of authentic scientific breakthroughs is simply a consequence of the fact that the Rules are not designed to seek cosmic understanding but, rather, to resolve legal disputes.

951 F. 2d 1128, vacated and remanded.

Blackmun, J., delivered the opinion for a unanimous Court with respect to Parts I and II-A, and the opinion of the Court with respect to Parts II-B, II-C, III, and IV, in which White, O'Connor, Scalia, Kennedy, Souter, and Thomas, JJ., joined. Rehnquist, C. J., filed an opinion concurring in part and dissenting in part, in which Stevens, J., joined.

Frye

The following is a synopsis of the *Frye* case:

Frye v. United States

54 App. D. C. 46, 293 F. 1013

No. 3968

Court of Appeals of District of Columbia

Submitted November 7, 1923 December 3, 1923, Decided

Before SMYTH, Chief Justice, VAN ORSDEL, Associate Justice, and MARTIN, Presiding Judge of the United States Court of Customs Appeals.

VAN ORSDEL, Associate Justice. Appellant, defendant below, was convicted of the crime of murder in the second degree, and from the judgment prosecutes this appeal.

A single assignment of error is presented for our consideration. In the course of the trial counsel for defendant offered an expert witness to testify to the result of a deception test made upon defendant. The test is described as the systolic blood pressure deception test. It is asserted that blood pressure is influenced by change in the emotions of the witness, and that the systolic blood pressure rises are brought about by nervous impulses sent to the sympathetic branch of the autonomic nervous system. Scientific experiments, it is claimed, have demonstrated that fear, rage, and pain always produce a rise of systolic blood pressure, and that conscious deception or falsehood, concealment of facts, or guilt of crime, accompanied by fear of detection when the person is under examination, raises the systolic blood pressure in a curve, which corresponds exactly to the struggle going on in the subject's mind, between fear and attempted control of that fear, as the examination touches the vital points in respect of which he is attempting to deceive the examiner.

In other words, the theory seems to be that truth is spontaneous, and comes without conscious effort, while the utterance of a falsehood requires a conscious effort, which is reflected in the blood pressure. The rise thus produced is easily detected and distinguished from the rise produced by mere fear of the examination itself. In the former instance, the pressure rises higher than in the latter, and is more pronounced as the examination proceeds, while in the latter case, if the subject is telling the truth, the pressure registers highest at the beginning of the examination, and gradually diminishes as the examination proceeds.

Prior to the trial defendant was subjected to this deception test, and counsel offered the scientist who conducted the test as an expert to testify to the results obtained. The offer was objected to by counsel for the government, and the court sustained the objection. Counsel for defendant then offered to have the proffered witness conduct a test in the presence of the jury. This also was denied.

Counsel for defendant, in their able presentation of the novel question involved, correctly state in their brief that no cases directly in point have been found. The broad ground, however, upon which they plant their case, is succinctly stated in their brief as follows:

"The rule is that the opinions of experts or skilled witnesses are admissible in evidence in those cases in which the matter of inquiry is such that inexperienced persons are unlikely to prove capable of forming a correct judgment upon it, for the reason that the subject-matter so far partakes of a science, art, or trade as to require a previous habit or experience or study in it, in order to acquire a knowledge of it. When the question involved does not lie within the range of common experience or common knowledge, but requires special experience or special knowledge, then the opinions of witnesses skilled in that particular science, art, or trade to which the question relates are admissible in evidence."

Numerous cases are cited in support of this rule. Just when a scientific principle or discovery crosses the line between the experimental and demonstrable stages is difficult to define. Somewhere in this twilight zone the evidential force of the principle must be recognized, and while courts will go a long way in admitting expert testimony deduced from a well-recognized scientific principle or discovery, the thing from which the deduction is made must be sufficiently established to have gained general acceptance in the particular field in which it belongs.

We think the systolic blood pressure deception test has not yet gained such standing and scientific recognition among physiological and psychological authorities as would justify the courts in admitting expert testimony deduced from the discovery, development, and experiments thus far made.

The judgment is affirmed.

For many years, the admissibility of expert scientific evidence was governed by law known as the *Frye* test, after a 1923 decision by the District of Columbia Court of Appeals in which it was first addressed. Under the *Frye* test, expert scientific evidence was admissible only if the principles on which it was based had gained "general acceptance" in the scientific community.

Despite its widespread adoption by the courts, this general acceptance standard was viewed by many as too restrictive because it sometimes barred testimony based on intellectually credible but somewhat novel or new scientific methods.

In *Daubert*, the Supreme Court was asked to decide whether the *Frye* test had been superceded by the adoption, in 1973, of the Federal Rules of Evidence. After all, Federal Rule of Evidence 702, the rule broadly governing the admissibility of expert testimony, did not even mention general acceptance, but simply provided: "If scientific, technical, or other specialized knowledge will assist the trier of fact to understand the evidence or to determine a fact in issue, a witness qualified as an expert by knowledge, skill, experience, training, or education, may testify thereto in the form of an opinion or otherwise" *Daubert v. Merrell Dow Pharmaceuticals*, 509 U.S. 579 (1993).

The majority opinion in *Daubert*, authored by Justice Blackmun, held that Rule 702 did indeed supplant *Frye*. This did not mean, however, that all expert testimony purporting to be scientific was now to be admissible without further ado. Rule 702 did require, after all, that the testimony actually be founded on "scientific knowledge." This implied, according to the Court, that the testimony must be grounded in the methods and procedures of science—also known as "the scientific method." Evidence thus grounded, said the Court, would possess the requisite scientific validity to establish evidentiary reliability.

The Court also noted the requirement for Rule 702 that expert testimony assist the trier of fact. This, according to *Daubert*, was primarily a question of relevance or "fit." The testimony must be sufficiently tied to the facts of the case, the Court held, to aid in the resolution of an issue in dispute.

The Court explicitly refused to adopt any "definitive checklist or test" for determining the reliability of expert scientific testimony, and emphasized the need to be flexible. The Court did list several factors listed in Rule 702 that it thought would commonly be pertinent:

- whether the theories and techniques employed by the scientific expert have been tested;
- whether they have been subjected to peer review and publication;
- whether the techniques employed by the expert have a known error rate;
- whether they are subject to standards governing their application; and
- whether the theories and techniques employed by the expert enjoy widespread acceptance.

The Court emphasized that the admissibility inquiry must focus "solely" on the expert's "principles and methodology" and "not on the conclusions that they generate."

To assuage fears that its ruling would result in a "free for all" in which juries would be confounded by "absurd and irrational pseudoscientific assertions," the Court emphasized the continued availability of traditional tools under the adversary system, including vigorous cross-examination, presentation of contrary evidence, and careful instructions to jurors on burdens of proof. The Court also noted the availability of other mechanisms of judicial control, including summary judgment and the ability to exclude confusing or prejudicial evidence under Federal Rule of Evidence 403.

In response to the fear that its new evidentiary standards would sometimes stifle courtroom debate, the Court acknowledged that those standards would occasionally prevent juries from "learning of authentic insights and innovations," but concluded that such was the inevitable consequence of evidentiary rules "designed not for the exhaustive search for cosmic understanding but for the particularized resolution of legal disputes" (Table 8.1).

Table 8.1   States Using *Daubert* as Opposed to *Frye*

Daubert	Frye	Other
Connecticut	Alaska	Alabama
Delaware	Arizona	Arkansas
Georgia	California	California
Indiana	Florida	Colorado
Kentucky	Illinois	Hawaii
Louisiana	Kansas	Idaho
North Carolina	Massachusetts	Iowa
Ohio	Maryland	Maine
Oklahoma	Michigan	Montana
Oregon	Minnesota	South Carolina
Rhode Island	Mississippi	Nevada
South Dakota	Missouri	North Dakota
Tennessee	Nebraska	Texas
Vermont	New Hampshire	Utah
Washington	New Jersey	Virginia
West Virginia	New Mexico	
Wyoming	New York	
	Pennsylvania	

Source: By permission of Kristi Bugajski, PhD candidate.

Enhancement of Images

9

Introduction

We enhance photo images to make them more usable, more understandable, and clearer so that the story the images tell can be more readily interpreted. This may be to see the friction ridges better in a developed latent fingerprint, to be able to identify the facial features of an individual, or to see detail better in shadows.

While we may enhance, we may not change. When change is used in relation to photo images, it can be interpreted as actually changing the image to show something different from what existed at the time the image was taken. We may use words such as enhance or adjust but not change. A chiropractor adjusts a patient's back. If the chiropractor spoke of changing the patient's back, a whole new meaning could be inferred concerning the manner of treatment used.

Scientific Working Group on Imaging Technology

To enhance images, there must be direction and guidance; this is provided by the Scientific Working Group on Imaging Technology (SWGIT). Remember, the "endgame" or final purpose of the work we do as crime scene investigators (CSIs), law enforcement officers, forensic scientists, laboratory analysts, and others involved in the field of justice is a *court of law*. It is here that the arguments of law, the introduction of evidence, and testimony are used in our criminal justice system.

History

The Technical Working Group on Imaging Technology was formed by the Federal Bureau of Investigation in December of 1997. In 1999, the name of the group was changed to the Scientific Working Group on Imaging Technology (SWGIT). From the beginning the group has been comprised of individuals from federal, state, and local law enforcement agencies, the American military, academia, foreign law enforcement agencies, and other researchers. Those selected for membership in the group are experienced professionals working in the field of imaging technology or a related field and demonstrate the willingness to participate by consulting on the release of best practices and guidelines for the use of imaging technology in the Criminal Justice System. All SWGIT documents represent the consensus opinion of this membership and should not be construed as the official policy of any of the represented agencies. (SWGIT, Section 1, 1.2 Version 3.2 2010.01.15)

The Mission Statement of SWGIT

The mission of the Scientific Working Group on Imaging Technology (SWGIT) is to facilitate the integration of imaging technologies and systems within the criminal justice system (CJS) by providing definitions and recommendations for the capture, storage, processing, analysis, transmission, and output of images. (SWGIT, Section 1, 1.1 Version 3.2 2010.01.15)

Admissibility of Digital Images

Digital imaging is an accepted practice in forensic science, law enforcement, and the courts. Relevant, properly authenticated digital images that accurately portray a scene or object are admissible in court. Digital images that have been enhanced are admissible when the enhancement can be explained by qualified personnel. (SWGIT, Section 1, 1.4 Version 3.2 2010.01.15)

The SWGIT document is a "living" document. This means that it changes as technology changes. It also reflects applicable court decisions. The SWGIT document is updated periodically as needed. The latest version of the document is posted online. I would suggest that you check the Web site (http://www.theiai.org/guidelines/swgit/) to see if there are changes that affect a particular question.

"Doctored" Images

When digital imaging was introduced as a possible replacement for film cameras, many individuals were skeptical that the images could be used in court because it was so easy to modify, change, and "doctor" the images. With software programs such as Photoshop, ACDC, Picasso, and many others, it is easy to insert or remove items that would change the entire meaning of the image.

Photo images could have people or items removed or inserted, which could easily fool a juror, a savvy prosecutor, or even an expert.

Film, on the other hand was accepted. It was said that it was extremely difficult to modify or change a photograph and even more difficult to modify or change the negative. Let me assure you that with the access to a well-equipped photo lab, modifying or changing a photograph is relatively easy. Things or persons can be removed or added. While working as a criminalistics investigator, experimenting in our photo lab, I placed my partner's head on a male model's body so seamlessly that my partner could not believe it. It can be done. With film, it is a long and laborious job.

With digital images, the same thing can be done, much faster, with much less training, and much better. Should digital photo imaging be banned in forensic work? Of course not. That would be like banning jet planes because they are faster, fly higher, and are more comfortable than propeller planes.

There are several "protections" in place to make digital photo images acceptable to the courts. First, there is the testimony of the photographer, such as the following:

Prosecutor: Detective, do these images that you have examined here today truly and accurately represent the crime scene on the day and time in question?
Detective: Yes sir, they do.

Your testimony under oath makes these photo images evidence. Second, a set of guidelines and recommendations set up by experts in their field, if followed, make the images conform to the laws and applicable court decisions.

Cover Letter, Richard W. Vorder Bruegge, Former SWGIT Chair

A cover letter of great significance was written on April 27, 2004, and signed by Richard W. Vorder Bruegge, the then-chair of the SWGIT:

Dear Colleague,

A number of law enforcement officials in North America have approached the Scientific Working Group on Imaging Technology (SWGIT) requesting guidance in developing policies and procedures to acquire and protect their digital image evidence. Many express concern regarding potential challenges to the integrity of digital images. With those individuals in mind, the SWGIT is pleased to present the attached document "Digital Imaging Procedure, Version 1.0," to the forensic community at large.

This document was published by the United Kingdom's Police Scientific Development Branch (PSDB), which has agreed to let us distribute it through the Forensic Science Communications. We are doing so because this document addresses the issues of digital image acquisition and integrity in a straightforward manner that is consistent with the guidelines and recommendations of SWGIT.

SWGIT strongly encourages agencies to incorporate the recommendations provided in this document within their own policies and procedures as they see fit. In doing so, agencies will be taking an important step to ensure the integrity of their digital image evidence.

Among the most critical fundamental ideas presented in this document is the concept of a "Master Copy," which serves as the digital equivalent of an original film negative or video tape. A "Master Copy" represents either a bit-for-bit duplicate of original digital files or as a digital copy of an analog recording that has been written to removable media, such as a compact disc or DVD-R. Once such a "Master Copy" has been generated, it can be handled using the same policies and procedures an agency would use to protect and preserve the integrity of an original film negative or video tape. As this "Digital Imaging Procedure, Version 1.0" points out, although it is commonly accepted that a credible manipulation of digital image files can be accomplished relatively easily, it is very difficult to conceal manipulation when the manipulated file is compared to the "Master" file. Thus, creation of a "Master Copy" represents the most critical step in any procedure involving digital image files.

Another important concept discussed within this document is the fact that imaging devices—whether they are film, video, or digital still cameras—do not duplicate (or clone) reality, but merely generate a visual representation of a subject. The degree to which an image represents a "life-like" simulation of reality will be a function of many factors, including such things as the type of camera used, the processing applied to the image, and the means by which the image is displayed. Agencies and personnel utilizing images should be cognizant of the capabilities and limitations of different technologies. Furthermore, agencies must develop policies and procedures and utilize technology that will enable them to generate images of sufficient quality to accomplish their given mission.

SWGIT notes that some of the guidance provided in this document may only apply to agencies operating within the United Kingdom. Agencies planning on implementing the guidelines within North America or elsewhere should take care to ensure that they meet statutory requirements within their jurisdiction.

The SWGIT will continue developing guidelines for the use of imaging technology in the criminal justice system. We will also continue to reach out to our international partners to identify similar documents and guidelines that will be of benefit to our local community. We hope you find this document of assistance in your work.

Sincerely,

Richard W. Vorder Bruegge
SWGIT Chair

The "Master Copy"

Enhancing an image is perfectly acceptable as long as you document what you do during the enhancements and you work from a copy. The master copy must remain untouched. The master copy is created by

- Uploading the images to a computer file folder.
- After they are uploaded to this folder, "burn" the contents of that file folder to a CD-R or DVD-R.
- Once this CD-R or DVD-R is created, checked to see that the burn was successful.
- Mark the CD with the case number, date, case name, and your signature or initials. Mark "Master Copy" on this disk.
- Place the master copy disk into an evidence envelope.
- Mark the appropriate information as required on the evidence envelope.
- Seal the envelope with evidence tape.
- Write your initials or signature across the tape and envelope, across both overlaps of the evidence tape, and on the bottom glued flap.
- Place this evidence in the evidence room.
- Additional copies made from the file on the computer should be labeled: Copy 1, case number, date, case name, and your initials.

Image Categories

The following is word for word from the SWGIT document (www.swgit.org [2010]):

SWGIT recognizes two fundamental categories, end uses for images encountered in the legal system.

Category 1

Category One images are used to demonstrate what the photographer or recording device witnessed but are not analyzed by subject matter experts. These can include, but are not limited, to the following:

- General crime scene or investigative images
- Surveillance images
- Autopsy images
- Documentation of items of evidence in a laboratory
- Arrest photographs, such as mug shots

What documentation is necessary? SWGIT recommends: When enhancing Category One images, one need only document the techniques with a standard operating procedure that describes the typical enhancement processes. If an original image previously treated as a Category One image is to be subjected to scientific analysis, it becomes a Category Two image.

Category 2

Subject matter experts use Category Two images for scientific analysis. These can include, but are not limited, to the following:

- Latent prints
- Questioned documents
- Impression evidence

- Patterned evidence
- Category 1 images to be subjected to analysis

What documentation is necessary: SWGIT recommends: The use and sequence of any enhancement techniques in Category Two images should be documented in every case.

Documenting image enhancement steps should be sufficient to permit a comparably trained person to understand the steps taken, the techniques used, and to extract comparable information from the image. Documenting every change in every pixel value is discouraged because it adds nothing of value to the analysis.

The degree to which procedures used in image enhancement should be documented will depend on the intended end use of the image. Furthermore, the nature of such documentation will depend on the procedures used. (SWGIT, Section 11, Version 1.3 2010.01.15)

SOPs: Standard Operating Procedures for Enhancing Photo Images

SWGIT recommends that a SOP (standard operating procedure) be instituted for the enhancing of photo images. If in court you are asked if you follow any specific procedures and you answer that you have an SOP, as recommended by SWGIT, the defense will have to attack the evidence from a different direction. A sample of a SOP is found in the SWGIT document, Section 11, Appendix—Sample Standard Operating Procedure.

Sample

Standard Operating Procedure

Title: Latent Print Image Processing Approval Date _____

Reviewer Signature _____

Technical Leader Signature Forensic Services Director Signature _____

Purpose: To establish a list of actions to enhance latent print images requested by latent print analysts.

Procedures:

1. Log into the agency-approved software application for processing latent prints.
2. Select the case containing the images to be processed.
3. On the menu bar, click Image, Enhance. The program will make a copy (working image) of the original image and import the copy and the enhanced image history into the agency-approved enhancement software application.
4. Process the working image using enhancement techniques. All processes applied to the working image are recorded using the enhanced image history tool. Approved processing techniques for use on working images are those that have direct counterparts in traditional darkrooms including brightness and contrast adjustment, dodging and burning, and color balancing. The tools include Brightness/Contrast, Levels, Curves, Color Balance, Hue/Saturation, and Invert. Using Mode, Channels, and Fast Fourier Transform filters (FFT) are acceptable. The following tools are prohibited: Rubber Stamp, Airbrush, Paintbrush, Paint Bucket, Eraser, and Blur.
5. After the working image is processed and the processes are recorded, save the changes to the processed working image. Import the processed working image back into the latent print processing application.
6. The operator may now process additional images, export a processed image for printing, or exit the application.

Safety Considerations: None.

Limitations: Based on existing equipment and technology.

Quality Control: Perform appropriate equipment maintenance to ensure proper capacity and quality performance.

(*SWGIT Section 11, Appendix—Sample Standard Operating Procedure*, Version 1.3 2010.01.15)

Note: Check the Web site (http://www.theiai.org/guidelines/swgit) for most current version of the document.

A sample of your agency's logging requirements should be included in your SOP.

Photo Image Enhancement Log

SWGIT advises that a number of ways can be used to document the enhancements: handwritten notes, logs, electronic recording, and automated logging tools in the software you use. I recommend that you use an enhancement log. The log is one more item that can be introduced as evidence in court. SWGIT states: "Documenting image enhancement steps should be sufficient to permit a comparably trained person to understand the steps taken, the techniques used, and to extract comparable information from the image" (SWGIT Version 1.3 2010.01.15). The use of a log can allow just about anyone to take the enhanced image, and by following the log in reverse, one can get back to the original unenhanced image (Table 9.1).

Photoshop

Photoshop is an excellent software package with which to enhance digital images. It is a bit pricey, but worth it. The new versions of Photoshop CS5 and Photoshop CS5 Extended are available and can be downloaded (you can get a 30-day free trial, after which you will have to purchase it; http://tryit.adobe.com/us/cs5/photoshopextended/).

George Reis has written a guide for Photoshop CS3, *Photoshop CS3 for Forensic Processing*. It is available from Amazon.com (ISBN 978-0-470-11454-4).

ACDSee Pro

ACDSee Pro is another software package that offers many of the same features (not all) as Photoshop. It is significantly less costly. It designates increments of change in numerical values. It is extremely easy to work with it.

Enhancing a Latent Fingerprint

We need to understand that there must be something there to work with in enhancing a latent fingerprint. In the old "wet" darkrooms, if we had a "light" negative (underexposed), it was difficult to make, from the negative, a good photographic print of the latent. If, on the other

Table 9.1 Photo Image Enhancement Log/Worksheet

| Worksheet for Image Number: _____ Case Number: _____ |
| Technician's Name: _____ Technicians Initials: _____ |
| Description of Image: _____Date: _____ |
| Software & Version Used: _____ |
| *Note:* Use one sheet for each photo image. |

Enhancement Number	Enhancement Type[a]	Amount of Enhancement	Imaged Save as	Notes
1				
2				
3				
4				
5				
6				
7				
8				
9				
10				
11				
12				
13				
14				
15				
16				
17				
18				
19				
20				

[a] Basic: Brightness and contrast adjustment, including dodging and burning, resizing (file interpolation), cropping, positive-to-negative inversion, image rotation/inversion, conversion to grayscale, white balance, color balancing or color correction, basic image sharpening and blurring (pixel averaging), deInterlacing, exposure. Advanced: Frame averaging, Fourier analysis (including the use of fast Fourier transformation [FFT]), deblur, noise reduction, image restoration, color channel selection and subtraction, perspective control or geometric correction, advanced sharpening tools, such as unsharp mask.

hand, we had a "thick" print (overexposed), the image was on the negative and was enhanced by "dodging" (holding back light in specific areas) while printing to the photographic paper.

If the digital image is so light, that there is nothing there, you cannot create something out of nothing.

When imaging latent lifts or developed latents, photo image in color, not black and white. With color, you have much more basic data to work with, and you can always convert to black and white in software.

Latent Lift

Let us begin with a dark print (Figure 9.1), a dark latent lift. We begin by adjusting the exposure, adding +100 increments. We enter the adjustment on the enhancement log and save the image as "latent_print_1_+100_exposure" (Figure 9.2).

Next, we increase contrast by +50. We enter that information in the log and save the image file as "latent_print_1_+100_exposure" (Figure 9.3).

We have considerable improvement, but we can do more. We increase fill by +66. Again, we enter the data in the log and save the image as "latent_print_1_+_66_fill_light" (Figure 9.4). We now add +53 more contrast to the image and record that information on the log and save the final image as "latent_print_1_+_53_contrast" (Figures 9.5 and 9.6). After we have completed our last adjustment, on the next line of the log write "end" and draw a single diagonal line (from left to right) from under the word *end* to the bottom right side of the log sheet. This prevents someone from entering data in the lines left blank (Figure 9.7).

Figure 9.1 Image of developed latent DCS2343.

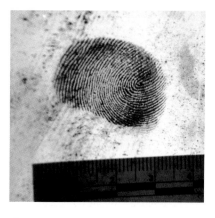

Figure 9.2 Image of developed latent +100 exposure.

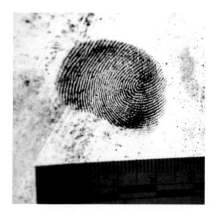

Figure 9.3 Image of developed latent +50 contrast.

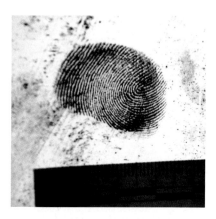

Figure 9.4 Image of developed latent +66 fill light.

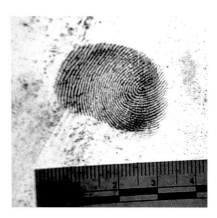

Figure 9.5 Image of developed latent +53 contrast.

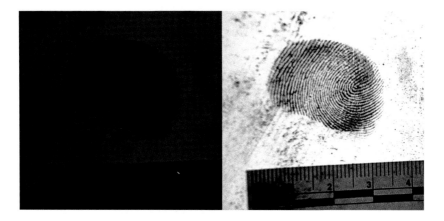

Figure 9.6 Image of original next to enhanced latent.

Bare Footprint Developed with Ninhydrin

We have a barefoot print developed by the ninhydrin chemical method. It is okay, but it could be a lot better. Examine Figure 9.8, DCS46781. We use our log again. We try adding and subtracting exposure. Neither does anything significant. If we do not apply it to the image, we do not have to log it. Next, we add 40 contrast. The image improves. We log it on the sheet and save the image as "footprint 1 +40 contrast" (Figure 9.9).

Next, let us subtract fill, −36 fill. We log the adjustment and save as "footprint −36 fill light" (Figure 9.10).

Now, under "levels," we adjust by +136 shadows. We log this and save as the image as "footprint 1 +136 shadows" (Figure 9.11).

The next step is modifying the color image to a grayscale image (black and white). We log the modification and save as the image as "footprint 1 grayscale" (Figure 9.12).

We next proceed to unsharp mask. We adjust the amount from +100 to +281. We again write the data in the log, then save the image as "footprint 1 unsharp mask from 100 to 28" (Figure 9.13). Last, we go back to shadows and set +107 to that adjustment. We log the data and save the image as "footprint 1 shadows +107" (Figure 9.14).

Photo Image Enhancement Log/Worksheet

Worksheet for Image Number 9-1 latent print 1 Case Number: 123456
Technician's Name: Your Name   Technicians Initials: YN
Description of Image: Latent Fingerprint Lift   Date 12-10-XX
Sofware and Version Used: ACDSee Ver. 10
Note: Use one sheet for each photo image

Enhancement Number	Enhancement Type*	Amount of Enhancement	Imaged save as	Notes
1	Exposure	+100	Latent_print_1_+100_exposure.png	Still dark
2	Contrast	+50	Latent_print_1_+50_contrast.png	More definition
3	Fill	+66	Latent_print_1_+66_fill_light.png	Define ridges
4	Contrast	+53	Latent_print_1_+53_contrast.png	
5	END			
6				
7				
8				
9				
10				
11				
12				
13				
14				
15				
16				
17				
18				
19				
20				

*Basic Brightness and contrast adjustment, including dodging and burning, Resising (file intergalation). Cropping. Positive to negative inversion, Image rotation inversion, Conversion to grayscale, White balance, Color balancing and/or color correction. Basic inage sharpening and blurring (pixel averaging.) De-Interlacing, Exposure
*Advanced Frame averaging. Fourier Analysis (including the use of FFT) Deluxe Noise reduction, Image retention, color channel selection and subtraction. Perspective control and/or geometric correction. Advanced sharpening tools, such as unsharp mask

Figure 9.7 Enhancement log for image of developed latent DCS2343.

You may have to go back to areas you previously adjusted. There may be 2 to 3 adjustments, or there may be over 20 (in which case you will need a second log sheet). You continue with the adjustment until you reach the results you are want.

After we have completed our last adjustment, on the next line of the log write "end" and draw a single diagonal line (from left to right) from under the word *end* to the bottom right side of the log sheet. This prevents someone from entering data in the lines left blank (Figure 9.15).

Figure 9.8 Image of developed ninhydrin footprint DCS4678.

Figure 9.9 Image of developed ninhydrin footprint +40 contrast.

Figure 9.10 Image of developed ninhydrin footprint –36 fill light.

Figure 9.11 Image of developed ninhydrin footprint +136 shadows.

Figure 9.12 Image of developed ninhydrin footprint convert to grayscale.

Figure 9.13 Image of developed ninhydrin footprint +181 unsharp mask.

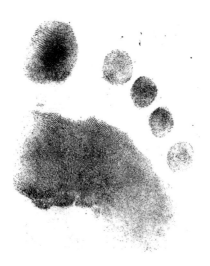

Figure 9.14 Image of developed ninhydrin footprint.

Photo Image Enhancement Log/Worksheet

Worksheet for Image Number 9-8 DSC4678   Case Number: 123999
Technician's Name: Your Name   Technicians Initials: _____ YN _____
Description of Image: Bare footprint - Ninhydrin   Date 12-10-XX
Sofware and Version Used: ACDSee Ver. 10
Note: Use one sheet for each photo image

Enhancement Number	Enhancement Type*	Amount of Enhancement	Imaged save as	Notes
1	Contrast	+40		
2	Fill	+36		
3	Shadows	+136		
4	Grayscale	Black and White		
5	Unsharp Mask	From 100 to 281		
6	Shadows	+107		
7	END			
8				
9				
10				
11				
12				
13				
14				
15				
16				
17				
18				
19				

*Basic Brightness and contrast adjustment, including dodging and burning, Resising (file intergalation). Cropping. Positive to negative inversion, Image rotation inversion, Conversion to grayscale, White balance, Color balancing and/or color correction. Basic inage sharpening and blurring (pixel averaging.) De-Interlacing, Exposure

*Advanced Frame averaging. Fourier Analysis (including the use of FFT) Deluxe Noise reduction, Image retention, color channel selection and subtraction. Perspective control and/or geometric correction. Advanced sharpening tools, such as unsharp mask

Figure 9.15 Enhancement log for image of developed latent DCS2343.

Footwear and Tire Impressions 10

Introduction

Photographing footwear and tire impressions is not as easy as it seems on TV. Remember, that is drama, and this is the real world. The TV crime scene investigator (CSI) walks up to the footwear impression, takes three or four pictures (at the same angle and with the same lighting), then moves on to the next shot. It does not work that way. We are not just trying to capture a picture of a footwear impression but, it is hoped, an artifact in the impression that will change it from a class identification to a unique identification. We have to deal with real lighting, real temperature, and real weather.

Your agency should have a standard operating procedure (SOP). Having a SOP will be a plus when you testify and can say, "I followed the SOP." The SOPs also give you a checklist that you can use when working. Checklists are great. They keep you from forgetting important details, and they give proof that you completed a specific task and all subtasks associated with that job.

Casting

You will want to cast the footwear or tire impression; however, you only get one chance, and if for some reason the casting material is bad, the water or dental stone (plaster) is not correct, or it is just a bad day, you could end up with nothing. Before you cast, photograph.

Equipment

The question regarding equipment needed is, "How large is your storage area for equipment?" I have always wondered about the TV CSI who walks into the crime scene caring one small equipment case. Whatever he or she needs happens to be in that case. This CSI never has to go back to the car to get something else—another bit of the drama.

- Digital camera. The Scientific Working Group on Imaging Technology (SWGIT) recommends a digital single-lens reflex (SLR) camera with at least 8-megapixel native resolution (SWGIT, Section 11, Version 1.3, 2010.01.150).
- Shutter release.
- Macro lens.
- Tripod. A tripod that allows the camera to point straight down (90 degrees to the footwear or tire impression) is appropriate.
- Strobe. Include a strobe that can be operated off the camera; this can use a slave, pc cord, radio, or in the case of Vivitar 283 and others similar to it, a cord that

allows the sensor to remain on the hot shoe of the camera, triggering the strobe off camera.
- Flat scales.
- Notebook.
- A white foam board approximately 18 × 18 inches. This board can be used to reflect light (additive lighting) or to block light (subtractive lighting).
- Small level.
- A large umbrella. You have to protect the impression if it starts to rain. Your camera also needs protection. You, on the other hand, need a rain suit or, if you are not prepared, you will get wet. A golf-style umbrella works well. Try to find one that does not have metal in it. Metal draws lightning.
- Fingerprint powder, fluorescent.

Footwear

After you have taken your overall shots, establishing shots, and perspective shots of the scene, set up your tripod so that the footwear impression is centered underneath the camera. You will want to turn off the autofocus. Manual focus gives you much more control over the camera.

Set your camera (using the menu) to the highest possible resolution. Also in the menu, set the camera to record images in a lossless format (e.g., TIFF or RAW).

Focus the camera on the bottom of the impression (Figure 10.1). This gives you the greatest depth of field. You should also close down your lens to f/16 or f/32; this also increases depth of field.

Remove the strobe from the camera, and either hold the strobe in your hands or use a small auxiliary tripod to place the strobe in an oblique position (approximately 45 degrees to the footwear impression). In Figure 10.2, a Vivitar 283 is in use. The strobe is connected to the camera by a cable. The cable runs from a trigger on the hot shoe (which also halos the sensor) to the strobe. This allows the flash (in the automatic mode) to read the light level from the camera regardless of where the actual strobe is located.

A number of shots should be taken. The ability to see the completed shot in the viewer of the digital camera is a great advantage. Remember, do not delete bad, out-of-focus, or unusable shots.

Figure 10.1 When focusing on a footwear impression, focus on the bottom or lowest portion of the footprint.

Figure 10.2 Camera setup for footwear impression in dirt, with flash off the camera.

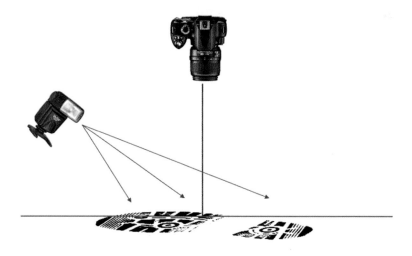

Figure 10.3 Camera setup with light from left.

Rotate the light in 120-degree increments (at a minimum). Continue to rotate the light source until you have the images that you want (Figures 10.3–10.5). Not only are you recording the print for class comparison, but also you are attempting to photo record an artifact (something that does not belong), such as an embedded stone in the sole of the shoe or a cut or gouge. If an artifact exists and can be recorded, it is possible that a *unique* identification can be made (Figure 10.6).

Other lighting techniques should also be employed. A plain white foam board that you can obtain from any office supply store makes an excellent reflector and an excellent shield. The board should be approximately 18 × 18 inches. There are times even when you are using the strobe off the camera, if there were additional light coming from another direction, it would light the footwear perfectly. (It is never going to be perfect, but we strive for perfection.)

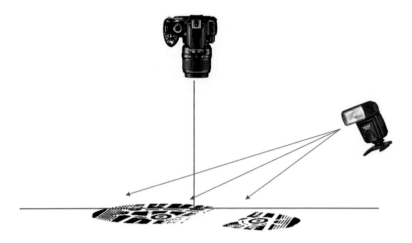

Figure 10.4 Camera setup with light from right.

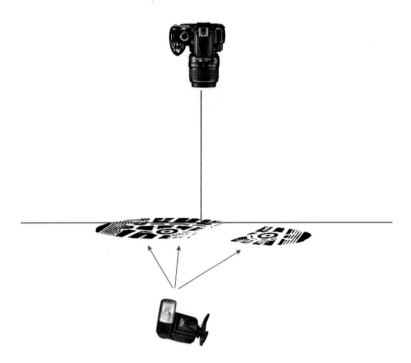

Figure 10.5 Camera setup with light from bottom.

Position the white board so that it acts like a reflector (see Figure 10.7). It takes the sunlight and redirects and focuses it on your target object. This is called *additive light* (Figure 10.8). Anytime you use additional light from a light source to assist in the ambient light, it is additive light. Remember, ambient light is the light that exists around your subject or object.

Just as we can add light, we can take it away. There are times that the sun may create too bright or harsh lighting to adequately image our footwear impression. In this case, we can use our white foam board again. This time instead of reflecting the light, we block the light (Figure 10.9). This is called *subtractive lighting*.

Figure 10.6 Footwear impressions with light coming from the right with scale.

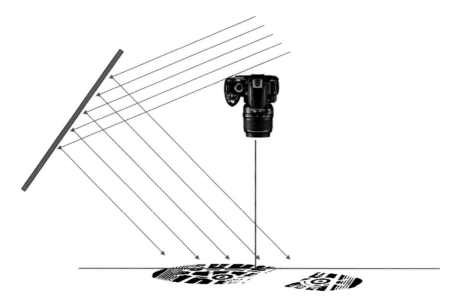

Figure 10.7 An example of reflected light.

These types of lighting are the same types that movie and portrait photographers use. You may have seen in documentaries in which a person is holding a large board, either reflecting or blocking the light from the subject of the camera.

After successful photography of the footwear impressions, you cast them as well. You can now use bench photography in the lab to photograph the castings; in the lab you can control the light and conditions much better than at the scene. As shown in Figure 10.8, you can use specific lighting, halogen/fiber optic, to highlight artifacts on a casting. You can rotate the casting instead of the lighting, which gives you much more control of the shot.

In the lab, you can both examine the casting and in addition to an overall shot of the footwear casting, you can move in for close-ups of specific areas. You will notice that in Figure 10.10 there is a scale, but it is not covering any part of the casting, only the bench. There is no exculpatory evidence on our bench, so we do not have to shoot it without a scale.

Figure 10.8 A setup using bench or rephotography in the lab to photograph a plaster cast. The light source is a fiber-optic multihalogen light.

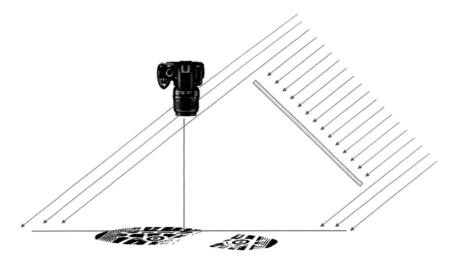

Figure 10.9 Subtractive lighting. The board is used to block the light coming from the right.

Figure 10.10 Image of a complete footwear plaster cast.

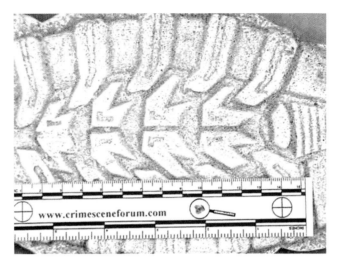

Figure 10.11 Close-up image of a partial plaster cast of a footwear impression with scale.

Figure 10.12 Close-up image of a partial plaster cast of a footwear impression without scale.

In Figures 10.11 and 10.12, we are imaging only a small area of the casting. There could be exculpatory evidence under the scale. We therefore shoot both with and without scale.

Also, please remember that evidence, this type of evidence especially, must be photographed at 90 degrees (Figure 10.13). If photographed at any other angle, there will be some distortion.

Tire Impressions

For photo imaging of tire impressions, we can actually say the previous discussion pertains with only several exceptions. A footwear impression displays itself as either a left foot or a right foot. Each footprint is about a maximum of 12 inches (unless the individual is in the National Basketball Association, in which case, it is slightly bigger). When we are searching for artifacts on footwear, we are basically relegated to two areas that are 12 × 5 inches (left and right feet).

Figure 10.13 Imaging at a 90-degree angle.

With a tire impression, there is a minimum of four wheels, and if it is an impression from a truck, it could mean even more. Another issue is the fact that a tire impression is not just the small area where the tire meets the road, but the entire circumference of the tire. So, if the diameter of the tire is 28 inches, we use the equation ($c = \pi \cdot d$.); then, the circumference is 87.96 inches (Figure 10.14). If from the tire impressions you are attempting to determine the type of tire used, then just the small area where the tire meets the road is good (Figure 10.15). A class-type identification can be made from this area. If, however, you are attempting to make a unique identification, a match, then you must photo document a minimum of 88 inches of the tire impression. This will allow a much better chance of finding an artifact (nail in tire, gouge, rip, tear, or other unique characteristic).

Figure 10.16 shows 87.96 inches of tire track (an inked impression of a tire with a diameter of 28 inches) taken from a suspect's vehicle. This is the known standard. An artifact exists in this standard.

A photo image of the entire tire track that was photographed at the scene is shown in Figure 10.17. If only the area between the two red lines in Figure 10.18 were photographed, comparison to the known standard would only yield class characteristics. If only the area between the two red lines in Figure 10.17 were photographed, one could make a unique

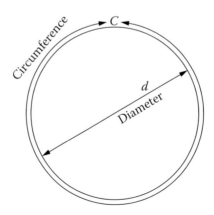

Figure 10.14 Circumference and its equation.

Figure 10.15 A plaster cast of a partial tire impression with scale.

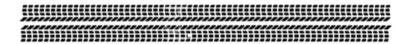

Figure 10.16 The complete tire track, 88 inches.

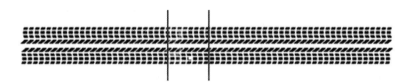

Figure 10.17 The complete tire track, 88 inches, the area or partial seen between the two red lines, with artifact.

Figure 10.18 The complete tire track, 88 inches, the area or partial seen between the two red lines, with no artifact.

identification due to the fact there is an artifact present that can be compared to the artifact from the known standard shown in Figure 10.16.

Fluorescent fingerprint powder can be used to highlight areas in tire impressions. I prefer green fluorescent powder; however, most other colors work just as well. It is best applied by using a device such as an atomizer or a method I developed at Purdue University that uses compressed air to evenly blow powder onto a surface (Jones Brush System) (Figures 10.19 and 10.20). The SWGIT recommends that if the impressions are processed with fingerprint powder or chemicals, the impressions should be rephotographed after each process (SWGIT, Section 9, Version 1.2, 2010.15).

Figure 10.19 Tire impression with scale.

Figure 10.20 Tire impression with scale treated with green fluorescent fingerprint powder.

Digital Panoramic Camera Scanning

11

Scene Scanning

I would be remiss if I did not address a budding technology that is rapidly inserting itself into the forensic photo imager's bag of tools. Laser technology used to be the only game in town to provide panoramic scene images and virtual scenes, but now digital photo imaging has invaded the field.

Laser systems are used to capture complete and detailed data, scanning locations to make virtual video images and stills of crime scenes. These systems are expensive, in most cases $25,000 and up. Several companies have produced an alternative to the laser systems. They use specialized digital cameras to accomplish the same goals with a number of advantages, one of the biggest being cost.

The Panoscan MK-3 is one such unit (Figure 11.1). The MK-3 is a third-generation panoramic camera. The MK-3 can scan a full 360-degree image in less than 8 seconds. MK-3 images can be presented as flat panoramic images. They can also be presented in most virtual reality players, such as QuickTime VR, Flash VR, or JAVA-based players.

This method of documenting a crime scene will not replace the digital still images that are taken at scenes, but in complicated and unusual situations, use of the Panoscan MK-3 has many advantages.

The System

The camera is set up on a special tripod, and two panoramas are scanned (Figure 11.2). Next, the images are processed to ensure geometric accuracy. Finally, the images are loaded into PanoMetric for measurements. The user simply points to any pixel in the scene, and accurate distance and spatial data are displayed. Point-to-point measurement is fast and accurate.

Once the points and measurements have been collected, the results can be saved in DXF format for use with popular computed-aided design (CAD) programs and three-dimensional (3D) modeling applications such as Cad Zone, AutoCAD, Maya, Lightwave 3D, and many more.

Photogrammetry

Photogrammetry is the practice of obtaining surveys by photography. The camera commonly is airborne with its axis vertical, but oblique and horizontal (ground-based) photographs also are applicable. Many industrial and laboratory measurement problems are solved by photogrammetry. Data reduction is accomplished by stereoscopic line-of-sight geometry with use of both analytical and analog methods.

Figure 11.1 Panoscan digital scanning camera. (Courtesy of Panoscan.)

Figure 11.2 Panoscan digital scanning camera with both upper and lower sections mounted on the tripod. (Courtesy of Panoscan.)

PanoMetric is accurate to fractions of an inch over a 25-foot radius. The high resolution and repeatability of the Panoscan system is most accurate relative to spatial measurement. Since the PanoMetric application is based on image data, surface details such as skid marks or blood spatter can be measured accurately. The entire scene can be captured and brought back to the lab for measurements. New measurements can be added at any time. It is not necessary to be on location to take the measurements.

The Scene

A body is found in a home. It will take many individual images to "tell" the story of the crime scene. The outside of the residence (Figure 11.3) shows the configuration of the structure. The next images depict the body in the kitchen, as well as the rest of the kitchen area (Figures 11.4–11.7).

There is a gun, a knife, a bloody towel, and an overturned pet dish in the kitchen area. Each has an importance in the scene that must be documented. There are a number of other pieces of evidence, such as blood drops and spatter.

Figure 11.3 Sample image from Panoscan digital scanning camera, outside. (Courtesy of Panoscan.)

Figure 11.4 Panoscan digital scanning camera interior, kitchen, with body on floor. (Courtesy of Panoscan.)

Figure 11.5 Panoscan digital scanning camera, other end of kitchen. (Courtesy of Panoscan.)

Figure 11.6 Panoscan digital scanning camera, kitchen dining area. (Courtesy of Panoscan.)

After the scene images taken by the MK-3 are processed by the technician, each piece of evidence is linked to the overall picture of the crime scene. A technician, investigator, or other user, utilizing one of the software programs to display the combined image, can "click" on various pieces of evidence, and the program will enlarge each piece for individual viewing (Figures 11.8–11.11).

An operator can take someone or a group (such as a jury) on a tour of the crime scene. This can be done in the courtroom as opposed to transporting the entire court to the scene. The operator can stop at various "points of interest" in the virtual crime scene and point out objects or pieces of evidence. Each piece of evidence can be enlarged for better viewing and study. At each point, the operator can "turn around" and look at the opposing wall. For example, a person or an entire courtroom of people can see what the victim saw and what the perpetrator saw.

Figure 11.7 Panoscan digital scanning camera, kitchen. (Courtesy of Panoscan.)

Figure 11.8 Panoscan digital scanning camera, gun. (Courtesy of Panoscan.)

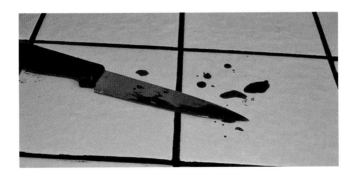

Figure 11.9 Panoscan digital scanning camera, knife. (Courtesy of Panoscan.)

Figure 11.10 Panoscan digital scanning camera, bloody towel. (Courtesy of Panoscan.)

Figure 11.11 Panoscan digital scanning camera, overturned pet dish. (Courtesy of Panoscan.)

Each room or area can be linked with a drawing, which allows the user to toggle between rooms to see a pathway of entry or exit (Figure 11.12). The user can click on a room and immediately be transported to that location.

Panorama Imaging: Ultraviolet/Infrared

The Panoscan MK-3 has a unique interchangeable filter system that allows for alternate-spectrum photography. While most digital cameras have a permanent filter (a hot filter) that blocks all infrared (IR) light from reaching the CCD (charge coupled device), the MK-3 has a removable filter. The removable filter allows near-ultraviolet (UV) and near-IR energy to reach the CCD sensor if desired.

This unique feature also allows the MK-3 to be fitted with specific-wavelength filters (band block and band pass) for forensic applications. In the examples in Figures 11.13–11.16, the IR filter has been replaced with various yellow and orange filters, and an alternate-spectrum light source was used to reveal hidden stain evidence. The MK-3 can also be fitted with a visible light-blocking filter (such as a Tiffen 87) to produce IR images. This removable filter system is unique to Panoscan.

Surveillance

Because of the resolution of the MK-3 camera, it can also take incredible pictures at extreme distances. We had mirrored lenses that could reach up to several blocks away and get a good

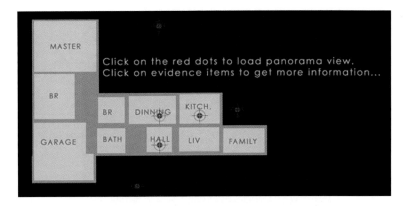

Figure 11.12 Diagram of room locations. (Courtesy of Panoscan.)

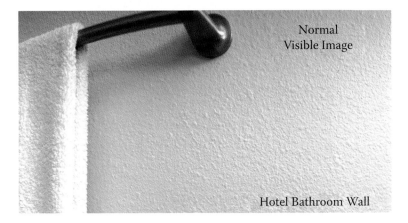

Figure 11.13 Image of bathroom wall taken with visible fluorescent light. (Courtesy of Panoscan.)

Figure 11.14 Image taken with UV light source (405 nm) and yellow filter (500 nm). (Courtesy of Panoscan.)

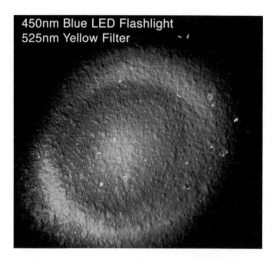

Figure 11.15 Image taken with forensic light-emitting diode (LED) blue flashlight (450 nm) and yellow filter (525 nm). (Courtesy of Panoscan.)

Figure 11.16 Image taken with blue LED flashlight (450 nm) and (590 nm) orange filter. (Courtesy of Panoscan.)

enough picture, although grainy, to read a license plate. One could see faces, but because of the magnification in the lens and additional enlargement in the darkroom, identities could not be discerned with any degree of surety.

In Figure 11.17, you see a panorama image of a mountain in the distance. Please note the red arrow and the area to which it is pointing. Figure 11.18 shows the house to which the red arrow is pointing. The amount of magnification is incredible, and the quality is superb. I really wished that we had this type of equipment back in the days before I entered the forensics field, when I was working controlled substances cases.

This image was shot on April 8, 2006 at 5:33 p.m. in Calabasas, California. Although the air quality was not perfect, the picture shows amazing detail. It is one of the largest images

Figure 11.17 Very long panorama of mountainside. Note the red arrow. (Courtesy of Panoscan.)

Figure 11.18 Image of home on mountainside. This is the home to which the red arrow is pointing in Figure 11.18. (Courtesy of Panoscan.)

ever captured on a Panoscan camera. The original 180-degree image was captured at 9,000 pixels high by 59,000 pixels wide. The exposure was made using the Mamiya 150-mm f/3.5 lens set at f/11.0, ISO 202 at 1/240 second/line. The file is 533 megapixels.

Preventive Measures

Violence in schools and other public places is a disturbing reality of modern life for law enforcement officials. First responders need to be prepared for these emergencies, and a plan should be in place to minimize loss of life and property.

Let us discuss an example of a school where every room and outdoor space was captured in a single day by one police officer from the Kern County Sheriff's Department. First, an aerial photo was taken. It was linked to the specific rooms and areas in Figure 11.19.

Next, all the rooms were linked to adjacent rooms and outdoor spaces, allowing officials to determine hiding places, locations of dangerous chemicals, methods of safely entering and exiting the scene, and the best way to get students and school employees out of harm's way. It would also be a way to brief special operations to be able to plan a rescue if necessary. This type of intelligence is most valuable in operations of this nature. To be able to have quick access to the layout for a potential rescue mission could mean success or failure. We often see this type of valuable information as "hindsight" when we should have been considering foresight (Figures 11.20–11.23).

Figure 11.19 Aerial photo of a school. (Courtesy of Panoscan.)

Figure 11.20 A room inside the school pictured in Figure 11.20. (Courtesy of Panoscan.)

Figure 11.21 A classroom inside the school pictured in Figure 11.20. (Courtesy of Panoscan.)

Figure 11.22 Another view of the classroom inside the school pictured in Figure 11.20. (Courtesy of Panoscan.)

Figure 11.23 Still another view of the classroom inside the school pictured in Figure 11.20. (Courtesy of Panoscan.)

Death Investigation 12

Introduction

This chapter is titled "Death Investigation," not homicide investigation, suicide investigation, accidental death investigation, or others. Isn't homicide investigation most important? Actually, all death investigations are important. But, every case to which we are assigned involving a death is a death investigation. Whether there is a man shot 38 times on a street corner or a man who has apparently died in his sleep at home, it is a death investigation.

We need to process the scene with no prejudice, no preconceived notions, or any specific mind-set. We have to be open to consider only the evidence that we see, feel, smell, and hear and what we can document, photo image, collect, and analyze.

Only the medical examiner or coroner (based on the autopsy performed by a forensic pathologist) can identify a death and assign a *manner* of death to the case. There are five manners of death: homicide, suicide, accidental, natural, and undetermined. The manner of death is a category, one of the five. Cause of death can be just about anything from blunt force trauma to cancer or kidney failure.

As an investigator, a crime scene investigator (CSI), a criminalist, or others involved in the investigation, we treat all death investigations *as if* they were the most heinous of killings, doing our absolute best and using every bit of expertise that we have to document, both photographically and verbally, information that can be used to make the final determination and, if a crime was committed, to prosecute the person responsible.

The Coroner or Medical Examiner

The medical examiner is a medical doctor (MD) who has had additional training in pathology. The medical examiner is appointed by a governor or county board. He performs autopsies and determines cause, manner, and mechanism of death.

The coroner is an elected position, usually voted on in a county election. The coroner is not required to have any training in death investigation. He or she uses the services of a forensic pathologist, a medical doctor, to perform the autopsy, and based on the doctor's report (the protocol), the coroner makes a ruling on the cause, manner, and mechanism of death. The coroner may appoint deputy coroners. They also do not have to have special training when they are appointed. Most states require at least the deputy coroner to go through some type of training after the appointment.

Official Photos of the Scene

If at all possible, do not allow anyone to take photo images of the scene before you, the CSI, do so. There are several reasons why following protocol is so important. You, as a CSI, are trained and have experience as a technical photographer. For example, you will take images of evidence at 90 degrees to the object to eliminate distortion.

On the other hand, images taken before you take yours may be ruled the official images of the scene because the court wants the "best evidence." Ask yourself, "Which photo is better, one taken 1 hour after the incident or one taken 3 hours after the incident?" The 1-hour photo is better because it was taken closer in time to the actual incident. Less could have changed in the 1-hour photo.

As an example, there was a fire in a residence. The fire was struck (put out) by the fire department. One of the firemen took two pictures, one overall of the bedroom and one of an apparent victim (Figures 12.1 and 2.2, respectively).

Figure 12.1 Overall image taken at a fire/arson.

Figure 12.2 Victim located in fire/arson seen in Figure 12.1.

When the CSIs arrived, we took well over 100 photo images. The court could look at the two images and say that they more truly and accurately represented the scene on the date and time in question. More time had elapsed between the incident and when we took our images.

The Scene

Before you begin taking pictures, it is a good idea to do a walk-through of the scene. Get an idea of the scope of the case. Determine what you will need to properly photograph the scene. Is there any special equipment you will need? Once you have completed the walk-through, you are ready to begin photo documenting the scene.

We begin by taking a photo ID card shot to identify the set of images that will be taken for this case. The next shot is, of course, the *N* or north card shot. This helps you or others involved in the case to be able to identify directions in this photo and others.

We have to tell the story. Because a death investigation is more serious than a burglary, we need to tell it with more detail. Plan on taking many images; remember there is no "shoulda, woulda, coulda" (I should have taken more pictures, I would have taken more pictures, and I could have taken more pictures). You cannot go back.

Unlike TV depictions, we do not collect evidence while we photograph the scene. We completely photograph the scene, then collect evidence. The first thing that is done is the photography. *This is important.* For example, if you photograph a knife on a desk in an office, then immediately collect it, later when you are photographing "overall photos" and perspective shots, the knife would be missing from the picture (Figures 12.3 and 12.4). The defense could ask, "Officer, does this picture truly and accurately represent the scene on the date and time in question?" You would have to say no because there is no knife in the picture. The defense could request that the image not be placed in evidence. Then, the

Figure 12.3 Overall image of room, knife on desk.

Figure 12.4 Overall image of room, knife missing from desk.

defense can ask that all the photos not be allowed into evidence because if one image is bad, then they all could be bad.

The scene should have overall images taken before any numbered tent cards or number cones are placed. These items are foreign objects and actually contaminate the scene. Once the overall photos are taken, the cones or numbered tent cards help identify objects and thereby show perspective (the relative position of one item to another).

Overall or Establishing Photos

Overall photos are images that show a large angle of the scene. If you have a wide-angle lens, it should be used for these shots. If you have a zoom lens, zoom all the way out for these shots. Note: Do not use a "fish-eye" lens or and extreme wide-angle lens. These will cause unacceptable distortion in the images.

Initially, shoot the "four corners" of the compass. Standing in the center of the scene, shoot from north to south, from south to north, from east to west, and from west to east. Then, standing from the edge of the room or, if outdoors, from the scene tape, shoot from north to south, from south to north, from east to west, and from west to east. The barest minimum of images that should be taken at a crime scene is 10 (ID shot, north shot, 4 images in from the outside, and 4 images out from the center).

Perspective Photos

We take perspective photos to show the relative position of one or more objects to another. In Figure 12.5, we see the body, a garrote, and two cups. The evidence (the garrote and the cups are evidence) should be imaged separately, but in telling the story, we need to know their positions in relation to the body.

Figure 12.5 Perspective image shows man's relative position to the two cups and to the garrote.

Unexpected Objects and Evidence

Just when you have followed all the rules, photo imaging first, then collection of evidence, you discover a piece of evidence that was hidden under, around, or on top of some object at the scene. This is where your listing of images comes into play and helps you. Take the image with and without scale, and when listing this evidence indicate that it was discovered after overall and perspective images were taken. The fact that it is in the report shows that

1. You are aware of proper procedure.
2. You are not trying to hide anything.
3. You documented it in the report so that there is no confusion.

When this information is documented, it takes away the issues introduced by the defense and clears the way for the prosecution to object to any motion not to allow the images into evidence.

Types of Images Taken during a Death Investigation

As a rule of thumb, the types of photographs that you will be taking during a death investigation are as follows:

1. Photo ID card (identifies the group of images)
2. Overall or establishing shots (shows the "big picture")
3. Perspective shots (shows relative position of objects)
4. Objects and evidence with scale (shows size; shot at 90 degrees)
5. Objects and evidence without scale (eliminates exculpatory evidence claim)

6. Rephotography at the lab (using controlled lighting to better document objects)
7. Morgue photography (imaging at morgue of wounds, evidence, clothing, standards from victim)

Using this list will usually work to photograph a death investigation well. However, since death investigations are so diverse and unique, there will often be something that does not fall into one of these categories yet still requires photo imaging. In the immortal words of Captain Murphy, a U.S. Air Force safety officer: "If anything can go wrong, it will go wrong." I imagine that you have heard this saying. It continues, however: "So either fix it or prepare for it." The following discussion is of cases for which a specific type of imaging was needed and why it was needed. I do not show all the images from each case due to the number involved. Images most pertinent to the lesson to be learned are shown.

Cases

When teaching forensic photo imaging, my students enjoy when I tell a "war story," a tale about a case that I or an associate worked. While most of the stories are at least entertaining, I often use them to sneak in a lesson. Some lessons are obvious, while others are more elusive. In any event, enjoy the following stories.

A Snowy Night

The victim, a young girl, was discovered on the ground in an alley behind a residence (not hers) (Figures 12.6 and 12.7). The girl was dusted with snow. The snow covered her body almost completely, yet she was clearly recognizable as a human body. There was little or no blood at the scene. The girl had what appeared to be a wound to the chest.

The depth of the snow on the ground was about 2 inches. It was noted that she had 2 inches of snow completely under her body. There was approximately a half inch of new snow on top of her.

Figure 12.6 Image of girl on back in alley with snow partially covering body.

Figure 12.7 Different angle of girl on back in alley with snow partially covering body.

This is important. If we know when the new snow started, we could estimate, with a high degree of accuracy, when the body was dumped.

Because of the location (the alley), it was necessary to shoot pictures of both ends of the alley to show how the body was dropped off (Figures 12.8 and 12.9).

The lesson is the following:

- This was a homicide.
- The person may not have died here because of the snow.
- The body told us when it was dumped.
- *Mortuus docui victus*: "The dead teach the living."

Figure 12.8 Distance overall of entryway into alley (north to south).

Figure 12.9 Distance overall of entryway into alley (south to north).

A Locked Apartment

The victim, an elderly lady, was discovered by the police in her locked apartment, her face and chin on a chair (Figures 12.10 and 12.11). The position of the woman was suspicious. It looked like the woman had been made to kneel, then pressure was placed on her back until she stopped breathing. Figure 12.12 was important, decidedly a case breaker. The door was latched. It appeared that the door was forced by her attacker. This was a poor assumption. When we spoke with the first officer on the scene, he advised that he had forced the door. The door had been locked from the inside. This changed everything. We needed corroboration. We received it from the medical examiner. The cause of death was stroke. The woman apparently had a stroke and fell onto the chair in a position that indicated positional asphyxia. It was not. The medical examiner ruled the death as natural.

Figure 12.10 Woman's head and neck on chair in living room of her apartment. All doors and windows locked from the inside.

Figure 12.11 Different angle of woman's head and neck on chair in living room of her apartment.

Figure 12.12 Latch on door, broken. The first officer on the scene had forced the door to check for well-being.

The lesson is as follows:

- Do not have preconceived ideas of what happened.
- Do not let others affect your thinking by identifying the case as "just a natural" or "just a suicide."
- Talk to the officer on scene.
- *Operor non vindicatum*: "Do not assume."

Gun-Cleaning Mishap

In a six-flat apartment building, a neighbor heard a loud "boom" and called the police to check on the well-being of the person living in the apartment adjacent to the neighbor. On arrival, the building manager opened the door for the police officer, and a male subject was found in his apartment, sitting in a chair with a shotgun in his hand and most of his head missing (Figure 12.13).

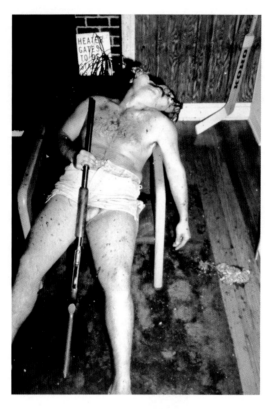

Figure 12.13 Man in chair. Shotgun was in his right hand; top of head missing. He was wearing little clothing and no shoes. His lips were intact.

Next to the chair on the subject's right was a small table with gun-cleaning equipment laid out. It appeared to be an accident. The photograph shows some interesting aspects.

- The gun, a pump action shotgun, had one shell, spent (fired) in the chamber.
- The subject was holding the shotgun in one hand, but all cleaning rods were on the table with the rest of the gun-cleaning equipment.
- No bottles of cleaner were open, and no cleaning patches were out of their package.
- The subject was barefoot.
- The subject was wearing a minimum amount of clothing.
- The lips of the subject were intact, while the top of the head was missing.

What does this mean?

- Most important, the lips were intact. This means that the barrel of the gun was in the subject's mouth when the gun fired. No one cleans firearms with the barrel in his or her mouth.
- The cleaning equipment was not opened. Probably, his intention was not to clean the gun.
- The subject was barefoot and had on little clothing. People who commit suicide have a tendency to want to be comfortable.
- The top of the head exploded. This is because the barrel was in the mouth. The tremendous amount of gases escaping from the barrel of the gun caused the head to pop. If the gun were positioned a short distance from the head, the lips would be destroyed as well as a greater portion of the front of the face, but the top of the head would not have popped. The brain came out intact (Figure 12.14). It bounced off the wall in back of the subject and landed on the floor to his left.

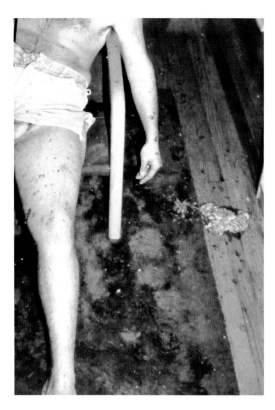

Figure 12.14 Brain on floor next to man in chair. We were able to locate a spot on the wall behind him that appeared to be where the brain struck, then ricocheted to the floor.

The lesson is as follows:

- The image tells the story.
- The medical examiner ruled the death a suicide.
- The scene was staged (most insurance policies do not pay if suicide is committed).
- *Probatur totus possibilities*: "Examine all possibilities."

The Man and His Neckerchief

A male about 20 years old was discovered by his parents; he was in his room on his bed with a .44-caliber magnum on his lap. There was no apparent entry wound, but there was an exit wound on the back of his head (Figure 12.15). The bullet went through the headboard and through the wall. It continued through the adjacent bedroom and into a third bedroom. The bullet was finally recovered from the third bedroom after it had penetrated four walls plus the subject's head.

The picture again shows us interesting aspects of the case:

- The subject is partially dressed. There was no shirt, and the subject was not wearing shoes.
- The barrel of the gun on the victim's lap was wrapped in a neckerchief.

What does this tell us?

- The victim wanted to be comfortable (no shirt or shoes).
- We discovered that he had had some dental work done recently and apparently did not want to damage or hurt his teeth, perhaps even thinking that the neckerchief would protect his teeth.

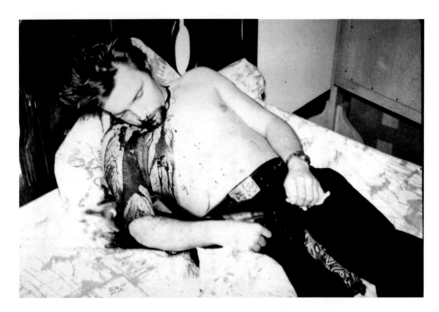

Figure 12.15 Man in bed with only an exit wound to the back of the head. A neckerchief was wrapped around the barrel of the gun, a Ruger six-shot .44 magnum. I expended the cartridge under the hammer; five live rounds. On looking in the mouth, the palate was missing, and a large cavity went upward toward the brain.

The lesson is as follows:

- Take plenty of photographs. Remember; you cannot "go back."
- Sometimes other information obtained by the detective helps to explain a puzzle piece.
- *Insequor quod persolvo novus:* "Pursue and explain the unusual."

Bomb Go Boom

On arrival at a scene, we found an area of about 3 to 4 acres. This was a huge crime scene. The other problem was that it was night. Apparently, a bomb had exploded in a vehicle on a four-lane divided highway (Figure 12.16). A man was believed to be carrying six to eight sticks of 60% dynamite under the driver's seat.

Note: When transporting dynamite safely, one should *not* keep the primer in close proximity to the dynamite. Also, electrical primers should be shunted (the lead wire small and closely wrapped around the primer as in Figure 12.17). It is believed that the man had the primer attached to the dynamite and the wires from the primer extended. When the electrical primer wires are extended, they act as an antenna (see Figure 12.18).

The entire crime scene (3 to 4 acres) was located under an electrical grid transformer. This grid produces a large amount of RFI (radio-frequency interference). This RFI triggered the primer, setting off the dynamite.

From the center of the blast (see Figure 12.16) to the ending point of the truck was about 75 yards. To photograph the entire scene at night, it was necessary to use a technique called "painting with light" (Figure 12.19). This technique is explained in Chapter 5. We could always come back the next day and shoot with daylight; however, that would not be the way it looked when the bomb exploded.

Part of the truck and part of the body were located on the road, close to the blast center. The truck continued on until it struck a fence (Figure 12.19).

The torso was recovered as well as the large body part from the road (Figure 12.20). Photo imaging the body at the scene was extremely difficult, so the majority of the body photography was done at the morgue.

Figure 12.16 Center area of blast. This was part of the asphalt road. It was the center of the explosion.

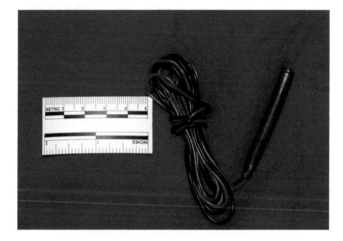

Figure 12.17 An example of an electrical blasting cap or primary explosive with wires shunted.

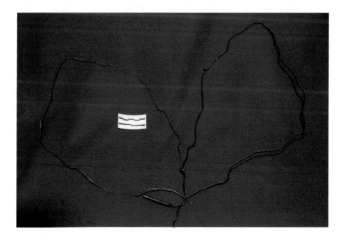

Figure 12.18 An example of an electrical blasting cap or primary explosive with wires extended. When the wires are extended, they act as a receiving antenna.

Figure 12.19 This image is an example of painting with light. This is a method to photo image large crime scenes after dark.

Figure 12.20 The image depicts a part of the body and part of the vehicle that kept moving after the blast. The distance between the body part and the part of the vehicle is about 35 feet. This was shot with a Vivitar 283, set on full manual. You can see that it is barely effective at the 35-foot mark.

Figure 12.21 These are artifacts removed from the body and body parts. Note the pieces of wire and remnants of the electrical blasting cap as well as the handcuff key.

Photographing a body at the morgue is similar to "rephotography" or "bench photography." After taking images at the scene, the body is taken to a place where there is a large amount of controllable light and controllable conditions. We were able to recover a number of pieces from the body in this case. The red arrows in Figure 2.21 point out the remains of the electrical blasting cap (primer). We found a handcuff key mixed in with some of the body parts. I thought that was somewhat interesting.

The lesson is as follows:

- Do not transport primers with dynamite.
- If there are explosives present, *call a bomb tech*. There may be a secondary device.
- Do not be afraid to try unusual techniques (painting with light).
- Be persistent. You may find evidence in the most unusual places (bomb parts in the body).
- *Nonnullus dies vos peto ambitus, quod nonnullus dies ciircus adveho vobis*: "Some days you go to the circus, and some days the circus comes to you."

The Man with the Latex Gloves

This death investigation was set up and looked like a suicide (Figure 12.22). A man was sitting on a couch. He had a gun in his right hand, resting at his side, with the gun loosely held in his hand. His shoes and socks were off, and his pants were unbuttoned and the zipper undone (he made himself comfortable). There were no apparent wounds on the body; however, when we looked in the mouth, we saw what appeared to be a gunshot wound. There was no exit wound in the back of the head. What was most disconcerting was the pair of latex gloves laying on the couch about 14 inches from the subject's left hand.

We asked the first responding officer if there was anyone else at the scene before we arrived. He replied, "No one except myself." There was a slight pause. Then he said, "Oh yeah, there were the two EMTs [emergency medical technicians] who checked the body for a pulse."

We asked why their names were not on the crime scene entry log. The officer replied, "I did not start it until I had a dead body. That was after the EMTs left."

As a CSI documenting the scene, you need to know if there has been any contamination, such as the EMTs' gloves. If such items are there, photograph them and indicate in your report and your photo listing that the gloves (or whatever) and where they came from. You may not remove the contamination because then the scene will not be as *you found it*.

This was a suicide. The latex gloves made it look like something else.

Figure 12.22 This image was taken of a man sitting on a couch. There is a pair of latex gloves on the couch next to him.

The lesson is as follows:

- There has to be communication between the first responder and the CSI.
- Everyone signs the crime scene entry log.
- While it is not a CSI's job to interview witnesses and others, in some cases the CSI has to at least talk to the first responding officer or the detective on the case.
- *Communications inter consors est paramount*: "Communications between comrades is paramount."

The Cal-Sag Canal

The Cal-Sag (Calumet-Sag) Sanitary Canal is a waterway in Illinois mostly used by barges to transport material from as far away as Louisiana. On a hot Illinois day, it was more than 90 degrees (Figure 12.23). A complainant had called our communications center to indicate that a 55-gallon drum was observed floating in the Cal-Sag. Uniformed officers, detectives, and the CSIs were dispatched. We all had a good guess of what was contained in the drum. On arrival, we watched the drum bob in the water. At this point of the canal, several counties came together, and location depended on what side of the canal the drum was located. This designated the jurisdiction of the drum and therefore who had to make the recovery.

After about 15 minutes of watching the drum bob in the water and drift to and fro, we decided it was not going to drift out of our jurisdiction. The dock workers assisted in recovering the drum using a small crane. My partner and I flipped a coin to see who did the photography and who opened the drum. I won (I chose the photography) (Figure 12.24). The body was a torso only, no legs, no arms, and no head. It was wrapped in black plastic. The torso seemed relatively fresh in that there was little decomposition. This was probably because the drum was under water, and the water temperature kept it cool.

It was believed that it had been caught up in some chains dragged by one of the barges. It could have come from as far away as Louisiana.

Figure 12.23 This is the Cal-Sag Canal in Illinois.

Figure 12.24 This is my partner removing the torso only of a female white victim from a 55-gallon drum.

The lesson is as follows:

- Always use a camera neck strap. The camera could easily drop into the canal or, worse, into the torso.
- Since the crime scene was actually the bobbing 55-gallon drum, there was no real scene. The torso was the scene. A much better job of photography could be done at the morgue, where the light could be controlled, the conditions could be controlled, and it was not 90 degrees Fahrenheit.
- No one should wear white shoes and light-colored pants to a recover body parts.
- *Vestio ordine pro officium*: "Dress appropriately for the job."

The Arcade

A call was received regarding a homicide in a game arcade. We immediately advised our dispatch center that this was a death investigation. On arrival, we found a teenage male on his back. The victim had numerous gunshot wounds to the neck and torso (Figure 12.25).

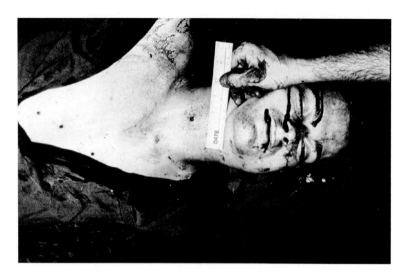

Figure 12.25 Victim in arcade shot 13 times.

It was noisy in the game area. There were dozens of pinball and other amusement games clanging, beeping, and ringing. There was a .22-caliber revolver on the floor. Later examination of the weapon revealed that is was a .22-caliber nine-shot revolver. It contained four spent (fired) rounds. On the floor, nine spent .22-caliber rounds were recovered.

We were advised that the local police had a suspect in custody. One of the CSIs drove to the police station and ran an AA (atomic absorption) gunshot residue (GSR) test on the suspect. Later, it came back positive for GSR.

The suspect confessed to the shooting. The suspect stated that he and the victim had been arguing about a female. The suspect drew the nine-shot revolver and discharged the gun at the neck of the victim. After the first shot, the victim went down to the ground. The suspect continued to shoot until all nine rounds had been fired. The suspect then ejected the empty shell casings and loaded the gun with four more rounds. He closed the cylinder and shot the victim four more times, dropped the gun, and ran out the door.

No one saw or heard the shooting because the gunfire was covered by the excessive noise in the arcade.

The suspect later recanted his confession (reversed it).

The photo images taken as well as the evidence recovered supported the original confession. In Figure 12.26, the image depicts a perfect example of stippling or tattooing. This is caused by still-burning particles of gunpowder as it escapes from the barrel of the gun. Test fires were made of the murder weapon, and it was determined that the barrel was approximately 4 to 6 inches from the victim's neck when the first round was fired.

The lesson is as follows:

- It is a good thing to have a basic idea of what went on at the crime scene (if possible).
- When an unusual phenomenon is observed (such as the stippling), photo document it well.
- Wear gloves when working with a dead body. It should be noted, however, that this case occurred prior to AIDS, knowledge about hepatitis, and any number of diseases that exist today.
- *Acsi commissio est in custodia, opus scaena ut sententia is erant non*: "Even if the perpetrator is in custody, work the scene as though he were not."

The Hit

Unlike on TV, we do not solve all of our cases. In this one, dispatch sent us to a suspicious circumstances call. The detective requested CSIs because he had a feeling something was wrong. A uniformed officer had run a "hot/cold" check on a car. It had come up hot (stolen). It had been reported only 6 hours previously. The detective on call advised the uniformed car to pull back and

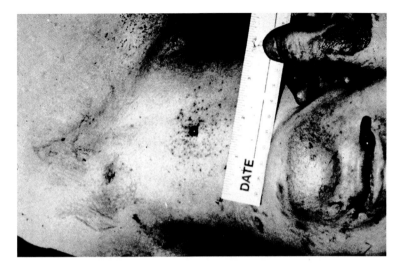

Figure 12.26 Close up of the stippling or tattooing on the victim's neck. It was caused by a .22-caliber nine-shot revolver at close range (4–6 inches).

sit on it (watch it) until he could arrive. He hoped the thieves might come back to pick up the car and maybe use it in another crime.

When the detective arrived and drove by the car for a quick "look-see," he observed about 50 to 100 flies in the back window. Something was wrong. It was at this time that he requested CSIs.

Unfortunately, when we arrived, we were greeted by the news media. Several of the local TV stations had investigative reporters maneuvering for a position to see into the trunk when it was opened. Both my partner and I concurred with the detective that there was something wrong. I retrieved a crowbar from the trunk of my car and told the detective to move the media people back from the trunk. If what I suspected was true, they would not want to be anywhere near the trunk. A cameraman started yelling that he had a right to be there; he was a member of the press. The detective winked at me and said "freedom of the press." I said, "Okay." The cameramen moved in closer.

I took a deep breath and held it (Figure 12.27). When I popped the trunk, the stench of heavy decomposition did not waft its way gently toward the cameramen and me but hit us like a brick wall. Both cameramen started to backpedal and tripped, falling, and their cameras struck the pavement. It turned out that both cameras were inoperable. I winked at the detective and said "freedom of the press."

On removal of the body from the trunk (Figure 12.28), we found two apparent bullet holes in the chest and one in the forehead. The bullet holes looked like a small caliber; however, you can never tell for sure until you get the remains to the autopsy suite. This looked like a professional "hit."

We processed the car completely (see Chapter 15 on auto processing), dusting for fingerprints and other evidence with no results (Figure 12.29).

The case was never solved.

The lesson is as follows:

- Other than the body, sometimes there is no evidence.
- The first officer on the scene should have put up crime scene tape to keep everyone back.
- We should have called a forensic entomologist.
- *Professio Interficio es difficile dictu solve*: "Professional murders are difficult to solve."

It's Complicated

I received a call regarding a death investigation. The deceased's wife allegedly found her husband dead on the stairs of their home at approximately 10:30 a.m. She stated that she had just found him when she got up and called 911. The police arrived at 10:33 a.m. On my arrival at 10:45 a.m.,

Figure 12.27 Man in trunk of car. August daytime heat. The victim was shot three times.

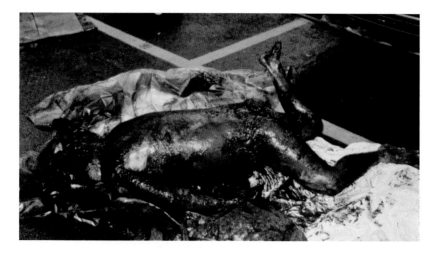

Figure 12.28 Victim on body bag after removal from the trunk. Victim was in advanced stage of decomposition.

the woman was in the kitchen speaking with the detective. I proceeded to examine the body (Figure 12.30).

The body was on the lower group of stairs, separated from the upper group by a landing. The body was lying face down, arms to the sides and bent at the elbows. The right leg was resting on the stairs, bent at the knee (Figure 12.31). The left leg was unbent and at an obtuse angle to the rest of the body. The victim was naked. He was cold to the touch and in full rigor. He exhibited obvious livor mortis consistent with the body position (see Figure 12.30). The livor mortis was not fixed. The victim had a fresh abrasion on his left inner thigh (Figure 12.32).

The stairs consisted of two groups, each pointed in the opposite direction, separated by a good-size landing (Figure 12.33). On the landing, a pair of glasses was discovered at the bottom of the upper group of stairs. They were not broken.

Figure 12.29 Senior Criminalistics Investigator Jones is dusting the vehicle for latent prints. The car had been wiped down.

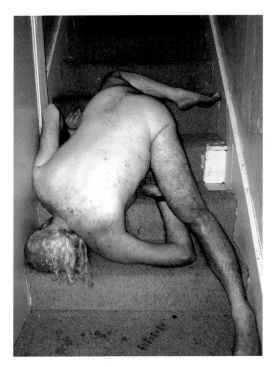

Figure 12.30 Man, stuck on stairs, in rigor and with livor onset, not set.

The wife stated, "He must have fallen down the two flights of stairs." If we look at both the upper and lower groups of stairs and the landing, this looks somewhat improbable (see Figure 12.34). The victim could have fallen down the top group, but he would have come to rest on the landing, probably at the point that his glasses were discovered. He could have fallen down the lower group of stairs and landed in the strange position in which he was discovered. But, then why were his glasses found at the bottom of the upper flight of stairs on the landing?

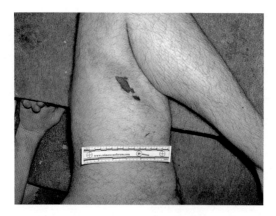

Figure 12.31 Abrasion on the rear of victim's right thigh.

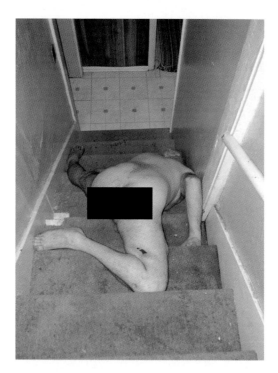

Figure 12.32 Man, stuck on stairs, as seen from the landing.

I decided to speak with and examine the wife. She was wearing shorts. I observed abrasions on her legs similar to those on her husband (they both appeared to be rug burns) (Figure 12.35). When questioned about the abrasions and told that her husband could not have fallen down the upper group of stairs, made a U-turn, then fallen down the lower group of stairs, she confessed.

She stated that her husband had fallen down the upper group of stairs, and she found him on the landing. Both she and her husband had been "doing coke" in their second-floor bedroom. There was still some coke in the bedroom. She decided that if he were found at the foot of the lower group of stairs, the police would not search their bedroom and find the coke. She decided to drag him down the lower group of stairs, but he was heavy and tumbled, then got stuck. She could not break him loose. She had several drinks and thought about her problem and decided she had to call the police.

Figure 12.33 Stairs down to landing from second floor. Notice victim's glasses.

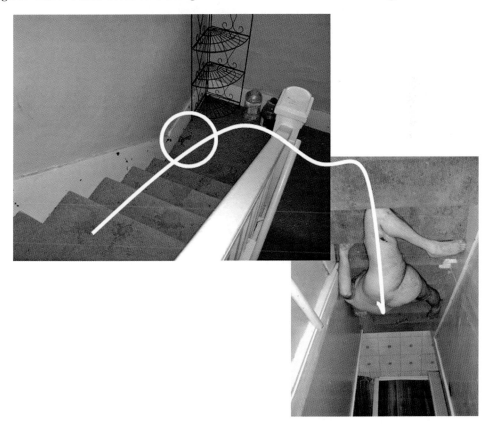

Figure 12.34 Path of fall from second floor of residence.

The lesson is as follows:

- Listen when the evidence speaks to you.
- Listen to the evidence even when an eyewitness states the opposite.
    - Eyewitnesses are not as reliable as physical evidence.
    - The eyewitness may be trying to deceive you.
- *Audio testimonium, is unus dico verum*: "Listen to the evidence, it alone tells the truth."
- Also see the comment in the "Bomb Go Boom example" about circuses.

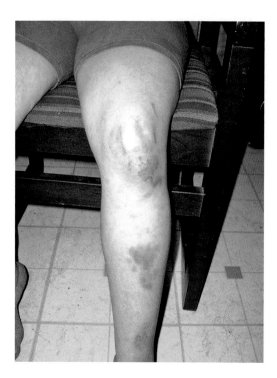

Figure 12.35 Abrasions on wife's leg, similar to victim.

A Note for Help

Dispatch sent us to the scene of a stabbing in an alley behind a restaurant. The body was laying face down in a trash pile in the alley. Next to the victim was the victim's car. On the trunk of the car was written

GOD
Help Me
I will call
the PD in time

On the trunk of the car was a Sharpie brand permanent marker. Note that this is one of those cases when a helpful police officer took three Polaroid pictures of the body and scene prior to our arrival, which made them the official pictures of the crime scene. Please note the detailed quality image of the body in Figure 12.36. (This is sarcasm.) The body and scene were processed. We took detailed images of the body, scene, and car. We collected and dusted the "Sharpie" for prints, with negative results.

As CSIs, we are sometimes asked to look at and interpret evidence (not analyze, but interpret, translate, give meaning to). These interpretations do not belong in our report. Our report contains true, accurate observations recorded in a document that is supported by the photo images, measurements placed in our drawing, and the written word based on our notes. But, we can look at the scene and speak with the detectives investigating the case.

Let us look at the writing. Look at jargon, slang, and language used by certain groups of people. Who uses the abbreviation "PD"? Most people would say police department, cops, or the like. Police refer to the police department as the PD.

Let us look at the writing instrument. It is not a black marker, it is not a crayon, it is not spray paint. It is a Sharpie. Who uses Sharpies? Lots of people, but police use them regularly; in fact, you will see them in many detectives' pockets, right next to their black ballpoint pens.

The investigation eventually revealed that a police officer was the perpetrator.

Figure 12.36 Message on the car trunk at alleged serial killing. Note: Sharpie permanent marker and the abbreviation "PD" (meaning police department) on trunk.

The lesson is as follows:

- Think logically.
- Base your observations not only on your training but also on your experience.
- *Quisquam can exsisto testimonium, vel orator vox*: "Anything can be evidence, even the spoken word."

My Husband Killed Himself? Or, My Husband Killed Himself.

Dispatch sent us to a 911 call for a death investigation. The wife said that her husband shot and killed himself in their mobile home. On arrival, the detectives were already speaking to the victim's wife. I was directed to the rear bedroom.

I was advised that the wife stated that she heard a gunshot from the bedroom. She ran to the room and saw her husband bleeding from the head. She further stated that she immediately called the police, who arrived less than 4 minutes later. She said that she did not touch or move the body.

I found the body of a man in the rear bedroom; he was on his back on the bed with the blanket pulled up to almost his chin (Figure 12.37). A handgun was loosely under the man's right hand, close to his head. A single bullet was present in the victim's right temple. There was no exit wound. There was blood pooled on the pillow. This was relatively consistent with the wife's story, except for the blanket. It is improbable that the victim would have pulled the blanket up to his chin before shooting himself in the temple.

The subject was beginning to show signs of rigor. There was tightening in the jaw, although the fingers were still loose. This was also inconsistent with the wife's story. She stated that she had called the police immediately. Rigor begins in approximately 2 hours.

The other issue I had was with the victim's face. As you can see in Figure 12.38, blood was draining from the nose in two different directions. This was not consistent with the wife's statement that she did not move the body.

I advised the detective in charge of the inconsistencies. He confronted the wife with them. She confessed to shooting her husband while he was asleep. She moved his head on the pillow and covered him with the blanket. She then placed the gun near his hand.

The lesson is as follows:

- Even though told that the scene was a suicide, it was a death investigation until all the evidence was collected.
- Work and communicate with the detective on the case. Sometimes information you can relay to the detective can assist in solving the case quickly.
- *Quis tangled webs nos weave, ut nos meditor frustro*: "What tangled webs we weave, when we practice to deceive."

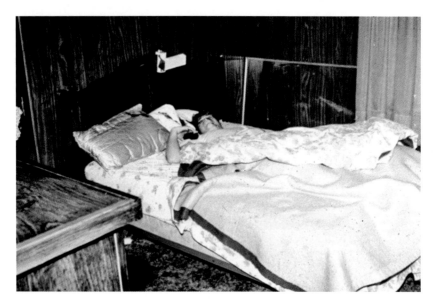

Figure 12.37 Overall of bedroom and victim in bed. Victim's wife said he shot himself. Wife said she did not touch the body.

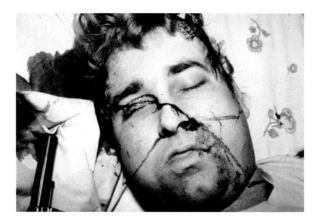

Figure 12.38 Close-up of victim's face. Note that it appears that blood has drained in two different directions.

Morgue Photo Imaging 13

Introduction

In documenting a death investigation, the crime scene is important. There is much evidence and lack of evidence and many items of interest to document. The investigation that takes place at the morgue and the evidence that is documented there are equally important. It is here that the victim "speaks to us."

In some jurisdictions, there is a photographer whose sole assignment is to take images of the autopsy and evidence recovered at this procedure. Many jurisdictions do not have such a photographer due to lack of funding. Regardless, I strongly recommend that, as a crime scene investigator (CSI), images of the autopsy and recovery of evidence during this procedure be taken by the CSI. Even if there is a morgue photographer, having an additional set of images available is certainly helpful.

At the Scene

Prior to leaving the scene, an image of the body in the body bag before it is closed should be taken. This shows the condition of the body as it was placed in the body bag (Figures 13.1 and 13.2). After the bag has been scribed with the body's name, the date, case number, and your initials, the bag can be zipped. It should then be sealed (numerical tag number should be recorded) and photographed (Figure 13.3).

Universal Precautions

You will be required to conform to the morgue's policy on universal precautions. Universal precautions are policies and procedures put in place to keep you, the CSI, safe from potential disease or contamination. The good news is that in applying universal precautions as a safety measure, we also reap the benefits in regard to the preservation of noncontamination of evidence. Depending on the specific morgue policy that is used, you may be required only to wear examination gloves. Other jurisdictions may require full Tyvek suits, gloves, booties, mask, and hairnets (Figure 13.4). Suits that are similar to those worn in "clean rooms" are also worn.

Working in a suit such as this reduces mobility. It is much more difficult to change memory cards in your digital camera or film in a 35-mm camera. It is more difficult, but it can be done. Remember that a medical doctor operates on a patient while wearing this type of protective equipment, and if the doctor can operate, you can take images.

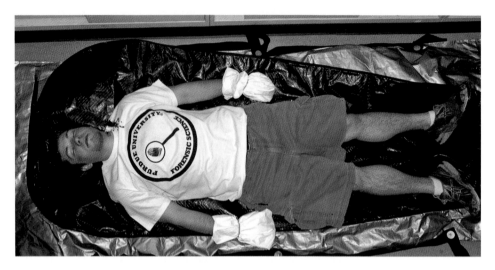

Figure 13.1 Photo of the body in the bag. Note that the victim has had his hands bagged to protect them for the examination at the morgue for trace evidence.

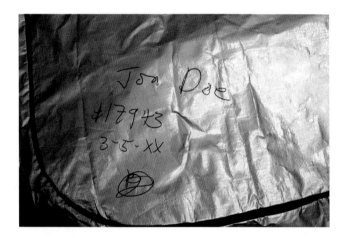

Figure 13.2 Photo of the body bag with the correct information on the bag.

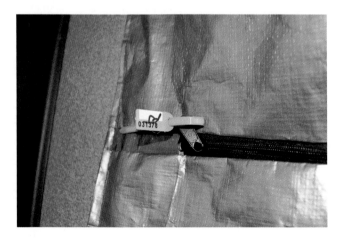

Figure 13.3 Photo of the signed seal (numbered) and initials on the body bag.

Figure 13.4 Image of man in what we call a "bunny suit." Sometimes, a complete suit is not necessary. This is up to the policies and procedures set by the morgue or your agency.

At the Morgue

The body has been transported to the morgue and, in all probability, will be posted (autopsied) the following morning. The body is still in the body bag, sealed, and will be waiting for you on a gurney or an autopsy table (Figure 13.5).

Your first picture is the photo ID card. This identifies the following images should they be misfiled or mismarked (Figure 13.6). The next image should be the cutting of the seal on the body bag. Showing, in sequenced images, that the seal on the body bag was intact and cut at the morgue confirms the continuity of any and all evidence recovered from the body at the morgue. It also ensures that no valuables or other items were removed in transit (Figure 13.7). Another overall photo of the body in the bag should be taken. This image should match the image taken of the body at the scene (Figure 13.8).

Sequencing

Sequencing is important. It is important to do things in order. If this order is circumvented, valuable evidence may be overlooked, not documented, or even lost. There are some images that should be taken before others. For example, there are many images that should be taken before the body is washed. Trace evidence especially needs to be imaged before the body is cleaned. These areas of the body should be examined carefully and documented with images.

Figure 13.5 This is an image of the autopsy table in the autopsy suite. The table is usually made of stainless steel and has running water and a drain.

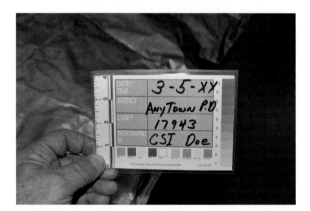

Figure 13.6 The photo ID card. This will identify the images that you take at the morgue.

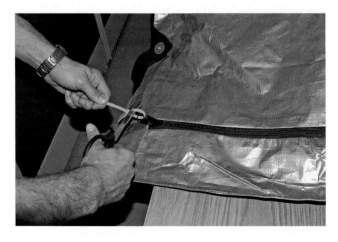

Figure 13.7 Photo of an investigator cutting the seal of the body bag at the morgue.

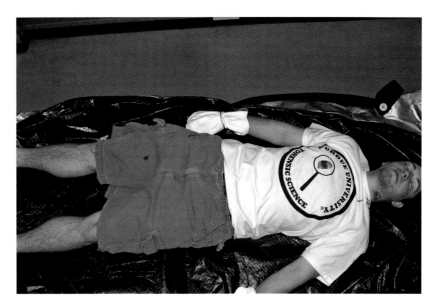

Figure 13.8 The body in the bag at the morgue.

Case Study

There was a case of a fire in a suburban town. The firemen, after striking the fire, discovered a female on the floor in the kitchen. The firemen called the medical examiner's office, and an MEI (medical examiner investigator) responded to the scene. He gave a quick examination of the body, took several Polaroid pictures, and told the firemen that it looked like an accidental death due to the fire, but he was going to send the body to the morgue for a CO (carbon monoxide) blood level. He then told the firemen to place the remains in a body bag and transport it to the morgue.

No additional processing was done at the scene by the local police department since the MEI was so positive it was an accidental death. No one followed up the case by going to the morgue, neither the local police department nor the fire department.

On arrival at the morgue the following morning, the morgue assistant read the brief report, glanced at the Polaroid pictures, and opened the body bag to prepare the body for examination by one of the forensic pathologists (Figures 13.9 and 13.10). To say the least, he was somewhat surprised to observe the handle of a carving knife sticking out of the subject's torso. The morgue assistant immediately called one of the forensic pathologists and explained the case, as reported, and his discovery. The forensic pathologist requested that I start a case on the deceased as an assist to the original agency. (At the time, I was at the morgue following up on another of my cases.)

I began a case, identifying it as a death investigation but treating it as though it were a homicide. Even if a case was apparently a natural or accidental death, it was our policy to treat it as if it were the most serious of cases. It is important to give all cases this type of attention and depth. Many times, these obvious natural and accidental deaths turn into homicides. The old adage "you can't judge a book by its cover" is true.

I also requested a team of CSIs to respond to the fire scene and attempt to salvage any evidence that may still have been there.

After a detailed examination of the body by one of the forensic pathologists and myself, and after many images were taken of the body and the protruding knife, the forensic pathologist carefully removed the knife. As he did so, he observed that there were carbon deposits on the entire blade, including the tip of the blade. All this was recorded by photography. The doctor observed that the blade had been exposed during the fire. On examination of the wound, the doctor further learned that the wound was postmortem (after death). When a CO level was run, it was found that the woman had a high level of CO in her blood.

When the doctor examined her lungs, a good deal of soot was discovered in both the lungs and the airway.

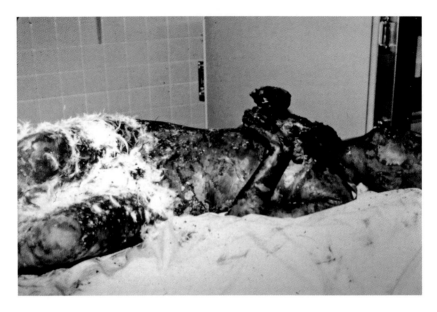

Figure 13.9 When the body bag was opened at the morgue, it was assumed that this was going to be an open-and-shut, by-the-book, easy case. *Never assume.*

Figure 13.10 The lady with the knife in her chest. The white material in the image is feathers from the feather bed in her room.

The other team of CSIs who went to the scene spoke with the firemen. When they had placed her in the body bag, they had not picked her up but rather rolled and pushed her into the bag. The CSIs at the scene found a number of kitchen knives on the floor. Apparently what had happened was that the woman had died as a result of the smoke and carbon monoxide. When the firemen placed her in the body bag, they had rolled and pushed the body, impaling her on the knife.

Good scene documentation and imaging would have saved a lot of work.

The documentation, the images taken at the morgue, along with the forensic pathologist's observations confirmed that this was an accidental death due to a fire.

At the crime scene, you can sometimes go back, but at the morgue, once the body is cleaned, you cannot go back and "image it dirty." You cannot take images of trace evidence, markings, and evidence transfers that have been washed away.

Lighting

The lighting at the morgue is quite different from most crime scenes. Unlike on television, there is no soft, blue, indirect, sexy lighting. The ambient light at the morgue is usually fluorescent. It is bright and intense.

Because of this bright, intense fluorescent light, you should ensure that your camera has been white balanced. Some digital cameras require manual initiation of the feature. I strongly recommend that you set the white balance as an automatic default, and when imaging with this type of light that you double check the white balance.

The Body

Once the bag has been opened and the body placed on the examination table, but before the body has had clothes removed or is washed, additional images should be taken. If, at the scene, the body's hands were "bagged" for the purpose of preserving trace evidence or for processing for GSR (gunshot reside), then the bagged hands should be imaged, showing that the hands arrived at the morgue bagged (Figures 13.11 and 13.12).

At this time, the body and its clothes should be imaged (Figures 13.13 and 13.14). There will be times that a ladder is not available. Remember that all wounds, evidence, objects of interest, and artifacts should be shot at 90 degrees to prevent distortion.

Any artifacts should be imaged that are in evidence. We see what appears to be a blood stain on the front side of the shorts worn by a victim (Figure 13.15). We also see what appears to be a knife in the right front pocket of the victim's shorts (Figure 13.16).

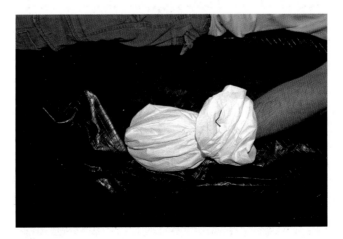

Figure 13.11 The left hand bagged. (I suggest that you use a Sharpie permanent marker to write R for right and L for left on the outside of the bagged hands.)

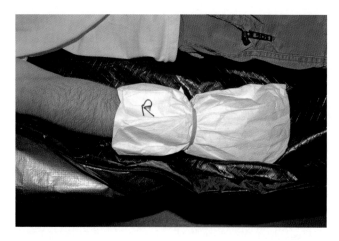

Figure 13.12 The right hand bagged. (I suggest that you use a Sharpie permanent marker to write R for right and L for left on the outsides of the bagged hands.)

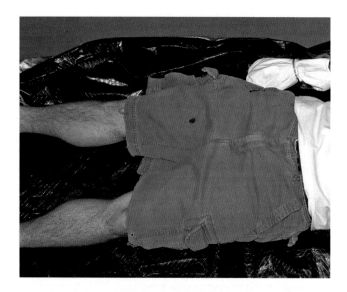

Figure 13.13 Bottom of body, front. It is nice if you can take a single image of the entire back and front of the body. If there is a ladder in the autopsy suite, then you can use that. If not, take the pictures in segments, making sure you overlap.

Remember, the body has a back side as well (Figures 13.17 and 13.18). Just like a gun or a knife, one has to photograph all sides.

ID Photo Image

A good image of the face is suitable for preliminary identification of victims. A good shot is taken at the morgue for this purpose (Figure 13.19). There are times that part of the face, the neck, or even a large part of the body is badly damaged. In this case, we would still like an image of the face for identification purposes, but we do not want to trauma-tize relatives or friends. You can take a second ID shot of the victim, but before you do,

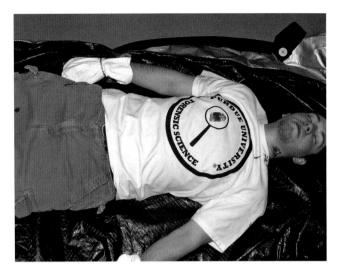

Figure 13.14 Top of body, front.

Figure 13.15 Suspect blood stain on pants with scale. (You already have an overall of the front bottom, so you will not have to take a "without scale" image of this area.)

cover the damaged areas with towels or sheets. In this way, we have done our best not to disturb the relatives and friends any more than is absolutely necessary (Figure 13.20).

Scales

Any artifact, wound, or item of interest should be taken with and without scale. A scale is a ruler used to attribute exact size to an item imaged. The scale can be straight or L-shaped (Figure 13.21). I recommend that the scale be of the type that can be written on. Plastic-coated scales work well. If one uses a "wet erase" marker, the case number and other pertinent information can be placed on the scale. This identifies every image in which the scale appears. The marking will easily come off with water or alcohol, and the scale can be reused and sanitized.

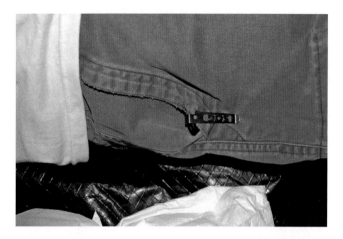

Figure 13.16 Right side, side pants pocket with what appears to be a knife.

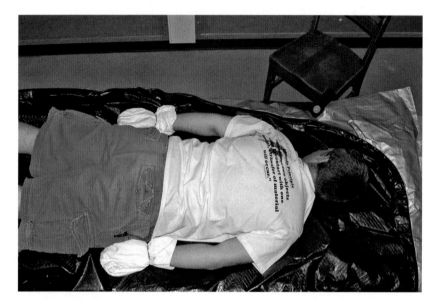

Figure 13.17 Top of the body, rear.

If we use a scale to "size" the subject's forehead in Figure 13.22, and if we only take the image with the scale, then what is potentially behind the scale (Figure 13.23)? If we take the image of the subject both with and without scale, we see that there is a scar behind where the scale was placed. It is important to image with and without scale so that there can be no accusation that you are "hiding" exculpatory evidence, evidence that can be used for the defense.

Hands

The hands are important. Both sides of both hands should be imaged, even if there is nothing there. The fact that there is not an artifact is also significant. Remember, negatives also

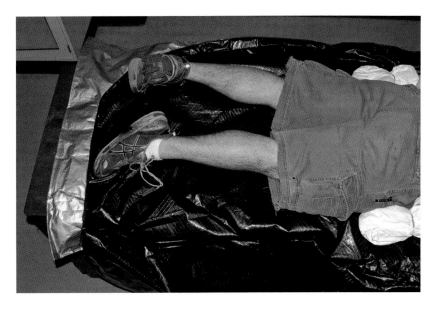

Figure 13.18 Bottom of the body, rear.

Figure 13.19 ID shot, face. This would be okay if the face, neck, or upper chest is not damaged. It is this ID shot that may be shown to the family to make a preliminary ID. Remember, a positive ID is only made by scientific methods (fingerprints, DNA, or dental x-rays).

tell part of the story. For example, they could show that there were no defensive wounds (Figures 13.24–13.27).

Any and all jewelry should be imaged. This can be important evidence, or the image can be later used to refute an accusation that a diamond ring worth $100,000 is missing (Figure 13.28). When describing jewelry, one should say "gold colored" rather than "gold" even if you know it is gold. Say "silver colored" even if you know it is silver. If the ring was a fake or copy, the owner may say, "You said it was a gold ring. Where is my gold ring?"

Next in your sequence are the overall images or full-body shots (after all clothing is removed). This can be accomplished best by using a small ladder. Many morgues have a

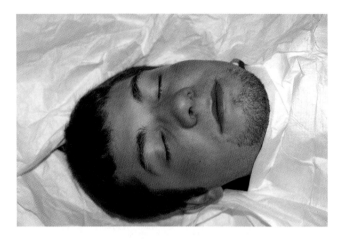

Figure 13.20 If the head, neck, or chest area is damaged, wrap the face in towels until only the undamaged area shows. This is not a forensic requirement but a compassionate one.

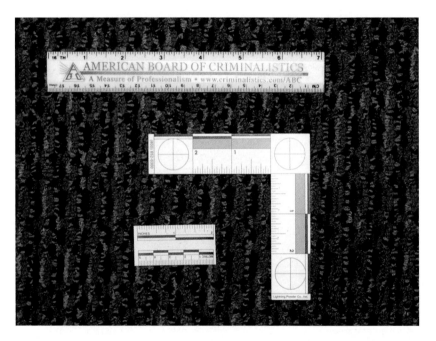

Figure 13.21 Several different types of scales: flat, two directional, and small adhesive backed.

device with stairs and a small platform on wheels that can be moved around the examination table. The reason the ladder or the platform device is used is that the body should be imaged with the camera at 90 degrees to the subject. If a ladder is not available, you may have to shoot in sections. If you must, make sure you overlap (Figures 13.29–13.32).

You should also photo image the back of the head to show any artifacts or the fact that there are no artifacts. Remember, we need to show negative as well as positive objects (Figure 13.33).

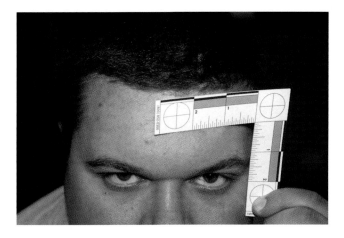

Figure 13.22 We shot wounds and artifacts with and without scale. Here is a subject with scale.

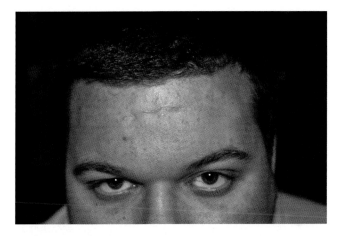

Figure 13.23 This is the same subject as in Figure 13.22 without scale. Notice the scar on the forehead? This was covered by the scale.

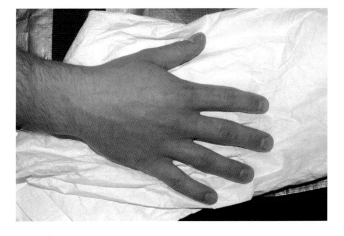

Figure 13.24 Right hand, back.

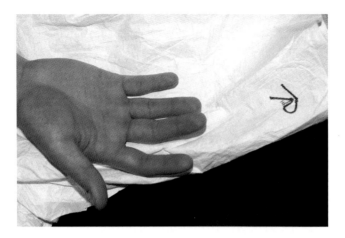

Figure 13.25 Right hand, palm.

Figure 13.26 Left hand, back.

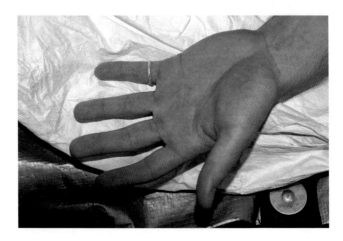

Figure 13.27 Left hand, palm.

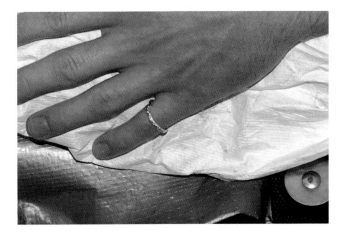

Figure 13.28 Left hand with silver-colored ring.

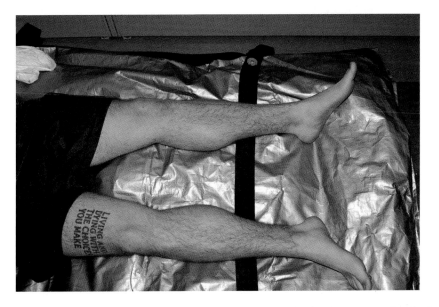

Figure 13.29 At this point, all clothes are removed, and the body is imaged naked. In the interest of my student who graciously volunteered to be my "dead body," he is wearing swimming trunks. Lower front body.

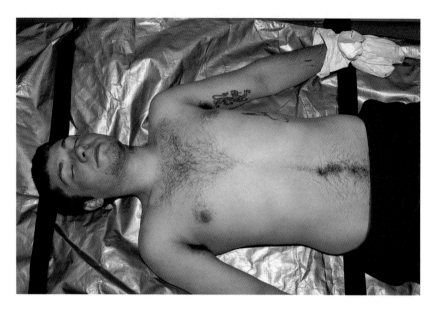

Figure 13.30 Upper front body.

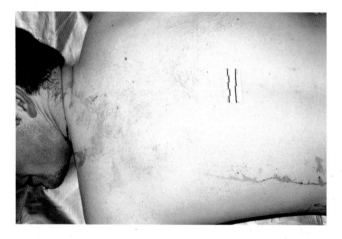

Figure 13.31 Upper back body.

Wounds

All wounds should be photo imaged separately (if possible—you may have a single sharp-force trauma wound extending from the front middle chest to the rear middle back, in which case it would be impossible to image separately). Photograph the wounds both with and without scale (Figure 13.34).

There are many different types of wounds. If an object is embedded in the victim, if it is wrapped or tied to the victim, or there are the remains of a medical procedure (Figures 13.35 and 13.36) (such as an endotracheal [ET] tube), these objects should be left embedded or attached to the victim. This is so that the forensic pathologist can see for

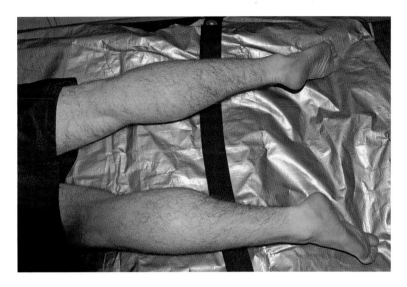

Figure 13.32 Lower back body.

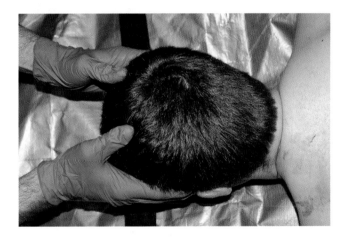

Figure 13.33 Back of head. Try to have your assistant, intern, or someone hold the head to be photographed.

him- or herself damage done by a weapon or medical procedure. These items should be photographed in place.

In Figure 13.37, the victim has a ligature wound around the neck. It is the electrical cord from a clock radio. It is also important to photo image any knots. In Figure 13.38, we can see the knot that was tied. This is important documentation. If the perpetrator took the time to tie a knot instead of just wrapping the cord around the victim's neck, this could identify intention as opposed to "heat of passion."

In some cases, you will be documenting several wounds at the same time. One type of wound melds into another. In Figure 13.39, the sharp-force trauma wound is evident. The wound was made by a hand axe. This is the primary wound. You should also note that

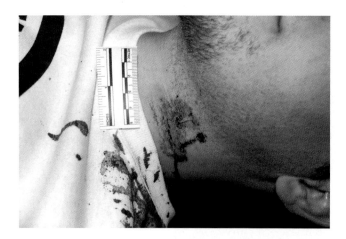

Figure 13.34 Wound on right front of the neck. Image this with and without scale.

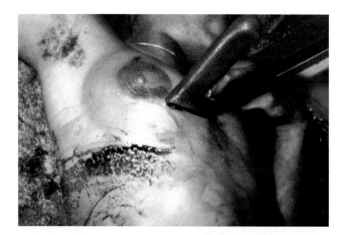

Figure 13.35 Knife in chest. This is a perspective shot showing several wounds in relative position to each other. You should also image them with and without scale at 90 degrees.

there was bruised eyelids or "racooning." This is the tertiary or secondary wound. This is caused by the force exerted to the head by the axe in addition to the cutting effect of the axe.

Many "top-of-the-head" wounds meld into this duality of wounds. Another example of the racooning effect is given by a gunshot wound to the forehead or the temple. This type of trauma creates bleeding in the head, and the blood flows to the eyelids. This is demonstrated in Figure 13.40. The victim was shot with a .22-caliber rifle at about 10 feet. The entry wound is indicated by the red circle.

Many individuals use firearms to commit suicide. The victim in Figure 13.41 committed suicide in front of a witness. If a shotgun or rifle is used, a good indicator that it is a suicide is that *the lips are intact*. An individual shooting him- or herself with a rifle or shotgun will place the muzzle of the gun in the mouth. When photo imaging the face, you should make every effort to get at least one image of the wound and the lips. The gas exiting the gun is what does the damage.

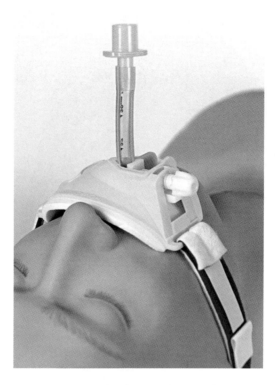

Figure 13.36 ET tube. This was a medical procedure performed at the hospital. After the subject dies, and if it becomes a coroner's case, nothing may be removed from the body. This includes a breathing tube, intravenous lines, chest tube, or any other object in or partially in the body.

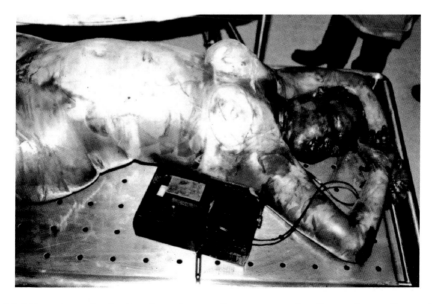

Figure 13.37 Body with electrical cord around victim's neck. The cord is still attached to a clock radio.

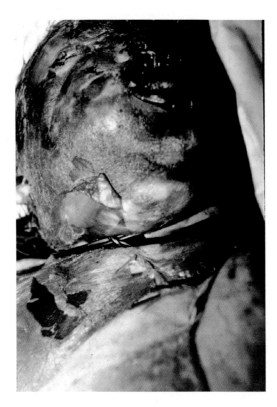

Figure 13.38 Close-up of the cord around the victim's neck showing the knot.

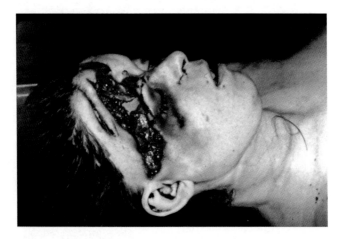

Figure 13.39 Victim with axe wound to right temple and forehead.

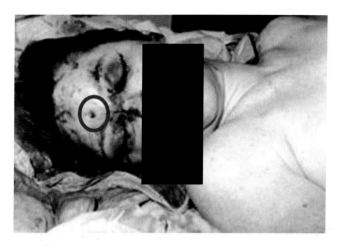

Figure 13.40 Victim with small caliber gunshot wound to forehead (see red circled area). This caused the phenomenon called "racooning." This occurs in head injuries. The blood from the gunshot wound seeped down into the eyelids. The victim was not beaten.

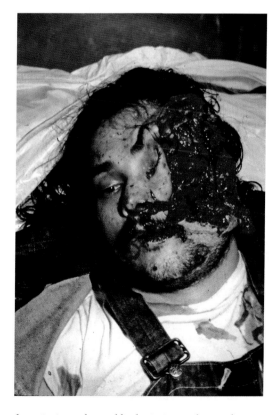

Figure 13.41 This is the victim of a self-administered gunshot wound. The shotgun was placed inside the mouth. Note that the lips are intact.

Figure 13.42 This image demonstrates livor mortis. Livor is the gravitational pooling of the blood after death. The plum-colored area is the livor. The white area is the area of the victim that was in contact with the floor. The blood was "pushed" out by the weight of the victim.

Lividity

Lividity is the gravitational pooling of the blood to the lowest part of the body after death. It is important to photograph the lividity at the scene and at the morgue to see if it has changed. If it has changed, then the body lividity may not have "set," which would assist in determining time since death. If it did not change, then lividity may have been set at the crime scene. In either case, it should be photo documented (Figure 13.42).

Scars, Marks, and Tattoos

There will be cases for which there will not be either a DNA or a fingerprint standard on file with which to compare to your victim. To make an identification, which will still need to be corroborated by another source, we can sometimes use scars, marks, and tattoos. Tattoos must be photographed with a scale. "Size is important," especially with tattoos. Make sure that images are taken both with and without a scale (Figures 13.43–13.46).

Scars can also be of help in establishing identity. Again, they must be shot at 90 degrees to the subject and remember to use the scale. In most cases, an on-camera flash will work well. If you find that you are getting a hot spot, you can try shooting with available light. A second option is to use indirect light or "bounce" lighting (Figure 13.47).

Birthmarks should also be documented with scale. Where they are located on the body should be listed in your photo log, which should be a part of your report package. The location can sometimes be seen in your overall pictures of the body; however, if they are small, they could be missed (Figure 13.48).

Anything unusual should be photo imaged. Too few objects, too many objects, or missing objects should be documented.

Figure 13.43 Tattoo of "Lady Justice" on victim with scale (overall photos were shot of the entire body without scale; you do not need to take the same shot without scale as these images have already been taken).

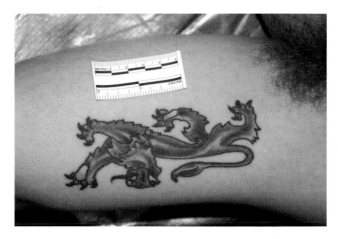

Figure 13.44 Tattoo of "griffin" on victim with scale (overall photos were shot of the entire body without scale; you do not need to take the same shot without scale as these images have already been taken).

Fingerprints

It is usually the procedure to take rolled, inked fingerprint impressions (10 print cards) from the victim to aid in identification. Due to the condition of the body, however, this is not always possible. We sometimes ask the forensic pathologist to remove the hands so that we can work on them in the lab, and if we are able to use techniques such as "gloving" or various "rehydration" techniques, then we do so. There are times when this is not an option. You can also attempt to photo image the fingers and attempt to recover the fingerprints with the aid of photography.

In all probability, when you work with a body at the morgue, there is an excellent chance that the body is going to be in rigor mortis (the stiffening of the body after death). You will

Figure 13.45 Tattoo "living and dying with the choices you make" on victim with scale (overall photos were shot of the entire body without scale; you do not need to take the same shot without scale as these images have already been taken).

Figure 13.46 Tattoo "my word is my bond" on victim with scale (overall photos were shot of the entire body without scale; you do not need to take the same shot without scale as these images have already been taken).

need to break rigor. This can be accomplished by moving the arm at the joint between the shoulder and the upper arm as though exercising. Then, after this joint becomes easily movable, do the same at the elbow joint. Next, do the same thing at the wrist. Finally, exercise the phalanges (fingers). This works relatively well. You will at least be able to move the fingers.

I have found that even though you have worked the rigor out by exercising, the fingers still have a tendency to curl. If you are working alone (without a partner or assistant), keeping the fingers straight (on a single plane for good overall focus), ensuring that there is a scale in the picture, and operating the camera are difficult unless you are an octopus.

I use a woodworker's clamp with a scale secured to one of the clamp edges (Figure 13.49). I realize that it looks like an object of medieval torture, but (a) the victim is dead and will not feel pain, and (b) you do not need to tighten it to the point at which it might have caused

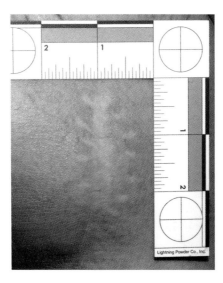

Figure 13.47 Scar, right knee with scale (overall photos were shot of the entire body without scale; you do not need to take the same shot without scale as these images have already been taken).

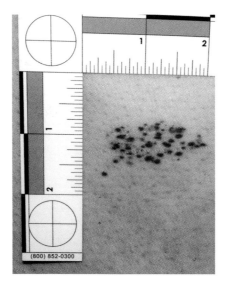

Figure 13.48 Birthmark on stomach (overall photos were shot of the entire body without scale; you do not need to take the same shot without scale as these images have already been taken).

pain in the living. Please note that I used one of my graduate students for the images taken, and I can assure you that no grad student was harmed in the making of these pictures.

After rigor has been reduced by movement in the phalanges, place one of the fingers in the clamp and "snug" it to keep the finger straight. In Figure 13.50, we have a good in-focus shot of the finger, but the ridges on the finger are not definitive. This is why, before you place the finger in the clamp, roll ink from a pad, glass plate, or stainless steel plate onto the finger. When photo imaged, the ridges can now be easily seen, as in Figure 13.51. When enlarged, ridges and in some cases the pores can be seen as in Figure 13.52.

Figure 13.49 Carpenter's wood clamp with scale affixed.

Figure 13.50 Subject's finger in clamp, with scale.

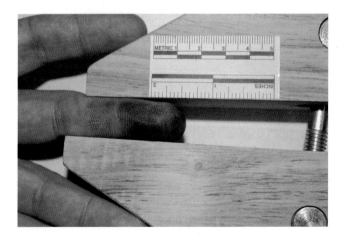

Figure 13.51 Subject's finger in clamp, inked, with scale.

Figure 13.52 Close up of subject's finger in clamp, inked, with scale.

Clothing

The clothing should be photographed after it is removed from the body. Each item should be imaged separately, front and back (Figures 13.53–13.58).

The personal property should be photographed (Figure 13.59). If currency (bills) is present, it should be fanned out and imaged also.

If additional detail is needed of a knife and wallet and its contents, for instance, the items can be photographed in the lab (see bench photography discussion in Chapter 7).

Figure 13.53 Victim's shirt, front with suspect blood.

Figure 13.54 Victim's shirt, back with suspect blood.

Figure 13.55 Victim's pants, front with suspect blood.

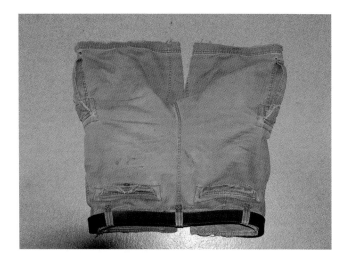

Figure 13.56 Victim's pants, back.

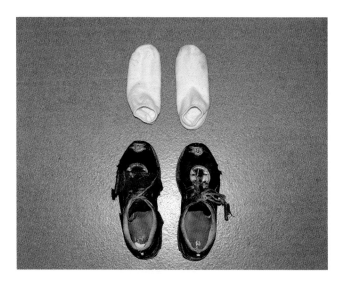

Figure 13.57 Victim's shoes and socks, front.

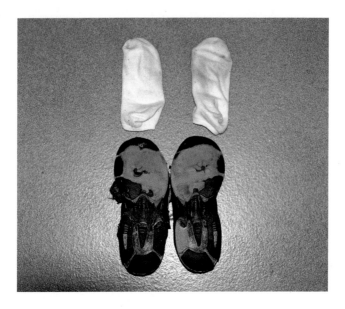

Figure 13.58 Victim's shoes and socks, back.

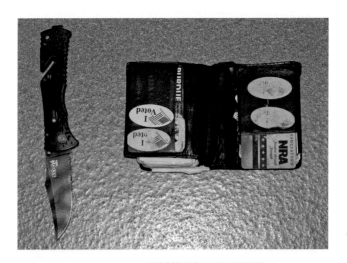

Figure 13.59 Victim's personal property.

Taphonomic and Entomological Imaging

14

Introduction

Taphonomy is the study of organisms after death. Taphonomists study the effects of many different forces on the organism that directly and indirectly affect decomposition. These forces include, but are not limited to, heat, cold, moisture, soil, scavengers, climate, insects, soil, vegetation, and more.

Entomology is the scientific study of insects. There are approximately 900,000 species of insects that have been recognized and documented. In the United States, there are considered to be 91,000 described species (*Smithsonian Encyclopedia*, 2009).

The Scene

The taphonomic scene is similar to that of a death investigation scene; however, additional care must be taken to include and photo document any and all insect activity as well as images of soil and vegetation. This image documentation must include not only the body itself but also the surrounding area.

Scavenging may occur; small- and medium-size wildlife may dismember and carry off parts of the body. It is important to locate the missing parts, document them, and document their relative position to the main body (perspective images).

As always, the first image should be the photo ID card. This will include the date, photographer's name, case number, and location. This image can be a close-up of the card showing the information only. This is important for record keeping and filing as well as identification of images in court.

The second image should be a photo indicating the north direction. This image should include a good portion of the background with the *N* card held by an assistant or propped up so that the *N* appears in the image. This is important so that you or others looking at this image, perhaps years after the incident, can determine which direction is north. You can then apply it to other images taken, thereby establishing compass direction in all photo images.

The Body

Approach the center of the scene (the body) from a direction that appears to be pristine. In this manner, you will preserve any footprints that may exist near the body. This is a path where you will see the vegetation standing straight. Areas that have been trampled may have evidence, so avoid walking in areas that have signs of walking by other individuals. We must show the lack of an artifact as well as artifacts. On your route to the body, photo image this area to show that there are no tracks. Photo image any area that has been

Figure 14.1 The path leading to the crime scene.

trampled. This will give an indication of how the perpetrator entered the scene to commit the crime or dump the body (Figure 14.1). It will also give you perspective of where the location is, how difficult it is to see from a distance, and how difficult it was to bring the victim to this place or to dump the body here.

Insects

There are a number of insects of interest to forensic entomologists. One of the most important, however, is the blowfly (*Phormia regina*) (Figure 14.2). When a death occurs in animals, including humans, the body chemistry changes, and an odor or pheromone is given off that is a signal to the blowfly that there is a prime area for ovaposition, or laying of their

Figure 14.2 The blowfly (*Phormia regina*).

Figure 14.3 The flies on the body began to arrive only minutes after death or when the body is "dumped."

Figure 14.4 Individual groups or concentrations of flies should be photographed. Also, take perspective shots to show the various groups and their relative locations on the body.

eggs. The blowflies come within 1 minute of the death (Figure 14.3). If the organism dies in place or the organism is dumped, the blowflies begin to lay their eggs after several minutes (Figure 14.4). Groups of flies should be photographed along with perspective shots showing the various collections of groups.

The blowflies will seek out body openings (e.g., the mouth, nose, eyes, vagina, penis, and rectum) in which to lay their eggs (Figures 14.5 and 14.6). They will also seek wounds inflicted on the body, such as gunshot or knife wounds. Figure 14.7 shows that wound openings are also a desirable site for the blowfly to lay its eggs. The eggs themselves appear as a white sawdust-type material. Figure 14.8 shows an egg mass behind the ear of a pig.

Before any collection of insects is made, photo image the body. Photograph clusters of insects so that the area of the body on which they are present can be determined from the image. Collect the insects from several areas (Figure 14.9). Remember to photo image

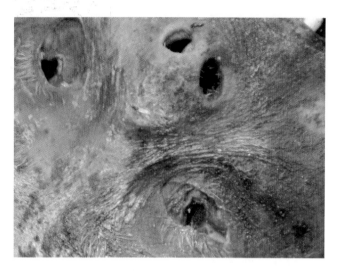

Figure 14.5 The missing eyes were probably removed by scavengers (crows as an example). This is also a prime location for the blowfly to lay eggs.

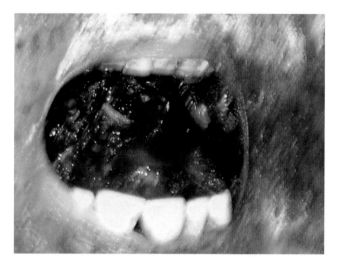

Figure 14.6 The mouth, a natural body opening, is also one of the desirable locations for ovapositioning the fly's eggs. (Photo image by Clayton Nolting.)

both with and without scale. Photo image the collection process. These images are often not taken. They do provide valuable evidence in court if there is a question involving the proper collection and the location of the insects on the body. They also aid the forensic entomologist if the entomologist is not at the scene.

Use a body diagram to identify where the insects were photographed and recovered from the body (Figure 14.10). For example, link the maggots in Figure 14.9, the flies in Figure 14.7, and the eggs in Figure 14.8 to the body diagram (Figure 14.11).

Photograph the small bottles and the rearing container (maggot motel). The "maggot motel" consists of a Styrofoam cup containing a small amount of vermiculite in the bottom with an aluminum foil pocket containing about 1 ounce of liver. Maggots are placed in the container and reared to adulthood.

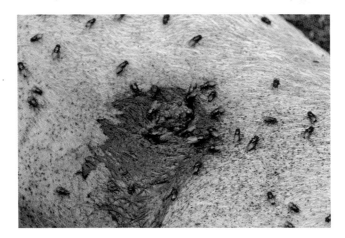

Figure 14.7 This gunshot wound is an unnatural opening in the body. This is a desirable location for the blowflies to lay their eggs. (Photo image by Clayton Nolting.)

Figure 14.8 The off-white sawdust-like material is a group of blowfly eggs. (Photo image by Clayton Nolting.)

Figure 14.9 A cluster of maggots.

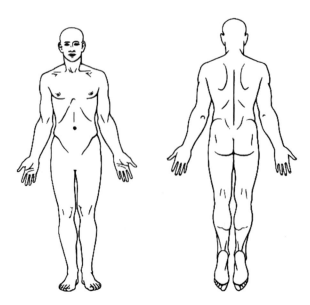

Figure 14.10 Body diagram used to plot clusters of insects.

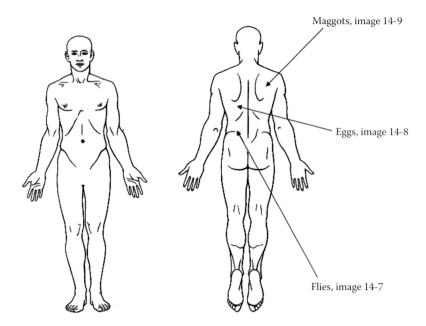

Maggots, image 14-9

Eggs, image 14-8

Flies, image 14-7

Figure 14.11 An example of a completed diagram.

Adult flies and other flying insects may be collected with the use of a net. These collections should also be photo imaged, as should the packaging of these samples (Figure 14.12).

Photo image from the center of the scene outward. Shoot images from the four points of the compass: from the south out, from the north out, from the east out, and from the west out. You can shoot from the southwest in, from the southeast in, from the northeast in, and from the northwest in.

Figure 14.12 Collection of insects. The individual in the photo is collecting maggots for the "maggot motel," a rearing chamber for the maggots. The maggots will be reared to adulthood in the lab so that positive species of insects can be made.

If the body is not whole, if body parts have been carried or dragged off by small animals, then each location of the body parts should be photo imaged separately. Each area should be imaged with a north card and imaged from the four points of the compass. Do not forget perspective shots from where the scavenged parts were located to the main body site.

If body parts were recovered from the scene, they should have been collected and packaged separately. Each of the body parts should be photographed in detail at this time. Lighting at the scene if the body was discovered at night may have been fair at best, but the morgue is well lit and will provide a controlled environment in which to take photo images.

Maggot Mass and Maggot Migration

Depending on the extent of the decomposition of the body, there may be a "maggot mass." This is a large concentration of maggots; there may be thousands. Image this phenomenon (Figures 14.13 and 14.14). When the maggots have finished feeding, they will begin to migrate away from the cadaver and seek a place to pupate, the next stage in their life cycle. They normally follow the sun when they migrate. They will move in the same direction in a mass, a maggot mass migration. If this is seen, it should be photo documented (Figures 14.15 and 14.16).

After they arrive at their destination, they dig down in the soil and begin the next part of their life cycle, pupa (Figure 14.17). When this area is located, it should also be photo imaged. The pupa should also be collected for the forensic entomologist.

If a forensic entomologist is not available for the scene, it is even more important to have the insects and their recovery photo documented.

Figure 14.13 Maggot mass almost completely covering a pig carcass.

Figure 14.14 Another maggot mass. The maggots are approaching their end of feeding and will shortly migrate away from the food source to a location they can "dig in" to the soil and pupate. (Photo by Marissa McDonough.)

Containers

There are times that the body will be found in a container. Sometimes bodies in containers are found outdoors and sometimes indoors. If the container can be collected after the body is removed, it should inventoried as evidence and photographed (Figure 14.18). The container can be as simple as a plastic bag.

It could also be a sealed garbage container. Figure 14.19 shows an experiment that was conducted at our remote research facility. A pig was placed in a 55-gallon plastic garbage container to study the effects of decomposition in a closed container. We use pigs because they closely mimic the human body in decomposition studies. We do not kill pigs for our experiments. When a pig dies at one of the local pig farms, the farms call us,

Figure 14.15 A maggot mass migration. After the maggots have completed their feeding, they will set or start their migration. They do it all together in one giant mass. When they reach their destination, they will bury themselves in the soil, preparing to pupate (move to the next stage of their life cycle). (Photo by Marissa McDonough.)

Figure 14.16 Another image of the maggot mass migration. The maggots follow the sun (directionally). If it appears that the insects have already migrated, look to the west or east (they could have migrated in the morning or late afternoon). If so, dig around in the soil until you discover the puparia and photograph them. (Photo by Marissa McDonough.)

and we retrieve the carcass. We then either use it in an ongoing study, or we freeze it for future use.

Dr. Ralph Williams, professor of entomology and a board certified forensic entomologist, is seen in Figure 14.20 placing the can inside the fences of the research facility. This is the type of scenario that I have come across as a criminalistics investigator. We check and photograph the container and its contents daily.

Other things to look for are drag tracks. A container with a body inside is heavy and will make tracks even if it has wheels (see Figure 14.21) If no tracks are observed, the body and the container may have been carried in separately.

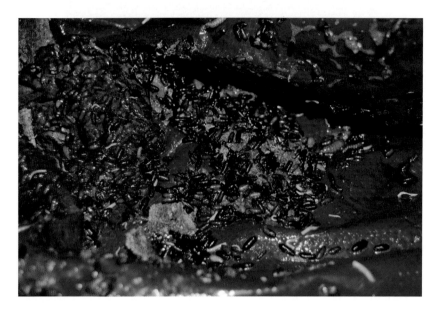

Figure 14.17 Image of the blowfly puparia.

Figure 14.18 A plastic bag as a container. The flies will lay their eggs on the bag. The bag does not mask the odor that calls to the blowfly.

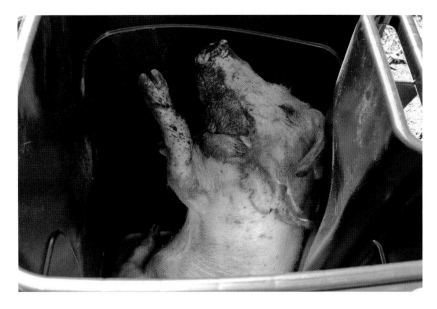

Figure 14.19 A 55-gallon garbage can containing a 125-pound dead pig. This was part of a decomposition study. Even though the garbage can had a snap lid, the flies still came.

Figure 14.20 Dr. Ralph Williams, professor of entomology and board certified as a forensic entomologist, places the garbage can in the research compound for a decomposition study.

Figure 14.21 Look for and photo image apparent drag marks. These marks were made by the wheels on the can. The drag marks could be heels (two parallel) or the head (if dragged by the heels). Photo image if there are none. This could indicate the perpetrator carried the victim, then carried the container in separately.

Vehicles

Vehicles are handy containers in which bodies are sometimes found. The body should be imaged before removal, as should locations of insect activity (Figures 14.22–14.24). After the body and insects are photographed, collect the appropriate insect samples. Do not forget to photograph the collection process.

Figure 14.22 Image of a man in the trunk of a car. Notice the presence of maggots even though the trunk was closed. Flies, when they are "called" by the odor, will get into all but the most perfectly sealed containers.

Figure 14.23 This image of the man in Figure 14.22 was taken at a different angle. A maggot mass can be observed at the lower legs.

Figure 14.24 A closer view of the man in the trunk from Figure 14.22. Note the black plastic tie wrap. This may have been used to secure the victim's hands or feet.

Water Recovery

Insect imaging when there is a water recovery involved poses some additional problems. For example, in Figure 14.25, the body shows several areas of insect masses. When imaging the body, of course we try to image the body in the water at an angle of 90 degrees. You have to stand in the boat to do this. Be careful. Have someone in the boat hold your belt from the back to give better balance. I have mentioned that we learn from our mistakes. Please learn from mine. *I fell in.* I did save the camera, however.

Take many images of the body while it is still in the water. This is because when you attempt to recover the body, it may break apart. After you have photographed the body, taken samples, and made notations of the location from which the samples were taken, recover the body. We used a "Stokes" basket. It worked well. We did not have dismemberment.

Figure 14.25 Body in water. Aquatic insects may be present, but because the body is floating, part of the body sticks out of the water. (The body floats because of the decomposition gases created and captured in the body's torso). Because of this, the part of the body out of the water will "call" the blowflies. Image the maggots and their location before a water recovery is attempted. Recovering the body from the water could disrupt the insect groups. Oh yes, and don't fall in.

Figure 14.26 shows the body from Figure 14.25 at the morgue. Note that the insect masses are different. This is why it is important to photo document the insects and their location on the body at the scene.

Bones

Often, you will get an assignment regarding a found body. On most of those occasions, it is in fact a body, skeletal remains, or body part. You must treat these cases as if the object is human remains, even if you are suspicious that they are not human. We received an assignment in relation to human remains near a river. On arrival, we found bones that a citizen had reported (see Figure 14.27). We initiated a grid search and discovered several other concentrations of bones.

The initial set of bones in Figure 14.27 appeared to be pig bones. The bone concentration in Figures 14.28 and 14.29, however, were identified as human bones. We were fortunate to have a medical examiner on the scene.

The moral to this story is as follows: Do not investigate a crime scene with preconceived ideas or prejudices.

The Autopsy

After all additional evidence is collected from the scene and the body is removed, attend the postmortem (autopsy). Normally, when the body arrives at the morgue, the body is

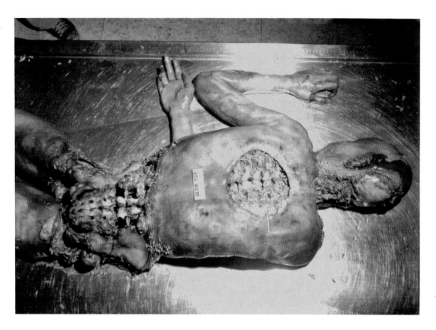

Figure 14.26 This is the body in water originally pictured in Figure 14.25 now seen at the morgue. You can see that many of the insects are missing from the pelvic area that was originally seen when the body was in the water.

Figure 14.27 The discovery of bones along a river was reported to the police. On arrival, the bones were pointed out by the citizen. They were identified as pig bones. However, see Figures 14.28 and 14.29.

refrigerated. This retards the growth and mobility of the insects. When the body is posted, take additional photo images. Some areas of the body may have insect activity that was covered at the scene. The body is normally not completely stripped until the forensic pathologist views the body. These additional areas may prove to be significant and should be thoroughly photo documented.

Figure 14.28 These bones were found in the same immediate area as the pig bones in Figure 14.27. These bones were identified as human.

Figure 14.29 These bones, well hidden by vegetation, were also identified as human bones.

Auto Processing

15

Introduction

Auto processing sounds simple, and it is, as long as you completely photo document the vehicle. The first and second images taken should be your photo ID card and the north card, respectively. After those are taken, we can start on the vehicle itself. Regardless of whether the crime involved is a homicide, theft of auto, or simply theft from auto, you should still photo document the vehicle as completely as possible.

A vehicle-processing report should be used. It is a checklist of items that should be documented when a vehicle is involved. It also has an area in which to record any evidence recovered, the photo images taken, and of course a narrative (Figure 15.1). If you do not have one in your department or agency reporting system, a simple lined sheet will suffice.

Exterior

Start from the outside and work in. Photo image the front side, driver's side, passengers' side, and rear of the vehicle. When describing the sides, use "driver's side" and "passengers' side." If you use left and right sides, this could be confusing depending on whether you are looking at the vehicle from the front or from the rear (Figures 15.2–15.5).

If there are any artifacts (objects that do not belong), photograph them and describe them in your photo listing. This would include damage to the vehicle, stickers, bumper stickers, and objects attached to the radio antenna.

Photograph the front license plate (Figure 15.6). Some states only issue one license plate, in which case it is displayed on the rear. If the vehicle is registered in a one-plate state, photograph the front plate holder or the decorative plate that some people display. Look for insect debris. This indicates that the plate was on the front of the vehicle for some time.

Photograph the real plate (Figure 15.7). Examine this plate for insect debris. If insect debris is found on this plate (displayed on the rear), this could indicate that the plate was recently on the front of another vehicle and may be lost or stolen.

Image the vehicle identification number (VIN). It is located on the driver's side dashboard and viewable from the exterior of the vehicle. Because you will have to shoot through the windshield glass, you may have a glare. This is a good time to use your polarizing filter. See Figure 15.8 for an image without a polarizing filter and Figure 15.9 for one with a polarizing filter. This is just like when you are wearing Polaroid sunglasses to cut down glare; the polarizing filter can be used to eliminate the glare so that you can get a clear image of the VIN. If the VIN is missing or if the owner has placed something on the dash to obscure the VIN plate, photograph it anyway. This may be important later if the owner is trying to hide ownership of the vehicle.

Vehicle Process Report

Report Classification [   ]　　Case Number [   ]

Date/Time [   ]　　Type of Location [   ]　　Agency [   ]　　Investigator [   ]

Victim's Name [   ]　　Victim's Address [   ]

Inventory Control Number [   ]　　Images Taken [   ]

Make [   ]

Model [   ]

Year [   ]

Color [   ]

Plate Number/State [   ]

VIN [   ]

Odometer [   ]

Clock/Time [   ]

Passenger Side　　**Top**　　**Driver Side**

Windows [   ]

Draw lines and clearly identify artifacts on the vehicle. Number them and describe in narrative.

Climate Control [   ]　　Blower/Fan [   ]　　Keys in Ignition [   ]　　Motor Running [   ]

Radio [   ]　　Exterior Temp [   ]　　Interior Temp [   ]　　Windows [   ]

Vehicle Length [   ]　　Front Bumper to Wind [   ]　　Front Window to Rear Window [   ]

Vehicle Width [   ]　　Rear Window to Rear Bumper [   ]　　Lights [   ]

Other Markings [   ]

Evidence Collected				Photo Images			
1		11		1		11	
2		12		2		12	
3		13		3		13	
4		14		4		14	
5		15		5		15	
6		16		6		16	
7		17		7		17	
8		18		8		18	
9		19		9		19	
10		20		10		20	

Signature

　　Note: Start listing photo images on this report - if additional space is needed use Photo Listing Sheet　　Page [   ]

Figure 15.1 Vehicle process report.

Figure 15.2 Vehicle, exterior, driver's side, overall photo.

Figure 15.3 Vehicle, exterior, passenger's side, overall photo.

Photo image any and all stickers located on the vehicle. There is a decal indicating where the vehicle was manufactured (Figure 15.10). If this sticker exists on the vehicle, it is most likely that the windshield has not been replaced. There appears to be a parking tag displayed inside the front windshield in Figure 15.11. Photograph such a tag. Because of the windshield, you may have to use a polarizing filter.

The rear bumper has some type of soil debris on it in our example. A sample should be taken for analysis; however, before the sample is taken, it should be photo imaged, both with and without scale (Figures 15.12 and 15.13).

Figure 15.4 Vehicle, exterior, front side, overall photo.

Figure 15.5 Vehicle, exterior, rear side, overall photo.

If the vehicle exhibits a specific pattern of mud spatter, it also should be photo documented. Samples should also be taken (Figure 15.14).

Interior

Now, we can move to the interior. I suggest that before you start taking photographs, without touching anything, you make a detailed inspection of the interior. Because of the

Figure 15.6 Vehicle, exterior, front license plate photo (tag).

Figure 15.7 Vehicle, exterior, rear license plate photo (tag).

potential for "booby traps," we have to be more cautious than we have been in the past. Open all doors: front, back, hatch or trunk, and hood, and examine the door frames.

Photo image the front, both driver's and passenger's sides (Figures 15.15 and 15.16). In this instance, when opened the driver's side door revealed an identifier sticker (Figure 15.17). The passenger's side door also had an identifying sticker (Figure 15.18).

The back seating area should be shot from both sides (Figures 15.19 and 15.20).

At this point, we should photo document the rest of the interior. Every effort should be made *not* to sit in the vehicle. Remember Locard's principle: Every contact leaves a trace. Photo image the gauges on the dash. You may have to start the vehicle if the gauges are digital. They are important, however. They can indicate quantity of fuel, mileage, or if there are any warning lights indicating problems with the engine or other car systems (Figure 15.21).

Image the console panel with the engine turned on and started. This can show if the radio was on, whether the heat or air conditioning was on, and the position of the blower selector (Figure 15.22). Note any accessories plugged into the cigarette lighter.

Figure 15.8 Vehicle, exterior, VIN through glass, no filter.

Figure 15.9 Vehicle, exterior, VIN through glass. A polarizing filter was used to photo image the VIN (vehicle identification number). The VIN is located on the driver's side dash, accessible only through the dash window. The use of the polarizing filter eliminates the glare on the window.

Figure 15.10 Photo of a decal on the passenger's side dash window.

Figure 15.11 Parking pass attached to the interior dash window, center.

Figure 15.12 Debris on rear bumper.

Figure 15.13 Debris on rear bumper, with scale.

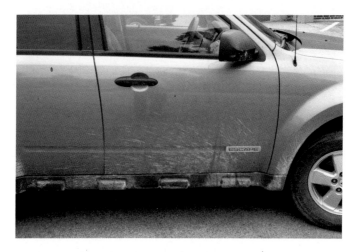

Figure 15.14 Mud spatter on passenger's side, front door.

Figure 15.15 Interior, front, driver's side.

Figure 15.16 Interior, front, passenger's side.

Figure 15.17 ID sticker, driver's side, front door.

Figure 15.18 ID sticker, passenger's side, front door

Figure 15.19 Interior, driver's side, rear seat.

Figure 15.20 Interior, passenger's side, rear seat.

Figure 15.21 Interior, driver's side dash, gauges with current mileage, 28291.3 miles, full tank of gas.

Figure 15.22 Interior, front dash console.

Compartments and Hidey-Holes

Examine the glove compartment. Photograph it and its contents (Figure 15.23). Some vehicles have a center console compartment. Photo image it, even if it is empty. Remember, we need to show negatives as well as positives (Figure 15.24). Again, some vehicles have a security area in the center console compartment. You may have to look carefully (Figure 15.25).

Today's vehicles have more and more storage places and hidey-holes. You need to check and photo document them all. Check the headliner. Open the compartments and photograph the interior of each area (Figure 15.26).

Examine under the seats. Under the driver's side seat in this example, we can see part of what appears to be a handgun. Before it is moved or examined, it was photo documented in place. You will notice in Figure 15.27 that a good part of the gun is dark while the butt is light. This is because the flash was on top of the camera and above the lens. The seat shadows the flash so that it does not completely light the gun. There is a simple solution. Turn the camera upside-down so that the flash is on the bottom of the camera and below the lens (Figure 15.28). It is a bit awkward, but it does not matter to the camera. Take the image. You can always rotate the image so the top of the seat is on the top of the image. Figure 15.29 is the same as Figure 15.27 except that the camera was turned upside-down. Note that this technique works well when shooting under beds, dressers, desks, and furniture. After a gun has been photo imaged in place, it can be removed, and an image with scale can be taken (Figure 15.30).

Figure 15.23 Interior, passenger's side, glove compartment.

Figure 15.24 Interior, center console.

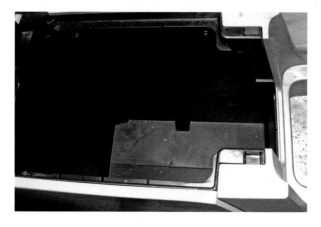

Figure 15.25 Interior, center console, security compartment.

Figure 15.26 Interior, front, headliner compartments.

Figure 15.27 Interior, front driver's side, under seat, gun butt. This image was taken with an internal flash (top of the camera).

Figure 15.28 Nikon D-40 with the camera inverted (flash on bottom of camera.

Figure 15.29 Interior, front driver's side, under seat, gun butt. This image was taken with an internal flash (top of the camera), but the camera was inverted. This places the flash under the camera, which will light under the seat better (see Figure 15.27).

Figure 15.30 Gun, with scale, photo imaged on pavement.

When you photo image areas of interest through a door, a window, or a hole, do not be afraid to change your format from horizontal to vertical. For example, in Figure 15.31 we see the backseat of the vehicle in the horizontal format. It is an image of the same area seen in Figure 15.20, but it has more area dedicated to the area of interest.

Trunk and Engine

The engine should be imaged just for the record to indicate that there is in fact an engine (Figure 15.32). Do not laugh. I was involved in a case in which we were processing a stolen auto. Fortunately, we photographed under the hood—there was no engine. At trial (the perpetrators were charged with theft of auto), the defense asked how the defendants drove the vehicle to the drop site where it was recovered. I replied, it did not have an engine, and that another method was used. The defense asked for an acquittal based on the fact that the vehicle could not have been driven, and therefore the defendant could not have driven

Figure 15.31 Interior, rear seat, passenger's side. This was shot with the camera in the vertical position. This allows the image area to be compatible to the object being imaged.

Figure 15.32 Engine area under front hood.

it to steal the vehicle. The acquittal was not granted. The prosecutor asked me on rebuttal how did I think it was stolen. I replied that I did not think; I knew. He asked me to explain. I said that when we opened the hood to photograph the engine (standard operating procedure), I found no engine. I photographed the empty space where the engine should have been. On further inspection of the vehicle, I found tool marks under the front bumper. I photographed them as well. With that information, the detective on the case was able to obtain a warrant to search the defendant's truck. The tool marks on the bumper matched the chain and hook that was discovered, as the result of the search warrant, in the bed of the defendant's pickup truck. Sometimes it is hard to keep a straight face in court.

You will also need to photograph the trunk or cargo area of the vehicle (Figure 15.33). Note that these cargo areas sometimes have lockable or hidden areas in which to keep things. You may have to lift up the carpet or mat in this area to discover the hidden storage area (Figure 15.34).

Figure 15.33 Interior cargo area.

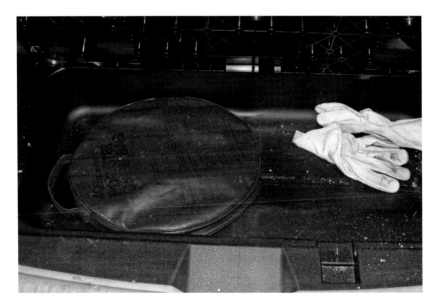

Figure 15.34 Interior, cargo area, security compartment.

Fingerprints

16

Latent Prints

Latent fingerprints are fingerprints that are invisible to the naked eye. In most instances, they must be developed before they can be photo imaged. The prints we are required to photo image are not always of the best quality. The fingerprints we see on TV and in movies I like to call "Hollywood prints." They are perfect in every way and are crisp and sharp (Figure 16.1). What we get to work with are "partials" or "partial fingerprints," which are far less perfect than the TV version. Thanks to the fingerprint examiners, comparisons can still be made, even with partials (Figure 16.2).

In photo imaging latents, we use a variety of techniques. If we have an object that has not yet been dusted, the object should be examined with a light source. A high-intensity flashlight is good, but in the lab, we have access to a variety of light sources. An excellent light source is the halogen fiber-optic unit. Its light is directional and can be adjusted to an infinite number of combinations (Figure 16.3).

General Rules

In general, it is always necessary to photo image fingerprints or friction ridge transfers with a scale. The fingerprint examiner needs to know the size of the print. It is also useful in printing a copy that is truly life-size. The image of the print should have as much contrast as possible.

Always image the latent at 90 degrees to the print so there is no distortion.

The best-case scenario is to take the object to the laboratory; however, that cannot always be done. Second best is to lift the print. Third best is to photo image the print. Before you move the object, you should photo image it in case it gets damaged in the process of taking the object. You should photo image the print before you lift it. No matter how good you are at lifting prints, there is always the possibility of a mistake.

When focusing on the print, turn the automatic focus off. Focus the camera at its maximum macro focusing and move the camera and your body toward the object and away until the object appears in focus. When doing close-up photo imaging, the automatic focus on most cameras will go crazy, moving one way, then the other.

Turn off your flash when imaging prints. Often, the surface will reflect, causing "flashback," which makes part of the image unable to be viewed.

Figure 16.1 This is an image of what I call a "Hollywood print." It is perfect. It appears as though it were "stamped" on the object from which it was recovered.

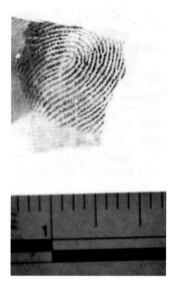

Figure 16.2 This is a developed "partial" print. This is an excellent print and suitable for comparison.

Fingerprints on Glass

Imaging fingerprints on flat glass is a relatively easy proposition. The problem is that glass is transparent. If you attempt to photo image the developed latent on the glass, the image is cluttered by the background, the other side of the glass (Figure 16.4).

A simple solution is to provide a contrasting, noncluttered background. This can be accomplished by taping a plain piece of white paper (if black powder was used for the fingerprint) to the other side of the glass (Figure 16.5).

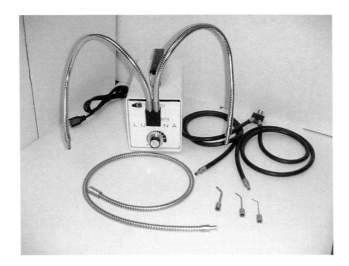

Figure 16.3 Fiber Lite. This is a halogen 100-watt light with fiber-optic gooseneck arms (two) that allow the light generated from it to be directed at specific objects.

Figure 16.4 This is a photo image of a developed latent fingerprint on glass. It is almost unreadable because of the background.

Fingerprints on Curved Glass

It is not as easy as flat glass to make a photo image of bottles, jars, and glasses (Figure 16.6). This is because the print is not flat (on a single plane) but rather on a curve (actually on a number of different planes). The problem is depth of field. This is the area that is in focus in front of the lens. The lens actually focuses on a single distance (Figure 16.7). There is an area of acceptable focus in front of and behind the focus (plane). This is approximately a third in front and two-thirds behind the plane of focus.

The *closer* to the object that you get, the *smaller the area of depth of field* becomes. This is not a real problem when you are 5 to 8 feet from your subject, but this has a great impact

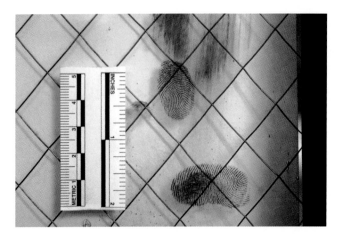

Figure 16.5 This is the same photo image of a developed latent fingerprint on glass as in Figure 16.4 except that a white piece of paper was placed behind the glass to add contrast. Now, it is easily readable.

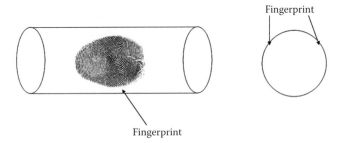

Fingerprint

Fingerprint

Figure 16.6 Drawing of a fingerprint on a vial (curved surface).

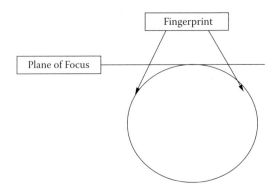

Fingerprint

Plane of Focus

Figure 16.7 The "plane of focus." Because this is a curved surface, the area of the curve that is tangent to the vial is in focus. The areas that are under the plane are not in focus. This means that only part of the fingerprint will be in focus. The plane of focus is determined by the depth of field, which is dependent on the aperture of the lens.

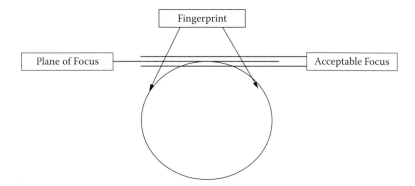

Figure 16.8 The depth of field (dependent on the aperture; the smaller the aperture, the more depth of field). The area of acceptable focus still does not cover the entire area of the latent. Use the smallest aperture setting (f/22 or f/32) for the largest depth of field.

on you when you are 2 inches from your subject. If you focus on the topmost portion of the curved vial, you can see from the diagram in Figure 16.8 that part of the print will not be in acceptable focus (it does not fall within the acceptable focus area).

One method that you can use is to set the aperture as small as possible. The *greater* the number (f/stop), the *smaller the opening* becomes. The f/32 stop is very small and allows a greater depth of field, and f/3.5 is large and allows a smaller depth of field. The *smaller the opening* on the lens, the *greater the area of depth of field,* the area that is in acceptable focus.

If a flash is used, a flashback occurs, making the print unreadable (Figure 16.9). Remove the flash and use a fixed light. This could be a professional photo light or a simple goose-neck desk lamp. I suggest a halogen if possible. It is an intensely white light. Set the lights up at oblique angles to the subject. Examine the subject from the position that the camera should be. If you see a reflection, move one or both of the light sources until you see no reflection. I have also used a set of "helping hands" to secure the vial (Figure 16.10).

Just as with flat glass, we have the same problem with transparency. This can be easily solved with the use of a small piece of white paper. Roll up a small piece of white paper and place it inside the vial. This will eliminate the transparency issue and provide a contrasting background (Figure 16.11).

Figure 16.9 Latent fingerprint developed with black powder and photographed with the internal flash. There is considerable flashback.

Figure 16.10 Light setup using fixed incandescent lamps will eliminate flashback. Placing a white piece of paper inside the vial will make the latent with black powder contrast against the background.

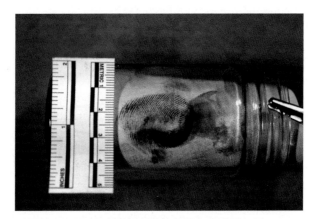

Figure 16.11 This image was taken with the light setup shown in Figure 16.10. A white piece of paper was also placed in the vial for extra contrast.

Feathers

Yes, feathers are helpful. As a criminalistic investigator (that is what we were called before the advent of TV and all the *CSI* programs), you will be called on to attempt to recover latent fingerprints from just about anything. On one occasion, I was asked to recover latent fingerprints and photo image them from a live monkey. I respectfully advised that I was unable to comply due to the fact that the monkey's hair was an unsuitable surface. Fur is *not* a suitable surface.

Feathers, on the other hand are much more realistic. Some tropical birds are worth thousands of dollars. Any object of value is also an object that could and will be stolen. The

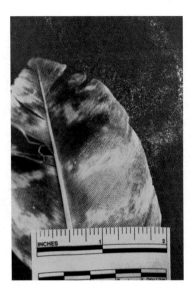

Figure 16.12 This is a latent fingerprint developed with green fluorescent powder and the Jones Brush System for the application and a UV light (365 nm). Additional contrast can be obtained by using a band-pass filter.

perpetrators, when making their grab for the birds, rarely wear gloves. The birds are not thrilled with the concept of being forcefully removed from their cages, so they flutter and lose feathers that drop to the bottom of the cage.

The latents on the feathers must first be developed. This can be done using the Jones Brush System that I developed while at Purdue University. It blows on the fingerprint powder rather than rubbing it on with a brush; the user therefore does not cross contaminate the objects for DNA and is able to dust small and fragile objects without the potential to "scrub" the print, destroying it (Figure 16.12).

I suggest using a fluorescent powder. Most colored powders blend in with many of the colors of the birds. Use an ultraviolet (UV; long-wave) light source. Turn off your flash and any other ambient light source. The results are impressive.

Prints on Pills and Capsules

Photo imaging pills and capsules is helpful in drug cases when possession of the actual drug is in question. First, latents must be developed with powder. This can be accomplished with the Jones Brush System. For the example here, two halogen gooseneck lamps were set up on the lab bench at an oblique angle (45 degrees to the pill). The camera can be set up on a copy stand or it can be handheld. Using a copy stand makes it easier to keep the camera at 90 degrees from the object (Figures 16.13–16.15).

Focusing is accomplished by extending the lens to its maximum close-up ability (best is 1:1), then raising and lowering it until it is in focus. Then, you can perform fine focus using the focusing ring on the lens.

Do not forget the scale. In close-up photo imaging, the depth of field is small. If you place the scale on the copy stand next to the capsule and focus on the capsule, the capsule will be in focus, and the scale will be out of focus. This is because of the extremely small area that is in focus. The

Figure 16.13 This is the light setup for the capsule imaged in Figure 16.18.

Figure 16.14 Because we are using a macro lens and are imaging at macro distances (1:1 ratio), even though we are using an aperture of f/32 the depth of field is still small. When we use a scale with our capsule, we focus on the top of the capsule where the developed latent is located. We must arrange the shot so that the surface of the scale is on the same plane of focus as the surface of the capsule. To do this, use a small piece of rope caulk. Build up the caulk so that the surfaces of the scale and the capsule are on the same plane.

Figure 16.15 The surface of the capsule and the surface of the scale are on the same plane.

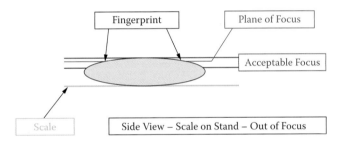

Figure 16.16 The area of acceptable focus if the surface of the scale is not on the same plane as the developed latent fingerprint on the capsule.

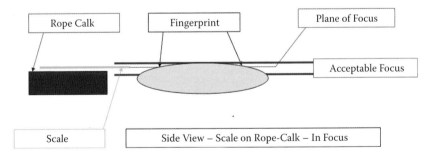

Figure 16.17 The area of acceptable focus if the surface of the scale is on the same plane as the developed latent fingerprint on the capsule.

field can be expanded slightly by "stopping down" the aperture (f/32 or f/64), but this may not be enough for both the scale on the stand and the capsule to be in focus (Figure 16.16).

The scale must be raised to the same level (plane) as the top of the capsule, so the top of the capsule and the scale are on the same plane. This can be accomplished by the use of some rope caulk. Tear a small piece from the roll (Figure 16.17). Manipulate the rope caulk so that it is the same thickness as the capsule. Place the rope caulk next to the capsule.

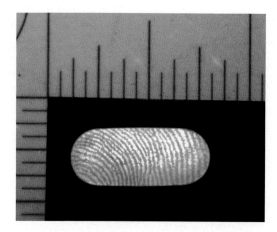

Figure 16.18 The image of the capsule with the developed latent fingerprint with scale, both in focus. The latent on the capsule was developed with black powder and the Jones Brush System.

Then, place the scale on top of the rope caulk. This raises the scale to the same plane as the fingerprint on top of the capsule, thereby making both in focus (Figure 16.18).

When imaging any object with a scale, the scale should be on the same plane as the object.

Prints on Stainless Steel

Unlike the ads on TV for appliances that are made from stainless steel that brag that the stainless steel objects do not show fingerprints, the stainless steel actually is an excellent suitable surface for fingerprints. After the latents are developed, before an attempt is made to lift them, photo image the prints.

The best method is to use ambient or available light. This assumes that the stainless steel and print are in an area with adequate light. If there is not enough available light, you will need fixed incandescent or halogen lamps. Use a scale, of course, and photo image at 90 degrees to the print. If you use a flash on the camera, you will get flashback (you will see the flash reflected back in the image) (Figure 16.19). You can see some of the print, but much of the print is obscured by the flashback (Figure 16.20).

Prints on Toilet Seats

Obtaining fingerprints on toilet seats is not one of my favorite practices; however, it is a good technique to have in your bag of tricks. This is important if a crime occurs and only females live in the residence in a home invasion or rape case. Perpetrators, who stop to use the toilet, will (sometimes) lift the seat to urinate. When this occurs, three or four fingerprints are left close together near the front of the seat. We can also sometimes get an idea whether the subject is left- or right-handed by what side of the seat the prints are found.

The two methods to use for lighting are the on-camera flash and available light (Figure 16.21). The on-camera flash works well as long as the toilet seat is not high gloss.

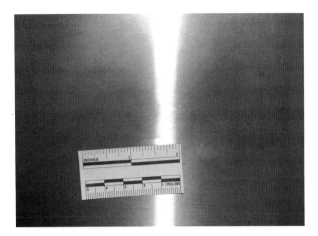

Figure 16.19 Latent fingerprint developed with black powder on stainless steel; shot with internal flash.

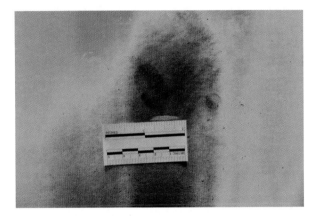

Figure 16.20 Same developed latent shown in Figure 16.19 but shot with available light (fluorescent and daylight from window).

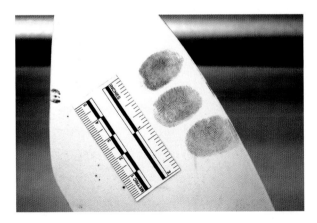

Figure 16.21 Developed latent fingerprint with black powder on underside of toilet seat.

If it is, you may experience flashback. If the seat is colored or a dull white or off-white the flash will do well.

If the seat is shiny or high gloss, the available light method may work better. If there is not enough available light and the seat is high gloss, you may need some fixed incandescent or halogen lighting.

In the "make it work department" (i.e., you do not have an incandescent or halogen light in your car as part of your equipment), see if there is a table lamp or a halogen torchiere floor lamp somewhere at the scene.

Burglary 17

Introduction

Burglary scenes are often not photo imaged. This is because many burglaries are not high-profile cases ($250 or less was stolen). If it is the policy of the department to photograph burglaries or if it is a high-profile case (involving thousands of dollars worth of objects stolen), then you should make every effort to do it well and completely.

Exterior

As with any scene, you should begin with the photo ID card. Your second image should be the *N* or north card. Remember, the ID card can be a close-up of the card, but the *N* card should include considerable background so that the viewer can determine north and acclimate the rest of the images accordingly.

As you begin to photo image the scene, you can start with an overall image of the structure. In this case it is a residence (Figure 7.1). Try to get the address number (if there is one) in the picture. Photo image the other three sides of the house. These images are for the record and completeness.

As you photo image the outside of the residence, you should be looking for a POE (point of entry). It may be obvious, such as a shattered window or a broken door. It could be a window left ajar (Figure 7.2). In Figure 17.3, we see a window ajar and what appears to be a footwear smudge under the window.

Interior

You should next look for the point of exit—usually a front, side, or rear door. The exit is not always easy to determine. Mud or debris at one of the doors is an indication, but this is not always the case. Image all of the doors. If one of the doors is the exit and it is later identified, then the prosecutor will have a photo image to use in court. Regardless, photo image all the doors to show that these points were not damaged; you should show negatives (i.e., those without evidence) as well (Figures 7.4 and 7.5).

Alarm

If the residence has an alarm system, photo image the alarm keypad. It should be inside one of the entryways (Figure 7.6). By photo imaging the keypad, you can sometimes tell if the alarm system is functional or is disconnected. Next, image the alarm panel. This is

Figure 17.1 Overall photo of front of house.

Figure 17.2 Photo of rear garage window slightly ajar.

normally located in the basement or a utility area (Figure 7.7). It is important to image this to show again if it has been "jumped," modified, or made inoperative. Even if you are not an expert in alarms, a good image of this panel will tell an alarm expert many things. If you have been able to identify the POE and there is an alarm system, photo image the inside of that location. This image is to show that there was or was not a sensor on this location. In Figure 17.8, we see that there is no sensor on this entry point.

Figure 17.3 Image of muddy footprint (not suitable for identification). This is a possible POE (point of entry).

Figure 17.4 Photo of front door showing no damage.

Figure 17.5 Photo of rear door showing no damage.

Figure 17.6 Alarm keypad inside front door. The keypad reads "zones faulted."

Locks

It is rare that a burglar will take the time to "pick" or "manipulate" a lock; however, one should check. When a lock is picked, there are often small metal filings in the keyway. The filings occur because the lock picks are made of much stronger metal than the pins. When the picks are used, filings are sometimes created.

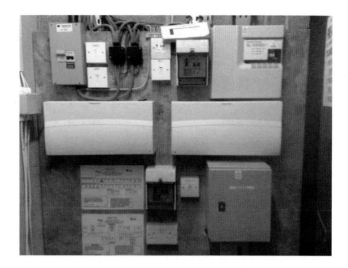

Figure 17.7 The insides of the alarm system panel (the brain of the system).

Figure 17.8 The interior garage window (ajar), our potential POE. The image shows that there are no sensors on this window.

To image the filings, you must first obtain them. Use a cotton swab and apply machine-type oil to the tip (Figure 7.9). Insert the tip into the keyway, then remove and inspect the swab (Figure 7.10).

If the lock was picked, there is a good chance that there will be small filings present on the cotton swab (Figure 7.11).

If the POE has not been located, examine the gap between the door jam and the door itself. If the gap is too great, then the door may have been "shimmed." Many door locks are easily shimmed. All that is needed is a flat piece of metal or plastic (see Figure 17.12). A plaster applicator knife is used. Credit cards can also accomplish the same goal; however, they break easily.

Some doors are equipped with an "antishim" device. The antishim device prevents the shimming of a door if the device is working. The object circled in red in Figure 17.13 is the antishim device. If present at your scene, press this into the latch. If working, you should not be able to press the latch into the lock. If when pressed the latch can be pressed into the door, the antishim device is inoperative.

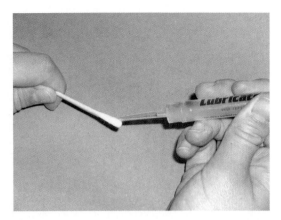

Figure 17.9 Placing oil on a cotton swab. This is a method to determine if a lock has been picked.

Figure 17.10 Swabbing the keyway in the lock with the oiled swab.

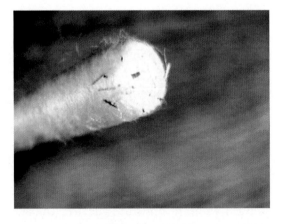

Figure 17.11 If, when examined, the swab has metal filings (more than just one), then there is a good chance that the lock was picked. In this case, take the lock as evidence.

Figure 17.12 An example of someone "shimming" a lock.

Figure 17.13 The antishim device (circled in red) on a door lock. The antishim device prevents shimming of the lock. These devices can be broken, the gap between the door and the jam can be too large, and the device can be removed. Check for these, and if one is found photograph it and document.

Items of Interest

Each room should be photo imaged. If there are items of interest, these items should be photographed in addition to the overall photos. Dressers, for example, can tell a great deal. If the dresser has had the drawers pulled out or dumped or some are closed and some opened, the burglar is unorganized and may be an amateur (Figure 7.14). Searching in this manner takes much more time. The burglar must either remove the drawer and dump it or push it back into the dresser to close the drawer.

A pro, on the other hand, wants to spend the least amount of time on the target necessary to conduct a search (Figure 7.15). The organized burglar will start at the bottom and open that drawer. The burglar will then move to the drawer above, but will not close the one below (which takes time). The burglar will then continue up the dresser until reaching

Figure 17.14 Dresser drawers opened and thrown askew. This is the sign of an amateur.

Figure 17.15 Removal "pyramid style." This is the sign of a professional. This method takes less time and is more efficient in a search.

the top. The burglar will not close any of the drawers. The more time spent inside the target, the better the chance of the burglar being caught.

Look for items missing that should be there. A good method to document this is with dust. If an object has been sitting somewhere for some time, often there will be an area free from dust under that object; when removed, the object leaves a telltale trace.

Figure 17.16 This desk has dust and a clean area with no dust. This indicates that something was there and is now gone. In this case, a computer was taken.

Figure 17.17 A desk without dust (all areas are without dust). This does not show what was shown in Figure 17.16.

Likewise, if the victim tells you that there was a computer on the desk and you see no clear area as in Figure 17.16, you may wish to question the victim further. (This is assuming, of course, that the victim has not just dusted the desk area.) Figure 17.17 does not show any areas that look like an object placed on the desk is missing.

Remember the rule of thumb: "You can never take too many pictures, but you can take too few."

Figure 17.18 This is an example of a photograph of an individual's room. It appears that the room has been ransacked by a burglar, which is not so. This is what the person's room looks like all the time—there was no burglary.

A final word is necessary on burglary. The old expression "perception is reality" is not necessarily true for us as crime scene investigators and a documenter of crime scenes. For example, Figure 17.18 depicts a bedroom that could be perceived as a room that had been searched thoroughly by a burglar. In reality, it is the dorm room of one of my students. The only crime committed is the condition of his room.

Storage of Digital Media

18

The Media

The storage of your digital media is important. This is because of how easy it is to change all, part, or parts of individual digital photo images. How the media is stored can make or break a case in court.

Storage

Films from cases were previously stored in the actual paper case files. Each film strip (negatives) was marked with the case number and initials of the photographer (Figure 18.1). This will not work for a CD that contains more than 200 images. We need to do the same thing as we did with the negative strips only adapt the method to digital images and storage media (CDs or DVDs).

First, there are some prerequisites. Set the number sequence of your camera (in the setup menu) to the on setting (Figure 18.2). This will ensure that there are no duplicate numbers. In the off setting, every time you remove the memory card from the camera and reinsert it, the camera will begin the numbering at 1. This can become confusing. If you attempt to upload to your master file on your computer, there may be duplicate numbers. The computer will ask you if you want to replace the old with the new. If you say yes, the images that you uploaded first will be written over and will be destroyed.

Remember, you may not delete any images. The opposition may allege that you removed exculpatory evidence if you do:

Attorney: Officer, the images skip from 0100.jpg to 0105.jpg. Where are images 0102.jpg, 0103.jpg, and 0104.jpg?
You: I deleted them because they were out of focus.
Attorney: What I believe is that you deleted images that would show my client to be innocent.
You: No, they were out of focus.
Attorney: Prove it.
You: Uhhh, uhhh.
Attorney: Your honor, based on the deleted pictures that may have proved my client innocent, I move that all of the images taken by this individual not be entered into evidence.
Judge: Motion granted.

Create a new file on your computer. Name the file using the case number, the victim's name, or both. It should have a unique name, however.

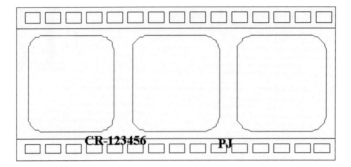

Figure 18.1 This is a drawing of a strip of negatives. This is how they would be marked for evidence. Each piece of the cut strip would have the case number and initials of the photographer.

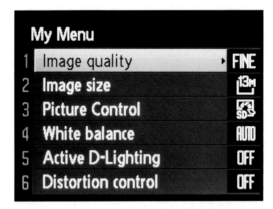

Figure 18.2 This is an image of the setup menu for a camera. One should always set the number sequence to off or continuous. This is so that the pictures continue the sequence even after the images are uploaded to a computer or the memory card is removed.

Upload all the images to this file. Now, burn all the images in this file to a CD (or if a truly large storage area is needed, to a DVD). Label this first CD or DVD that you burned from the computer the master copy (Figure 18.3). Use a permanent marker to write "Master Copy" on the disk. Also, place the case number and your initial or signature. Place the master copy in an evidence envelope (Figure 18.4). Seal and mark the envelope as you would any other evidence that you recover (Figure 18.5). Store this item in a safe place, such as a property control room.

Make a second CD or DVD. Mark this one as your master duplicate copy. Place this disk in your case file.

Maintain the folder in which you uploaded the images to your computer. Additional copies can be produced from the computer file. Duplicates can be made for the case detective, the defense (under the discovery rule), the medical examiner or coroner, the prosecutor, and others as necessary. Because the images are digital, every copy is an exact duplicate with no degradation or loss of quality.

The Scientific Working Group on Imaging Technology (SWGIT) has recommendations for electronic storage (see SWGIT Version 1.0 2007.06.04, Section 13).

The images on your personal computer should periodically be backed up based on the policies and procedures of your agency. Off-site backup is most desirable.

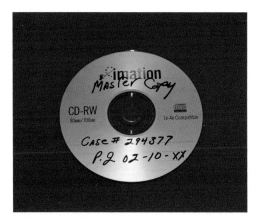

Figure 18.3 The "master copy." It is initialed and has the case number written on the disk.

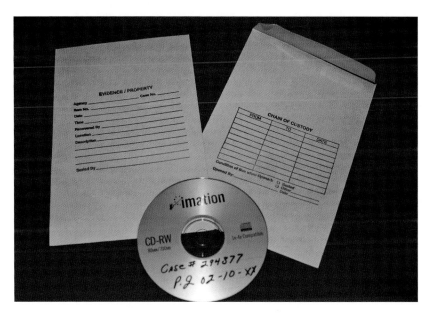

Figure 18.4 After the master copy disk is prepared, initialed, and has the case number written on it, it is placed in a standard evidence envelope.

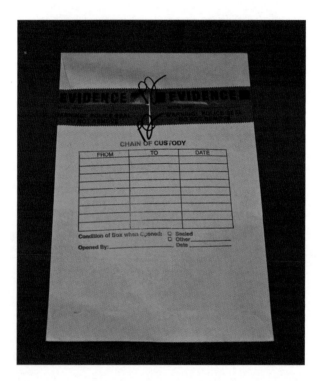

Figure 18.5 The envelope with the master copy is sealed and treated just like any other piece of evidence.

Fire and Arson Scene

19

Introduction

Photo imaging fire and arson scenes is somewhat difficult. There are entire books dedicated to arson scene investigation. While the books articulate many different areas to investigate and study, all of them agree that photo imaging documentation is one of the key methods to document the fire, the aftermath, and victims.

The Scene

Often, as crime scene investigators (CSIs), we are called to the scene of a fire only after it has been struck (extinguished). We do not often have the opportunity to photo image the fire in its fully engulfed stage. We are therefore relegated to photo imaging the aftermath.

On a good day, the aftermath of a fire is a structure or area that has had thousands and thousands of gallons of water poured on it. It consists of varying shades of dark brown and black, and it is difficult to identify any objects in the structure (Figure 19.1).

Because the structure looks like it has been in a toaster for the past few days, it is almost all black. Since the photographs our cameras are interested in recording are variations of reflected light, we appear to be off to a bad start. Light is reflected by objects. The darker the object, the less light is reflected. This is until we get to black. Black absorbs light. Very little light, if any, will be reflected into the camera.

Lighting

Due to the amount of water that has been poured on the fire, the power in the structure has probably been turned off by the firemen. This is done for safety. If live power comes in contact with the water, there is a potential for electrocution. Floodlights are helpful, when available (Figure 19.2). They do, however, require electrical power. Not only do they help with lighting the scene for the camera, but also they are helpful in lighting the scene when looking for evidence. Portable generators and light poles are not always available. There are battery-powered portable lighting units (Figure 19.3). They use battery power instead of connected power or generator power.

If a generator and light poles are available, this is the best-case scenario because they supply constant light, useful for photography and for evidence recovery.

Figure 19.1 Image of fire debris. (Courtesy of Det. Paul Huff, Lafayette, IN, Police Department.)

Figure 19.2 Portable lighting system with attached generator.

Figure 19.3 Portable lighting system with rechargeable battery.

Flash

You will have to rely on flash or strobe attachments. Most digital cameras have a built-in flash. For most crime scenes, they work well. Built-in camera flashes are not powerful. They are adequate but usually not effective over 20 feet. Have you ever watched a night baseball game and watched the pretty sparkle lights from the crowd? In Figure 19.4, spectators are using their on-camera flash option. They do not realize that the flash is only good for about 20 feet at best. This is due to the fact that light dissipates using the inverse square law (Figure 19.5). It really does make a pretty picture (of the crowd), though.

For the fire/arson scene, you need a much more powerful flash. You will probably need additional off-camera flashes, triggered by a direct connection to your camera, by a built-in radio-wave trigger, or by a light-activated slave (Figure 19.6).

Figure 19.4 An arena with flashes from cameras going off in the crowd. These flashes are good (for their images) for about 10 to 12 feet. They do nothing for their picture, but the image of the flashes going off is pretty.

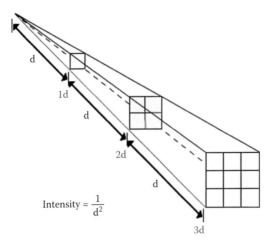

Figure 19.5 This is a drawing representing the inverse law.

Figure 19.6 A Nikon camera with two flashes, an on-camera Vivitar 283 mounted on the hot shoe and a second Vivitar 283 off camera operated by a "slave."

Marking Areas

Another problem with the aftermath of fire is that everything looks the same. It is either "ash or trash" (Figures 19.7 and 19.8). You should take a number of establishing overall images. These images should include recognizable objects. This is in addition to using a north card. The north card is used in an establishing shot to identify the direction north. The image with this card should include a substantial amount of the subject matter in the

Figure 19.7 Debris from fire. It is difficult to locate this particular area of debris and differentiate it from any other area of debris. (Courtesy of Det. Paul Huff, Lafayette, IN, Police Department.)

Figure 19.8 This is another image of debris from a fire. It is difficult to locate this particular area of debris and differentiate it from any other area of debris. (Courtesy of Det. Paul Huff, Lafayette, IN, Police Department.)

scene so that the north card image can be used to help identify direction in all the overall images. The other perspective or establishing shots should have something that is not "ash or trash" so that it can be used as a reference point.

Using bright-colored or reflecting markers, place one in a quadrant that corresponds to your sketch. If you later identify an object of interest in an image, you can use the

Figure 19.9 Debris from fire with fluorescent marker 4. This area can easily be located on a grid because of the marker number. (Courtesy of Det. Paul Huff, Lafayette, IN, Police Department.)

Figure 19.10 This is another image of debris from a fire with fluorescent marker 5. This area can easily be located on a grid because of the marker number. (Courtesy of Det. Paul Huff, Lafayette, IN, Police Department.)

marker to identify the area where it originated. Figures 19.9 and 19.10 are the same images as Figures 19.7 and 19.8 except that they have the bright markers.

Photograph mechanicals, such as pumps and motors (Figure 19.11). Make a photo image of negatives as well as positives. For example, image the electrical panel to show that there was no fire or burning associated with it (Figure 19.12).

Figure 19.11 Image of an electrical steam pump showing no damage.

Figure 19.12 Image of an electrical circuit breaker panel showing no damage.

One should always take some distance shots of the fire scene so that the structure in question can be located next to other nearby structures. This can be informative to investigators when analyzing the damage as it relates to other structures in the area.

Point of Origin

The POO (point of origin) is probably the most important point of the fire, whether or not it is arson. The POO is the "holy grail" of the fire scene. Once that is known, other information can be deduced using the POO as the starting point.

Photo document any burn pattern that you might see on the walls, ceiling, and floors. Locate them photographically and on a drawing. Look for the line of demarcation and photograph it. The line of demarcation can be found by looking for the line of soot on walls. Follow the smoke. Photo document the path it took to the point where it vents to the outside.

Artifacts

To the CSI or forensic scientist, the definition of an *artifact* is something that does not belong. Finding batteries and wire next to flammables indicates something that does not belong. Locating a fragment of a piece of pipe may indicate that a bomb was the initiator of the fire (Figure 19.13).

Objects such as lab glassware, specifically a separator funnel, could be used in the chemical initiation of incendiary devices (Figure 19.14). Other items that do not belong could be a group of matchbooks taped together with a cigarette, which could act as an ignition train (Figure 19.5).

Other items that do belong but are changed by the fire should be examined. The lightbulb in Figure 19.16 is a perfect example. The bulb is melted on one side. This one-side melting indicates that it was hotter on the side that is melted. The fact that it was hotter means that the point of origin was located in that same direction.

Figure 19.13 A piece of metal pipe located in the grass next to the blue building.

Figure 19.14 A separator funnel. This is a piece of laboratory glassware that can be used in an ignition train in starting fires.

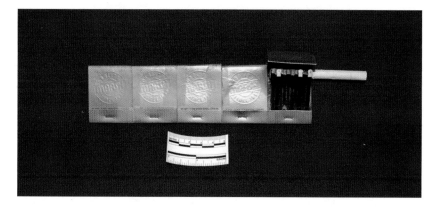

Figure 19.15 This is another example of an ignition train. The cigarette is the timing part of the device, and the matches are the igniter.

Other artifacts that should be examined and photo documented are any objects that are partially melted, especially if the object is melted more on one side than the other. The direction of the object and the degree of melting should be photographed. This could indicate the direction of the POO. Of course, obvious items such as gas cans, plastic containers, or broken wine or liquor bottles with small bits of fabric are artifacts.

Crowd

It has always been my personal thought to photo image the crowd that has gathered to "watch" the fire. If this is in fact arson and not an accidental fire, there was a fire starter or arsonist. If the perpetrator is not a professional arsonist, a "torch," but possibly a pyromaniac, one who not only likes to set fires but also to watch them, he or she may return to the scene of the crime. The additional minutes it takes to snap an extra couple of images may pay off. You may get lucky (Figure 19.17).

Figure 19.16 A lightbulb in its fixture. It was removed from a house fire. Note that the bulb is melted on one side only. This is the hottest part of the fire. The bulb points (to the right) of the hottest part of the fire, usually the POO (point of origin).

Figure 19.17 A picture of a crowd watching a fire/arson scene. Images of the crowd may provide you with an image of the arsonist.

Figure 19.18 Camera with the actual image that you just captured. The digital era is great because we know instantly if we have a good, correctly exposed picture.

Digital Imaging

The greatest advantage to using digital photography at a fire or arson scene is the ability to know that the last image that you took is composed properly and properly exposed (Figure 19.18). Because the aftermath of a fire or arson is one of the extreme conditions when working with film photography, in the past it was not known for sure if the images taken were good until they were developed and printed.

With digital photography, the images are immediately viewable. If they are out of focus, overexposed, or underexposed or if the composition is not what was wanted, another image can be taken immediately and adjusted to have the correct exposure. This can be done again and again until the desired image is obtained.

We may not delete the bad pictures as they could be considered exculpatory evidence. Images are numbered consecutively so that missing images would immediately be noticed.

Sex Offenses

20

Introduction

When we hear the words *sex offense*, most of us think of rape. We have learned that rape is not about sex, but it is about power and control. Sex enters into it only as a method to control the victim. The victim can be male or female.

As crime scene investigators (CSIs), it is our normal policy (except on TV, of course) not to talk to the victim. The sex offense is the only exception. In the case of a sex offense, the victim is often the evidence. It is crucial that the CSI talk with the victim, not as a detective, but in the interest of documenting physical evidence. We are not interested in which way the perpetrator escaped or even the description of the offender. That is the detective's job.

Dispatch

You will sometimes be dispatched to the scene of the crime or to see the victim at the hospital. You should of course process both, but you may have to make a decision which comes first. Think evidence: Is the scene outdoors or indoors? Has it been protected? Is there a uniformed officer or detective on the scene? Is the victim injured or deceased? I cannot tell you. You will have to make that decision yourself. Base your decision on the evidence. In what location is there entomological evidence or items that can be easily destroyed or washed away by rain? This location should be photographed first.

The Scene

If the victim is deceased at the scene, the scene is then handled as a death investigation. When processing the death investigation, remember to look at and photo document sex offense-related scenarios. For example, if a woman was involved who was living in the residence with no males, look in the bathroom at the toilet seat (Figure 20.1). If it is up, there may be fingerprints as well. If the woman lives alone, look for two plates or glasses. These should be documented as well. Photo image not only the room in which the attack occurred but also all the rooms, at least overall images. The meaning of a particular object in what appeared to be a room not connected with the incident may later come to light.

In the John Wayne Gacy case, we photographed all the rooms during the execution of the original search warrant. There was a Motorola 5 inch, black and white TV. It was just a part of the overall images of the rooms that were taken. Later, after evidence was reviewed by some of the detectives, it was discovered that one of the missing persons from the Des Plaines area had a Motorola set just like the one that was photographed in Gacy's bedroom.

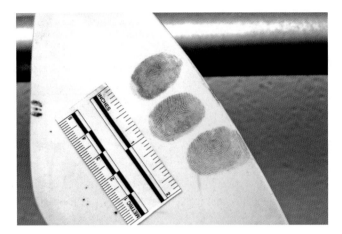

Figure 20.1 Fingerprints on the underside of the toilet seat. If there are no males living in the house and this is where the rape/home invasion occurred, if the toilet seat is up, check for latents under the seat. If the seat is glossy, use available light or a fixed incandescent light as your light source.

Victim at the Morgue

If the victim is at the morgue, you will photo image the victim differently from the way you would if the victim were alive at the hospital. The victim at the morgue should be imaged as any other deceased body. You will need to image the body both with clothes and naked. Pay particular attention to any wounds, which may be defensive in nature. Image the hands and wrists. They can show potential evidence from the perpetrator. Hands that look like they have had jewelry removed should be imaged. (See Chapter 13 for additional information on morgue photo imaging.)

Victim at the Hospital

There are different rules for the victim at the hospital. The victim of a sexual offense is usually female, but sometimes is a male. Sometimes, the victim is a child. This person represents evidence to us, but remember that this person is a living, breathing, human being who has undoubtedly gone through a horrible experience. Yes, we must get the evidence, but we must use every bit of our expertise and talent to put the victim at ease and not traumatize the victim any more than has already occurred.

In times gone past, the detective (no dedicated CSIs then) would speak with the victim and ask, for example, "All right, lady, give it to me from the top, what happened?" The woman had just been attacked, probably by a man, and as intimidating as a police officer can be, it would be even more intimidating to be questioned by a male officer because of his gender and position. He could then have said, "Take off all your clothes, including your underwear, and the nurse will bag it and give it to me." As violated as she was during the assault, she may feel equally violated for a second time due to manner and attitude of the officer.

Let me assure you that things are different today. There is a three-prong approach to working with the victim (Figure 20.2). There is law enforcement (the CSI), who processes

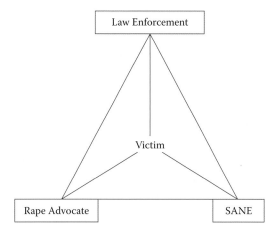

Figure 20.2 A diagram of the three-pronged attack in investigating a sexual assault/rape case.

the crime scene, interviews the victim, and collects and photo documents evidence. There is the rape advocate, who psychologically supports the victim. This specially trained person talks with and answers questions for the victim and facilitates the procedures that we use to collect and document the crime and to prosecute the offender. This person's prime duty is to the victim. Finally, there is the SANE (sexual assault nurse examiner), who is a qualified nurse with additional specific training in forensics. She is trained to properly collect evidence, properly photo document the victim's injuries, and work with law enforcement to successfully prosecute the perpetrator. There is also an association dedicated to forensic nursing (the International Association of Forensic Nurses, http://www.iafn.org/).

Meeting the Victim

As noted, in most sex offense cases, the victim is a female. It is helpful if you, the CSI, are also female; however, the preponderance of CSIs are male. When you are first introduced to the victim, do not have equipment cases in your hands; you do not want to look intimidating. Due to the incident, she probably is mistrustful, even afraid of all men. A notepad is okay. Speak softly. Ask about her condition. "How do you feel?" "Can you speak with me now?" The rape advocate will probably be with the victim. Allow the advocate to stay while you begin to speak with the victim. This allows the victim to feel that she has the strength of numbers, two of them to one of you.

After a bit of conversation and the victim is a little more comfortable with you, explain what you are going to do. There should be no surprises for the victim. Explain to the victim that not only do we want to apprehend the perpetrator, but also we want to prosecute him and send him to jail. If the victim does not want to prosecute, explain that we would like to continue anyway. Further explain that if she does change her mind, we then have the necessary evidence and documentation. In addition, the perpetrator may have done this before. That would make him a serial sex offender.

Begin with your report. Ask questions to complete the required information. Ask her to tell the story of what happened, in her own words, to the best of her recollection. Take notes, specifically where she may have received injuries or where she may have inflicted injuries to the perpetrator.

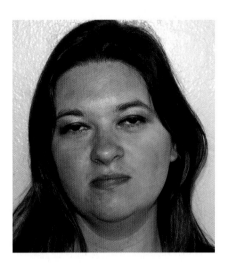

Figure 20.3 An example of a face ID shot. This is taken separately from any images of injuries. In this manner, the face does not appear in any of the injury images (unless the face itself is injured). This gives the victim more privacy. The images are all still connected to the face and other case photos because of the successive numbers of the pictures.

Photo Imaging the Victim

After the victim is somewhat relaxed, and in the presence of the rape advocate or SANE, advise her that you need to record and document any injuries. The first image should be the photo ID card. This identifies this group of images as from this specific victim. The second image should be a photograph of the head, face only (Figure 20.3).

Injuries

If some of the injuries are in nonprivate parts of the body, ask if you can see them. Examine them and take notes. Ask if you can photograph them. Ask, do not order. Explain to the victim that her face will not be in any of the images of her injuries unless, of course, there are injuries on the face (Figures 20.4–20.7.)

Now we must proceed to parts of the body that may be in private areas. These injuries must also be recorded and photo imaged. At this point, the SANE nurse can be of great assistance. It is hoped that she has received training in how to take forensic images. If not, give her a crash course of 5 minutes or less.

- Photograph 90 degrees to the wound.
- Photograph with and without scale.
- Do not erase any images, including bad shots.

The fact that we are shooting digitally is also a great advantage. After the SANE takes each image, have the nurse show you the image on the viewing screen. If it is okay, tell the

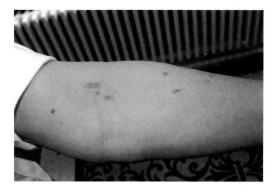

Figure 20.4 Wounds, left inside forearm and elbow.

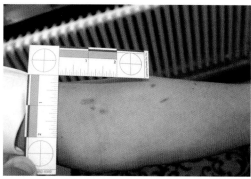

Figure 20.5 Wounds, left inside forearm and elbow with scale.

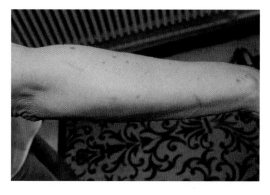

Figure 20.6 Wounds, right inside forearm and elbow.

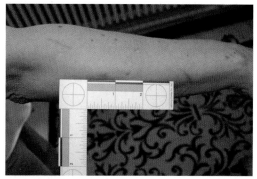

Figure 20.7 Wounds, right inside forearm and elbow with scale.

SANE to go on to the next wound. If not, have her retake the shot. Keep retaking until the image is good. In this way, images that are needed are obtained without further trauma and embarrassment to the victim.

Bruising

Bruising is an injury just like a cut or an abrasion. Bruising is slightly different, however, in that it changes color through its life cycle. One of my teaching assistants was a member of the fencing club. She was fencing with sabers and received a blow to her arm with the flat of the blade. She told me that it was going to be a beauty of a bruise. I told her that we should photo document it, and we did.

Note that everyone bruises differently; the bruise is also dependent on where on the body it is located and the physical makeup of the individual. The images in this chapter provide a guide. Each case of bruising should be looked at separately. If a bruise is similar in color and bears a resemblance to that of day 15 here, then it surely did not happen the previous day (Figures 20.8–20.19).

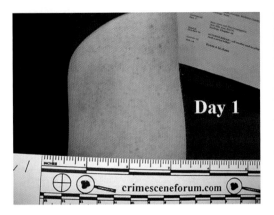

Figure 20.8 Bruise study, day 1.

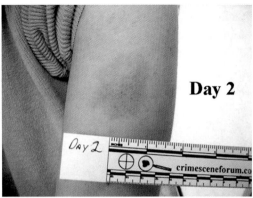

Figure 20.9 Bruise study, day 2.

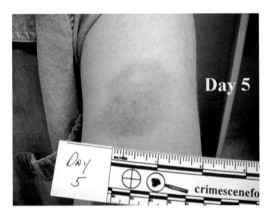

Figure 20.10 Bruise study, day 5.

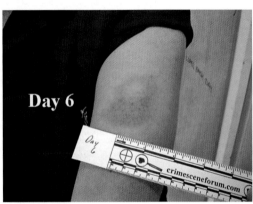

Figure 20.11 Bruise study, day 6.

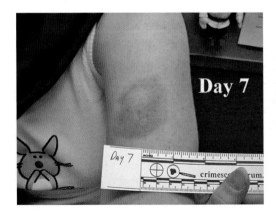

Figure 20.12 Bruise study, day 7.

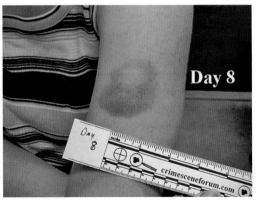

Figure 20.13 Bruise study, day 8.

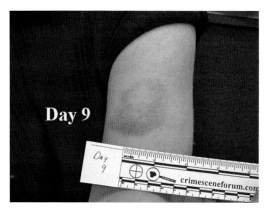

Figure 20.14 Bruise study, day 9.

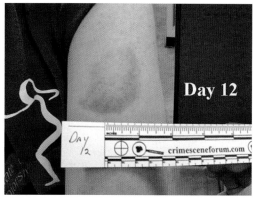

Figure 20.15 Bruise study, day 12.

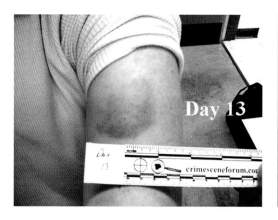

Figure 20.16 Bruise study, day 13.

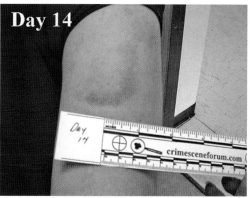

Figure 20.17 Bruise study, day 14.

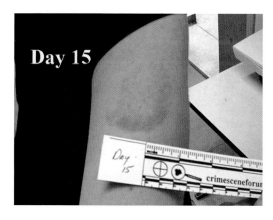

Figure 20.18 Bruise study, day 15.

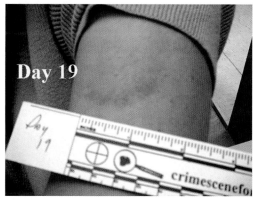

Figure 20.19 Bruise study, day 19.

Clothing

You will be collecting all of the clothing from the victim for serological and trace examination. When you return to the lab, you will want to photo image the clothing. This is a good place to photo document the clothing because you have much more control over the lighting and conditions.

Cut a fresh piece of brown kraft paper from a roll. Lay the piece of clothing on the paper. Place a scale on the paper but do not cover any part of the clothing (Figure 20.20). Photograph both sides (Figure 20.21). After each piece of clothing is imaged separately, fold the paper on which the clothing was placed. This keeps any trace evidence from being lost (Figure 20.22). Then, place the clothing folded in the paper into a paper evidence bag. Mark and seal the bag (Figure 20.23). Note that the images in Figures 20.22 and 20.23 are not needed in your photo image collection. These images are to show the next steps in the preservation of the clothing evidence.

Figure 20.20 Image front of blouse.

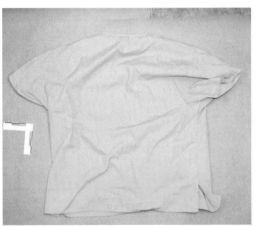

Figure 20.21 Image back of blouse.

Figure 20.22 Blouse partially folded in the brown kraft paper on which it was originally photographed.

Figure 20.23 Blouse completely folded in brown kraft paper and placed in evidence bag, ready to seal.

Children

Children are completely different. They still need compassion and trust, but they have legal rights different from an adult. When speaking with and working with the child, one or both of the parents should be present in addition to the SANE and rape advocate. There are two SANE certifications, SANE A (adult) and SANE P (pediatric). If the victim is a child, you should have a SANE P present.

There is an exception to having one or more parents in the room. This is if one or both of the parents may be a perpetrator. In this case, ethically and legally, the best interest of the child is paramount. You must therefore have someone there to represent the interest of the child. You should have a worker present from Children and Family Services, Child Welfare, or whatever the agency name may be in your jurisdiction to be in loco parentis (in place of the parents).

Trace Evidence and Microscopy

21

Introduction

Photo imaging trace is difficult at best. In this type of photo imaging, not only are we photo imaging small items, but also we are imaging minute items, in many cases microscopic.

To accomplish this, we will be using microscopes with cameras fitted to them and stand-alone engineered microscopes capable of photo imaging and in some cases video.

Images through a Microscope

Microscope Camera

There are several methods for photo imaging through a standard microscope. The first is by using a microscope camera (Figure 21.1), which replaces the ocular or eyepiece on a microscope. If the microscope is a stereo, the camera can be placed in one of the tubes, and the other ocular can still be used to view and focus. If the microscope is a compound scope, then the camera will be placed in the single ocular tube. The device comes with software that allows the user to view and to capture images to a computer. The device is connected to the computer via a USB (universal serial bus) port. Still, time-lapse, and full-motion video can be captured. The resolution is low, 640×480, but delivers a good image. The device with software is under $100 (Figure 21.2).

Another method is to obtain from the microscope manufacturer a camera attachment or adapter to fit the specific camera in your inventory. The scope must have the option of having this attachment fitted to it. The camera, digital single-lens reflex (SLR), then attaches to the scope, and images can be taken by the camera. This provides a much higher resolution.

A third method that works sometimes is to hold the camera to the ocular or eyepiece of the microscope, manually focus the camera, and shoot. Sometimes you get a good image, and sometimes you do not. The human hair was photo imaged with a Nikon D-50, manual focus, after about 15 attempts (Figures 21.3–21.6). The images are of a quality that we can see that the cut was made by a sharp object, in this case a razor (Figure 21.5). We can see the bulbous root with skin tag, which means that we can possibly obtain a DNA profile.

The Nikon Microphot

Promoted in the 1980s as one of the premier research microscopes, Nikon's Microphot-FX was originally designed to work with a film camera. It also has the availability of using a video camera. There are attachments as well as for quantitative transmitted light and fluorescence microscopy. When utilized in combination with the Nikon Microflex FX camera

Figure 21.1 Microscope camera. Attaches to one of the oculars of a stereomicroscope.

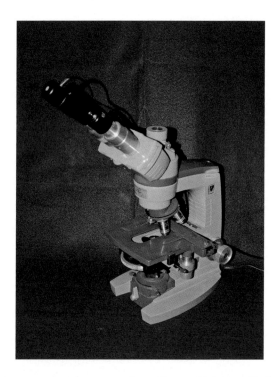

Figure 21.2 Stereomicroscope with camera from Figure 21.1 installed.

series, it becomes a photomicrographic system, and when coupled to a modern CCD (charge coupled device) camera, it becomes a digital imaging system (Figure 21.7).

To cope with the demand for highly technical epifluorescence microscopy, a high-performance vertical illuminator attachment was prepared for the Microphot series. The illuminator holds up to four interchangeable filter blocks, and turret rotation facilitates filter selection. A full line of 20 fluorescence filter blocks is available.

Figure 21.3 Hair under microscope. Note cuticular scale.

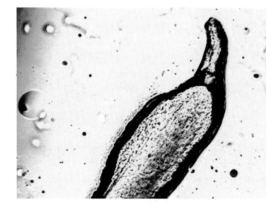

Figure 21.4 Hair under microscope. Note bulbous root and skin tag.

Figure 21.5 Hair under microscope. Cut hair (razor).

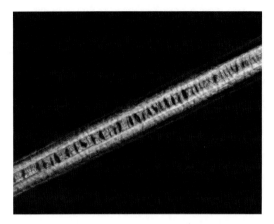

Figure 21.6 Hair under microscope. Note margins.

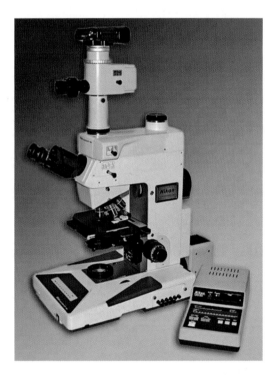

Figure 21.7 Nikon Microphot microscope camera. Has capabilities of multiple light sources, video, and still imaging.

Now that we are into the digital age, one can modify the unit slightly so that it will take any of Nikon's digital SLR cameras. I have tested the D-90, D-80, D-50, and D-40 with excellent results.

Modification

The first thing to do for modification is to find the 35-mm camera adapter that fits on the rear port of the top of the microscope. The adapter was made specifically for the film

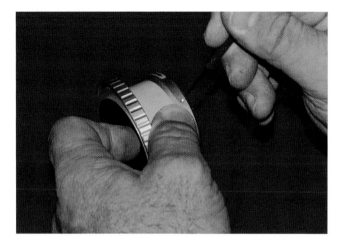

Figure 21.8 Modification made to Nikon Microphot so that scope can be attached to a Nikon digital camera, step 1.

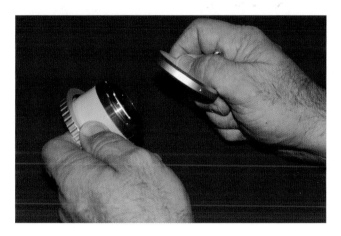

Figure 21.9 Modification made to Nikon Microphot so that scope can be attached to a Nikon digital camera, step 2.

camera that comes with the Nikon Microphot. Remove the three screws on the retaining ring (Figure 21.8). Remove the ring and set aside with the three set screws (Figure 21.9). The screws are small, so placing the ring and screws in a plastic bag may be wise. Attach the adapter ring to the top of the microscope. The Nikon digital SLR will now attach to the adapter ring (Figure 21.10).

The Nikon Microphot has an internal shutter. It must be opened. An easy way to open the shutter is to press "shift and manual" on the Microphot's keyboard. Next, type in "999," then enter. This opens the shutter for 999 seconds. Push in the lever marked "photo ob." This switches the view from the ocular to the camera.

Set the shutter on the camera to B (I suggest that you use a remote shutter release to reduce camera shake) and take the image. You may have to experiment with the exposure, but after a bit I was rewarded with good images (Figures 21.11–21.13).

Figure 21.10 Nikon D-80 attached to Nikon Microphot.

Figure 21.11 Nikon Microphot, animal hair. Photograph taken with a Nikon D-80.

Figure 21.12 Nikon Microphot, bird feather. Photograph taken with a Nikon D-80.

Figure 21.13 Patrick with Nikon Microphot.

Blood

22

Introduction

Photo imaging blood can be categorized into four different types and applications. The first type is blood imaged for the record. This imaging is to show the presence of blood on a particular object or place (e.g., traces of blood on a ceramic cup (Figure 22.1)). This image shows (in addition to testimony given by the recovering individual) a jury that blood existed on the cup.

The second type is blood spatter. This is the photo imaging of blood that has been moved by some type of force from one place to another. Examples of this type are spatter as a result of striking someone who is bleeding, causing the blood to leave the person and come to rest on a wall, ceiling, or some object; a gunshot wound that causes the blood to leave the person and come to rest on a wall, ceiling, or some object; or someone or something splashing in a pool of blood, causing that blood to leave the person and come to rest on a wall, ceiling, or some object (Figure 22.2). There are many possibilities of how this can occur. It must be documented by photo imaging. A blood spatter expert is not always immediately available, so a complete set of images should be taken. When you think that you have taken enough, take more. Remember that you can never go back.

When imaging the blood, remember to image it at 90 degrees to the spatter. Shooting at any other angle can distort the image. Remember to take images both with and without scale (Figures 22.3–22.12).

There is a phenomenon that occurs when a person or object is in the way of a spatter, causing some of the pattern to be blocked. This is called *shadowing*, *voids*, or *ghosting* (Figure 22.13). The absence of spatter may indicate that something was in place that is no longer there. This could be an object or a second person and must be documented by photo image.

A third type is blood drops. These drops, when found and photo imaged, can be used to compute angle and direction (Figure 22.14). The blood spatter expert can use these photo images to assist in unraveling what occurred at the crime scene. Blood drops should always be imaged at 90 degrees so that there is no distortion in the image (Figure 22.15).

It is important to take not only close-up images of these drops but also perspective shots so that a directional trail can be determined (Figure 22.16). The direction can be determined by the drop itself. The small "tail" points in the direction of motion of whatever or whoever dropped it. The use of cones or tent cards aids in demonstrating the direction and path in the perspective images (Figure 22.17).

The fourth method is for small droplets on fabric or carpet. This requires a macro lens and a digital single-lens reflex (SLR) camera. Since we need to get close to the droplets, the macro lens, as opposed to the camera macro capabilities, is desirable. The lens should be

Figure 22.1 Image of cup with suspect blood with scale.

Figure 22.2 Image of blood spatter.

Figure 22.3 Image of blood spatter, arterial spurt.

Figure 22.4 Image of blood spatter, cast off.

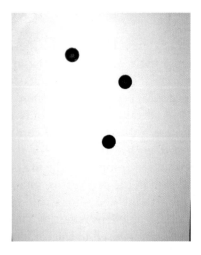

Figure 22.5 Image of blood spatter, passive drop.

Figure 22.6 Image of blood spatter, low velocity.

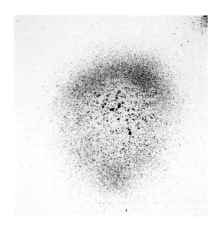

Figure 22.7 Image of blood spatter, medium velocity.

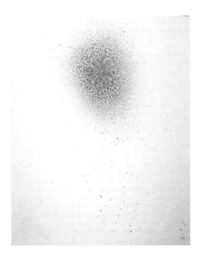

Figure 22.8 Image of blood spatter, high velocity.

Figure 22.9 Image of blood spatter, misting.

set to the smallest aperture possible. This allows the best depth of field. The focus should be set to manual and set to minimum focus. When focusing on the droplets, use your body to move the camera in and out rather than using the focus ring. To better identify the individual droplets, I use white reinforcement labels (Figure 22.18). These are small self-adhesive stickers with the center punched out. They can be placed on a piece of fabric to identify the location and apply a numeric identifier to each droplet. A midrange shot of the area of the fabric should also be imaged so that the relative position of each of the spots can be identified (Figure 22.19).

Figure 22.10 Image of blood spatter, patent print in blood.

Figure 22.11 Image of blood spatter, wipe.

Figure 22.12 Image of blood spatter, swipe.

Figure 22.13 Image of blood spatter, shadow, ghosting, or void.

Luminol

The use of luminol in detecting blood that has been washed, diluted, or hidden is a major piece of ammunition in the crime scene investigator's arsenal. The freshly mixed luminol is sprayed onto an area, and if there is blood present, it will glow in darkness. A good method is to set the camera on a tripod, then compose the image in the viewfinder. Take the image. With the camera still on the tripod and with the same composition, change the setting to "bulb," B, or its equivalent. This will allow the shutter to open and stay opened until it is closed. An electronic remote shutter release should be used. This prevents camera shake and possible blurring of the image due to pressing on the shutter release of the camera, then releasing it.

Have your partner spray the luminol on an area inside the precomposed zone. If the area glows, press the remote cable release and leave the shutter open for about 4 seconds.

Figure 22.14 This image indicates the various angles and their associated drops. Since the viscosity of blood is always the same, the drops always make the same impression when dropped at the same angle.

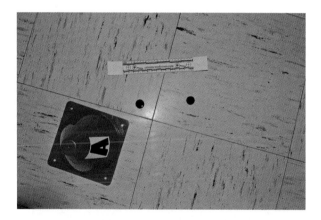

Figure 22.15 Blood dropped, passive at 90 degrees.

Spray another area of the precomposed image, and if this area also glows, take a second image. Continue until the entire zone has been examined with luminol (Figures 22.20 and 22.21).

Blowback: Blood in Gun Barrel

When a gun barrel is in contact with a body and is fired, the gases expended enter the hole in the flesh, and since they have nowhere to go, they "blow back" into the gun barrel. Samples should be taken, of course. Before the samples are taken, you should photo image the blood in the barrel (Figure 22.22).

Lighting is difficult due to the configuration of the gun and barrel. The best case is using a halogen light with a fiber-optic adjustable light source. The gun can be set up in a

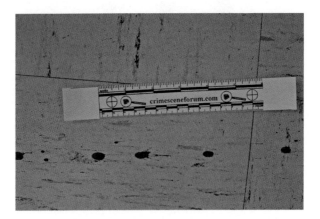

Figure 22.16 Blood dropped, nonpassive; the subject was moving. The direction is left to right. This is because the "tails" point to the right.

Figure 22.17 Using cones (or tents) to demonstrate the trail of blood as it proceeds down a hallway.

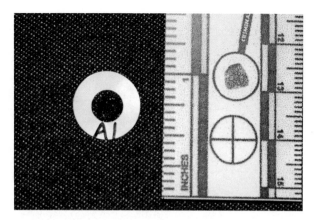

Figure 22.18 This is a macro photograph of a blood droplet on blue denim pants. The fabric is dark, and the blood is dark. A method to highlight and identify individual droplets is to use self-adhesive paper reinforcers. You can write the number on a small area on fabric or objects.

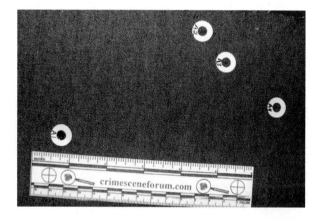

Figure 22.19 This is a close-up (not macro) photograph of several blood droplets in a cluster.

Figure 22.20 Photograph of kitchen floor. It is suspected that there may have been blood on the floor that has been wiped. (Courtesy of Det. Paul Huff, Lafayette, IN, Police Department.)

Figure 22.21 The same image after luminol (a presumptive test for blood) was sprayed on the floor. The shot was taken with a Nikon D-80, aperture 5.6, shutter set to B, exposed for 5 seconds. (Courtesy of Det. Paul Huff, Lafayette, IN, Police Department.)

Figure 22.22 Barrel of a Ruger 9-mm, semiautomatic pistol. Note the suspect blood in the barrel. This is a phenomenon called *blowback*. It occurs when the gun is placed in contact with skin. The outgoing pressure has to escape somewhere. If it cannot go into the body, it escapes the way it came out of the gun, blowing back some of the blood and sometimes tissue from the victim.

Figure 22.23 Halogen fiber-optic light setup for the image taken in Figure 22.21. Cost about $300.

hobby or table vise. Remember to use padding so that the handgun is not scratched by the imaging process. Adjust one of the arms of the fiber-optic light source to shine through the barrel from the chamber side of the gun. Take the image from the end of the barrel, and the light should light the blood (blowback) in the barrel. You may need to take several images to get the lighting just right. As a reminder, do not erase any of your less-than-perfect images (Figure 22.23).

Figure 22.24 Gooseneck, battery-operated flex light setup for the image taken in Figure 22.21.

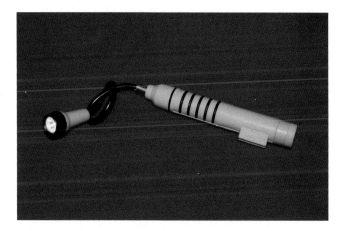

Figure 22.25 Gooseneck, battery-operated flex light; cost about $15.

In many cases, we cannot afford a $500 halogen fiber-optic light source. We do have options. At many hardware stores, a light is available that has an adjustable optical wire. It can be bent and even tied in a knot. It is available for under $15 and works almost as good as the halogen fiber-optic light. It can be used in much the same way the fiber-optic halogen light is used (Figures 22.24 and 22.25).

When I get an idea to do some strange kind of lighting or some type of apparatus to assist in my photo imaging, I often find the solution at my local hardware store. I look for a store where employees are always willing to spend time with me, giving me advice and finding unusual objects in their inventory to assist me in photo imaging.

Ultraviolet and Infrared Imaging

23

Introduction

Ultraviolet (UV) and infrared (IR) light have specific wavelengths, measured in nanometers (nm). Each is part of the electromagnetic spectrum, which contains wavelengths that are visible and invisible to humans. You can see in Figure 23.1 that only a small area of the electromagnetic spectrum is visible to humans. The visible spectrum extends from the UV (390 nm) to the IR (780 nm). A nanometer is 1 billionth of a meter. A meter is about 39 inches.

Some items fluoresce or glow under UV or IR light. The light excites a substance within the object, and under the specific light that excites, it glows. For example, using 532-nm coherent light (from a laser), rodent hair glows as seen in Figure 23.2.

We use fluorescent fingerprint powder to develop latent fingerprints. The powder has a substance in its composition that glows when exposed to UV light, 390 to 455 nm (Figure 23.3).

Inks that glow under UV light are used for security markings on everything from drivers' licenses to money. A thin Indiana driver's license, for example, when viewed under UV light reveals a third picture of the driver as well as his or her name printed across the main picture. U.S. currency (bills $5 and over) have security threads that will fluoresce under UV light. Both UV and IR light have some interesting properties beneficial to us as crime scene investigators (CSIs).

UV Light Sources

When working with UV light sources, make sure that you are using a true UV light. This is a source that emits light from 390 to 455 nm. For example, many "forensic blue lights" emit a blue light, but they are not UV light sources.

A true UV light source is pictured in Figure 23.4. The light source has two 4-watt lamps. It should also have a label on it that states its power or wavelength, as shown in Figure 23.5. Its cost is about $125. Size does not matter; it is the wavelength that counts. Figure 23.6 depicts a true UV light source. It uses a light-emitting diode (LED) bulb, but you will also notice the caution label stating that it is a UV light source.

You really have to read the label or specs. For example, I found a bulb (pictured in Figure 23.7) that stated it was a "black light." On reading the specifications, it stated that it emitted light at 455 nm. I obtained it from Menards for about $5. It works well but not as well as the light pictured in Figure 23.4.

Others are called UV lights, but they are actually a standard tungsten lightbulb with blue glass (Figure 23.8). This bulb is advertised as a "black light." It does not give off UV rays. It lights up psychedelic posters really well, but forensically, it is useless.

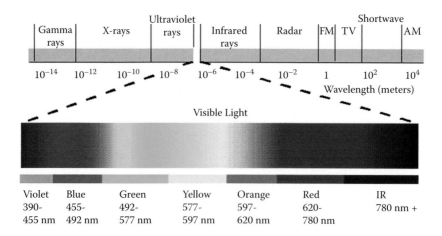

Figure 23.1 The electromagnetic spectrum. Notice the small area of the spectrum that is the visible spectrum.

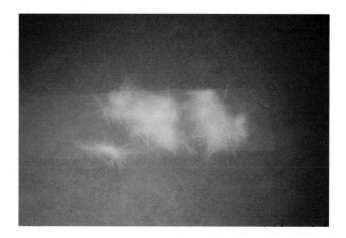

Figure 23.2 Rodent (rat) hair image made using a 532-nm laser light source. The rodent hair glows at this wavelength.

Body Fluids

Some body fluids fluoresce under UV light. Seminal fluid fluoresces under true UV light. The fluid does not have to have spermatozoa in it, just the fluid. For Figure 23.9, we used the true UV light to illuminate a known sample. Obvious positive results are seen. When photographing the samples under UV light, darken the room, turn off the flash, and shoot using the UV light as your only light source. If you have trouble with the autofocus, turn it off (in Nikons, it is on the lens, change *A* to *M*). Because of the low light level, you may have to put the camera on a tripod to prevent blurring from camera shake.

Figure 23.10 shows the same sample illuminated with the UV bulb I obtained from Menards. The response was positive; however, it was considerably less than seen with a true UV light source.

Figure 23.3 A latent fingerprint developed using green fluorescent powder.

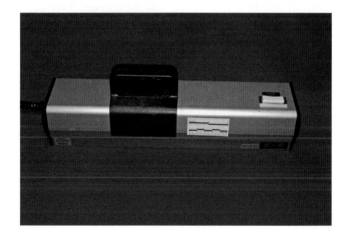

Figure 23.4 A true UV (ultraviolet) light source, with two florescent 4-watt tubes. Cost is about $125.

Figure 23.11 was taken using the black-light bulb. As you can see, the sample does not show any fluorescence. Leave these "black lights" to the dance clubs.

Urine gives a response similar to seminal fluid. The same type of fluorescence is evident when we look at a known sample of urine, shown in Figure 23.12.

Insects

Insects show, in many cases, different color characteristics—some bright and flashy and some subdued. In Figures 23.13–23.15, we look at the same blowfly under IR, UV, and white (halogen) light. In these images, it looks like three different flies, but it is not.

Figure 23.5 The label on the UV light source stating that its wavelength is 365 nm.

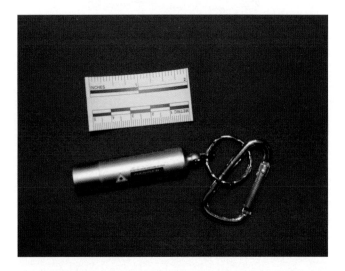

Figure 23.6 A small UV light source. This light source uses an ultraviolet LED (light-emitting diode) instead of a bulb. Cost is about $19.

Tattoos

Whether ink, natural pigmentation, or chemical makeup causes objects to look different under different wavelengths of light, forensic scientists, criminalists, analysts, and others involved with forensic science should use this characteristic as still another tool in the justice system.

Infrared Light

Infrared allows us to see still differently from white and UV light. Just as the flies are seen differently under different wavelengths, so do aspects of people. When an individual gets a tattoo, he or she has various colors of ink injected into the skin. Just as many inks appear different under UV and IR lighting, so do these tattoos (Figures 23.16–23.18). One of my

Figure 23.7 A fluorescent lightbulb. The label stated that there were UV light emissions. It was obtained from Menards home store. Cost is about $5.

Figure 23.8 A "black light" bulb. This does not emit UV light.

students, who graciously volunteered to have her tattoo photographed, has a medium brown complexion. This affects the images of the tattoos slightly; however, as we see in the images, each wavelength of light is a little bit different.

An example of an outdoor photograph is seen in Figures 23.19 and 23.20. Figure 23.19 is a photograph of scenery, normally exposed. In Figure 23.20, the image was taken using an 89b filter, a band-pass filter, which allows only IR light to pass through it to the sensor of the camera.

Fuji IS Pro UVIR Camera

The Fuji IS Pro is a camera that has been physically modified and has had software designed specifically for IR and UV photography (Figure 23.21). The IS Pro utilizes Fujifilm's Super

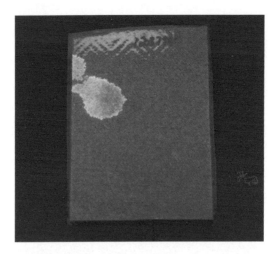

Figure 23.9 A sample of seminal fluid photographed with a Nikon D-80 using the UV light source pictured in Figure 23.4.

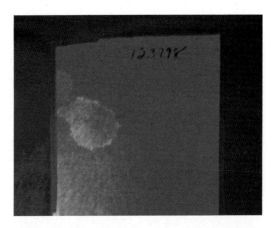

Figure 23.10 A sample of seminal fluid photographed with a Nikon D-80 using the UV fluorescent bulb pictured in Figure 23.6.

CCD Pro and Real Photo Processor Pro technology to see light from the UV, visible, and IR portion of the spectrum (approximately 380–1,000 nm). It is compatible with Nikon F mount lenses and Nikon's TTL (through-the-lens) flash systems, making it a cost-effective solution for law enforcement agencies that already have Nikon components.

This camera is designed for law enforcement and forensic imaging to utilize the benefits of a camera that works in these light wavelengths. This work includes, but is not limited to, the photo documentation of documents, trace location, body fluids, and much more.

Some features that make it useful to forensics are as follows:

- Dark opaque filters that cover the lens often render the viewfinder useless, so the IS Pro carries specialized features useful for investigative photography, such as live image preview. Imaging with IR with film photography literally "left you in the dark" because in the IR spectrum focusing is a small increment off. If you

Figure 23.11 A sample of seminal fluid photographed with a Nikon D-80 using the black light bulb picture in Figure 23.8. We cannot see the presence of the seminal fluid.

Figure 23.12 A sample of urine photographed with a Nikon D-80 using the UV light source pictured in Figure 23.4.

focus in the visible light spectrum, when the image was taken and recorded on film, you did not know if it was in focus until the film was developed and printed. With a digital single-lens reflex (SLR) camera, you know more quickly if it is out of focus. With live preview, you are able to focus while in the IR spectrum. The live preview can be activated with a single button and lasts for 20 seconds.

- The live image preview can be fed to a video input and viewed on a screen or on a personal computer (PC) monitor.
- The camera is Nikon lens compatible, allowing you to use existing Nikon lenses. This is a great cost savings.

Figure 23.13 Blowfly photographed with a Nikon D-80, with a macro lens, using an IR 100-watt light source.

Figure 23.14 Blowfly photographed with a Nikon D-80, with a macro lens, using the UV light source pictured in Figure 23.4.

Figure 23.15 Blowfly photographed with a Nikon D-80, with a macro lens, using a halogen fiber-optic white light source.

Figure 23.16 Tattoo photographed with a Nikon D-80 using a 100-watt tungsten bulb as a light source. The subject had a medium brown complexion.

Figure 23.17 Tattoo photographed with a Nikon D-80 using a 100-watt IR lightbulb. The subject had a medium brown complexion.

Figure 23.18 Tattoo photographed with a Nikon D-80 using an 8-watt UV light source, pictured in Figure 23.4. The subject had a medium brown complexion.

Figure 23.19 A scene photographed with a Nikon D-50, f/5.6 at 3/1,000 second. (Photograph by Venumadhav Margam.)

- The camera can be converted to a standard digital SLR with the addition of an IR/UV cut filter.
- It is compatible with Nikon's TTL flash systems.
- The "hot" filter, standard operating equipment for all digital cameras, has been removed and replaced with a specially formulated protective CCD (charge coupled device) glass filter that was designed to help protect the Super CCD Pro from dust and general maintenance damage while maximizing its UV and IR gathering potential.

Now the bad news: the cost of the body only is $2,599. But, for those who need the IR and UV capability, this is the best piece of equipment to use.

Filters for Use with the Fuji IS Pro Camera

- Digital Filter PECA 900 (Wratten filter 18A)   B&W 403
- Digital Filter PECA 902 (Wratten filter 70)
- Digital Filter PECA 904 (Wratten filter 87)
- Digital Filter PECA 906 (Wratten filter 87A)
- Digital Filter PECA 908 (Wratten filter 87B)   B&W 092
- Digital Filter PECA 910 (Wratten filter 87C)   B&W 93
- Digital Filter PECA 912 (Wratten filter 88A)

Figure 23.20 A scene photographed with a Nikon D-50, f/5.6 at 1 second using an 89b filter. (Photograph by Venumadhav Margam.)

Figure 23.21 Fuji IS Pro.

• Digital Filter PECA 914 (Wratten filter 89B)	Hoya R72
• Digital Filter PECA 916 (IR- and UV-blocking filter for visible light)	
• Digital Filter PECA 918 (IR- and UV-blocking filter for visible light)	Less red transmission than PECA 916
• Digital Filter PECA 700 (IR- and UV-blocking filter for visible light)	Slightly less red transmission than PECA 916

Other Considerations

In camras other than the Fugi IS Pro, when IR is the dominant source of light, the camera's autoexposure (AE) system may not operate properly due to the lack of visible spectrum light. It is recommended that manual exposure (M) be used in these situations. Program (P), aperture priority (A), and shutter priority (S) are likely to malfunction in the presence of high amounts of UV and IR light.

Under extreme IR lighting conditions, moiré patterns and other image problems can appear. Using an ISO (International Organization for Standardization number) above 200 can help reduce this effect but may not eliminate it completely.

Your lens is unable to sharply focus these very different wavelengths, resulting in a soft focus effect. Using filters (band pass and band block) to isolate or narrow the bandwidth of light you are trying to capture will greatly increase sharpness.

Bright hot spots and lens or aperture flare appears in the center of the image. This is a common IR problem encountered in outdoor daylight photography with both IR digital and IR film cameras. This can only be eliminated by manually holding a light deflector just to the side of the lens to help eliminate potential reflections. This is often caused by bright objects that create IR light reflecting off internal lens elements or even the IR filter itself. Often, the lens hood will not provide enough protection from such flares.

The CCD of the camera captures the light spectrum from the UVA (380 nm) through the visible portion of the spectrum and into the near IR spectrum (IR below 1,000 nm). It will not capture IR heat energy in ranges above 1,350 nm.

The camera cannot autofocus to objects in the UV or IR spectrum. To achieve proper focus, use the manual focus mode in combination with the live image preview mode of the camera to fine-tune your focus on a subject.

Sufficient UV and IR light is necessary before an image is displayed on the LCD. Ensure that the manual focusing mode of the camera is turned on. Increase or decrease the intensity of the LCD during live preview mode if nothing is visible.

Digital Photo Imaging Microscope

24

VHX-1000 and Forensic Inspection

In the past few decades, forensic inspection processes have shifted from qualitative observation, to detailed, validated, and sometimes quantitative observation and documentation (Figure 24.1). For any piece of forensic evidence to hold up in court, the documentation must be definitive. Until this time, the best documentation that was possible was through standard optical microscopic inspection with an attached camera. The VHX-1000 microscope takes a unique approach to this, allowing the direct recording and documentation of extreme trace evidence.

The VHX-1000 uses a 17-inch LCD monitor to view the objects on the microscope stage. Amazingly, it has a camera that can image up to 54 megapixels. The high-resolution optics available for the VHX-1000 have a magnification range from 1 to 5,000. The optics are interchangeable, allowing for one system to be used for imaging insects, identifying them for the purpose of PMI (postmortem interval); fingerprints (to look at individual pore configuration as well as the friction ridges); and exceedingly small particulates (chemicals and compounds).

A wide variety of lens types is available, from bright-field and dark-field zoom lenses and fixed lenses, to an entire lineup of bore scopes and fiber scopes (Figure 24.2). The unit itself provides several reproducible lighting scenarios. There are many lens adapters to optimize the lighting for any type of inspection.

Handheld Integration

One of the more challenging of applications that individuals in a DNA group may come across is being asked to find traces of some sort of fluid on a dark material (Figure 24.3). While the end result would be the eventual DNA testing of the fluid, with such low contrast between the material and the fluid, finding a patch of the target can be a tedious, time-consuming process. The VHX-1000 camera can be detached from the stand and can be used for handheld inspection (Figure 24.4). The lens and contact attachment can be pulled across the material as the analyst examines the live projected image onto the 17-inch monitor for any type of foreign material (Figure 24.5). A light shift function can also be used to cut off two-thirds of the light exiting the end of the lens. Changing this incidence of lighting can allow for different types of light reflections off the material to be noticed more easily, subsequently decreasing the amount of time needed for this type of forensic inspection.

When the fluid is found, an image can be immediately captured, time-stamped, and saved for documentation purposes. The VHX has a built-in 160-gigabyte hard drive to

Figure 24.1 Keyence's VHX-1000 digital microscope. (Photos courtesy of Keyence.)

store any image or video that has been captured and a networking capability that allows for easy transfer and sharing of files over the network. Images can also be transferred using the writable CD disk drive or one of the eight USB (universal serial bus) ports found on the unit (Figure 24.6).

Lenses

The lenses are optimized for depth of field, working distance, and resolution. While maintaining its high-resolution imaging, with magnifications from 20 to 200, the VH-Z20R lens provides a depth of focus of about 1 inch at ×20 magnification (Figures 24.7 and 24.8). With this large depth of field, an entire target can be observed in focus from the peaks to the valleys, giving the analyst the entire picture of the sample.

At higher magnifications, however, when the depth of field is lost, an algorithm, called "depth up," can be performed to dynamically compile a completely focused image. When the lens is mounted to the stand and depth composition is performed, the operator scrolls through the different planes of focus with the focus knob, and the lens is moved downward. The VHX captures only the focused pixel in each plane and dynamically compiles them into a fully focused image, even at higher magnifications. This solves the problem when, for example, imaging a blowfly. With other scopes with cameras, if the top of the fly is in focus, the bottom is not. With the VHX-100, the entire fly is in focus, allowing a clearer image to be documented, recorded, and presented in court.

The lenses are also designed to have relatively large working distances. The VH-Z50L, with a magnification of 50–500, has a working distance of 3.35 inches throughout its entire magnification range. Samples can be examined at high magnifications without the need for oil immersion or any type of contact.

Model		VHX-600	VHX-100	VHX-100N
Various controller funcions	Depth compositon function	Real-time depth composition / High-quality depth composition	Quick depth composition / High-quality depth composition	
	Hybrid D.F.D display function	Provided (Quick)	Provided	
	3-D illumination simulation function	Provided	—	
	3-D two-screen simultaneous comparison function	Provided (Combination/Comparison/Difference display mode)	—	
	Saving a 3-D 360° -rotation image	Enabled (3-D 360° -rotating observation after saving an image)		
	Real-time digital zoom	1.0x to 10.0x (100 steps)		
	Optical contrast function	Provided	—	
	Halation eliminating function	Provided	—	
	Noise eliminating function	Provided	—	
	Supercharge shutter function	Provided		
	Edge enhancement function	Provided (200 steps) For a moving image		
	Wide range view function	Provided		
	Gamma correcting function	Provided		
	Camera-shake correcting function	Provided(For a moving image)	Provided	
	Split function	Vertical split, Horizontal split, 4 part split		
	Moving image redording-reproducing function	28 frames/sec.max.Moving image size (800 x 600), Actual moving image size (800 x 480)	—	
	Timer recording function	Provided		
Measuring function	Automatic unit VHx-S15 control function	Provided	—	
	Hight-resolution dimensinal measurement function	Provided		
	Wide-visual-field automatic 2-point measurement	Provided	—	
	Distance,angle,radius,area,etc.	Various functions are provided		
	Automatic count/measurement function	Provided (Enables distance/area measurement through brightness/color extraction)		
	Scale display	Various functions are provided		
	Automatic edge detection	Provided		
	Auto calibratrion	Full-auto (Numerical input is net required)		
	3-D profile measurement	Provided (Enables height profile display along an arbitrary line on the 3-D screen)		
Measuring function (Optional function) (5)	3-D height color/scale display function	Provided (Enables X/Y/Z-axis height scale display and color bar display related to height)		
	2-point height difference measurement function	Provided		
	Auto-focus function	Provided		
	Cross-section profile measurement	Provided	—	
	3-D volume measurement	Provided	—	
	3-D plane distance measurement	Provided	—	
	3-D plane angle measurement	Provided	—	
Utility	Complete style covering Observation,Recording and Measurement	All-in-one system that enables all operations for Observation, Recording and Mesurement without using a PC		
	Mail transmission function	Provided		
	Pop-up guide	Provided		
	Bayonet-type attachment	Provided		
	keyboard entry	Enabled		
	Compatible with a foot switch	Enabled		
	Function guide	Provided		
Console/Front panel (One-touch operation)	Pause	Provided		
	Recording	Provided		
	shutter speed adjustment	Provided		
	Supercharge shutter	Provided		
	One-touch 2x zoom	Provided		
	Depth composition function	Provided		
	Quick 3-D display function	Provided	—	
	Frame rate switching	Provided (15 frame/sec.or 28 frame/sec.)	Provided (7.5 frame/sec.or 30 frame/sec.)	
	Light shift function(Height difference enhancement)	Provided (Full,Partial,Flanking illumination)		
	e-Preview mode	Provided (Automatically lists 4 types of images,allowing selection of the optimal image		
	Camera-shake correcting function	Provided	—	
	Optimal contrast function	Provided	—	
	Halation eliminating function	Provided	—	
	Sensitivity quick adjustment dial	Shutter speed and camera gain oan be adjusted with one trimmer		
	Halation eliminating function	Provided		
Accompanying software	PC communication software	Image data transfer between the VHX and PC can be performed easily.(LAN)		
	3-D reproduction software for the PC (Available free of charge)	The PC can reproduce a 3-D image saved in VHX.(Copy free)		

Figure 24.2 There are many lenses available for the VHX-1000, from zoom lenses, bright field, dark field, and fixed lenses to bore scopes and fiber scopes. (Photos courtesy Keyence's VHX-1000 Digital Microscope.)

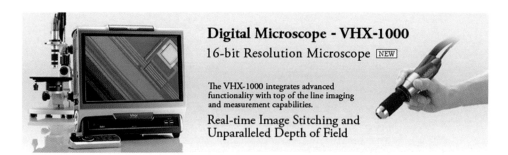

Figure 24.3 VHX-1000 handheld inspection scope optimized with integrated lighting and optics. (Photos courtesy Keyence's VHX-1000 Digital Microscope.)

Figure 24.4 The large depth of field of the lenses allows for detailed handheld inspection of materials. (Photos courtesy Keyence's VHX-1000 Digital Microscope.)

Figure 24.5 Foreign fluids can be identified on fabrics using handheld scope observation feature. (Photos courtesy Keyence's VHX-1000 Digital Microscope.)

Figure 24.6 The zoom lenses enable a telescopic-type zoom of the target even during hand-held observation. (Photos courtesy Keyence's VHX-1000 Digital Microscope.)

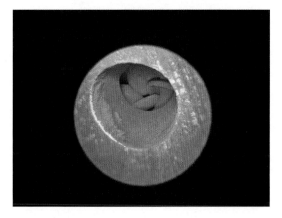

Figure 24.7 A bore scope attachment is used to look down the barrel of two different types of silencers: Silencer A. (Photos courtesy Keyence's VHX-1000 Digital Microscope.)

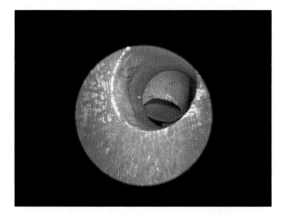

Figure 24.8 A bore scope attachment is used to look down the barrel of two different types of silencers: Silencer B. (Photos courtesy Keyence's VHX-1000 Digital Microscope.)

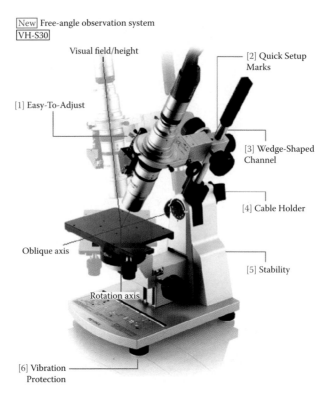

Figure 24.9 A multiangle motorized stage allows for full observation without touching or mounting the target. This also assists when small samples are viewed. (Photos courtesy Keyence's VHX-1000 Digital Microscope.)

Multiangle Stand

The need for samples to be imaged and examined without physically touching the sample is greater in forensic applications than for almost any other discipline (Figure 24.9). The Multiangle VH-S50 provides images of a sample all around the object in question without the need for object manipulation or mounting. The arm of the stand tilts 60 degrees to the left and 90 degrees to the right, while the stage itself rotates 360 degrees. The stage can be lowered to accommodate larger objects, and the lens holder attached to the arm can be swiveled to face the back to image a target that cannot be placed on the stage. Of course, for these applications for which the target cannot be placed on the stage, all imaging can be handheld without the need for a stage.

High-Resolution Imaging

The most useful of documentation features of the VHX-1000 is the high-resolution imaging capability (Figure 24.10). The VHX-1000 camera contains a 2.11-megapixel CCD (charged coupled device) but utilizes an advanced technique known as "pixel shift" to increase the pixel resolution to up to 54 megapixels (Figure 24.11). A set of piezocrystal actuators is attached to the sides of the CCD, and when supplied with voltage, these actuators expand, physically shifting the CCD. Using this method, the CCD is shifted three times to the right

Figure 24.10 High-resolution magnified imaging enables clear identification of bullet casing make, caliber, and tool marks created by the firing pin. (Photos courtesy Keyence's VHX-1000 Digital Microscope.)

Figure 24.11 These 54-megapixel three-CCD (charged coupled device) images reveal surface textures and properties of the bullet and tool marks. The extreme resolution allows enlargement of single striations without loss of definition. (Photos courtesy Keyence's VHX-1000 Digital Microscope.)

and three times downward to create nine subpixels within the original pixel. This effectively increases the pixel resolution from 2.11 to 18 megapixels. The pixel shift method is then used to reproduce the image color clarity of a three-CCD camera by exposing each pixel to a red, green, and blue (RGB) color filter. With a traditional three-CCD camera, each CCD is exposed to one of three color filters (RGB). The images are then superimposed onto one another to provide an image with high color clarity. With pixel shift, however, three CCDs are not needed to produce this level of color clarity. Each pixel can be exposed to each of the color filters by physically shifting the CCD under a Bayer filter containing all three colors. By imaging the sample three more times under each of the filters, the resultant image has the resolution and clarity of a 54-megapixel, three-CCD image.

Using a camera system with such high resolution and color clarity can make a huge difference in seeing the fine details that may go unnoticed with a lower-resolution microscopic imaging system. In any discipline that uses microscopy, there will be applications that require high-resolution imaging with a wide field of view. The VHX-1000 has an

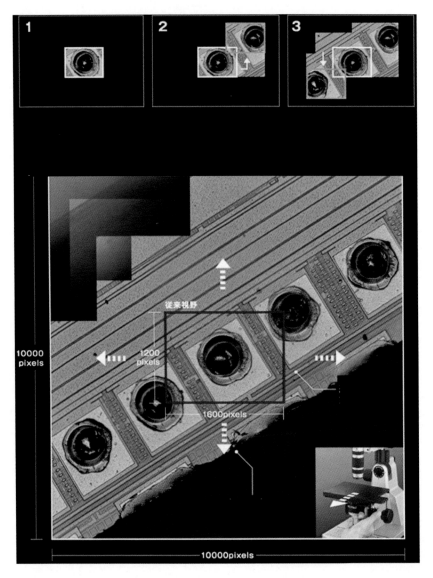

Figure 24.12 Images can be stitched in real time by moving the XY stage up to 10,000 × 10,000 pixels. (Photos courtesy Keyence's VHX-1000 Digital Microscope.)

advanced pattern-matching function that allows for the live stitching of two-dimensional (2D) and three-dimensional (3D) images up to 10,000 × 10,000 pixels from the standard size of 1,600 × 1,200 pixels. Larger targets can be imaged at higher magnifications without compromising the field of view (Figure 24.12).

High Dynamic Range

When examining latent prints on a material, a standard optical microscope may not provide enough contrast for adequate observation of the print (Figure 24.13). Different lighting adapters can help maximize the level of contrast. Sometimes, using a polarized

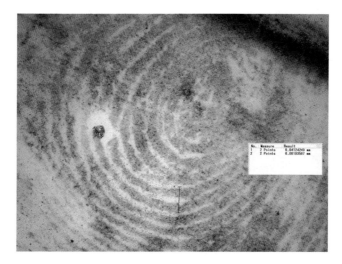

Figure 24.13 Combining different image enhancement techniques allows for the clear observation of latent prints. (Photos courtesy Keyence's VHX-1000 Digital Microscope.)

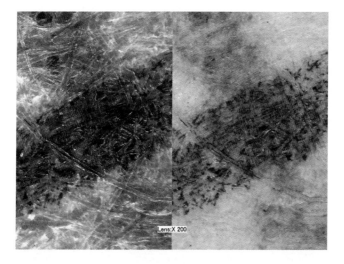

Figure 24.14 This questioned document was enhanced (left side) using HDR (high dynamic range). HDR increases the levels of observable color graduation and low contrast. Transparent items can be imaged with high levels of detail plus light shift functions, emphasizing the surface topography. (Photos courtesy Keyence's VHX-1000 Digital Microscope.)

lighting adapter can emphasize certain latent print features. Other times, using an adapter that can change the angle of incidence of the lighting can enhance the surface topography of the target, allowing for the observation of subtle surface features, like a latent print (without the benefit of development powder). Both of these methods can be enhanced, however, by using a function designed to increase the level of expressed color gradation in an image (Figure 24.14). A typical camera expresses brightness in 8-bit color resolution, or simply, 256 levels of color gradation. The VHX-1000 is capable of expressing color in 16-bit color resolution, thereby increasing the levels of color gradation to 65,000. The camera takes a series of images at varying shutter speeds (brightness levels), then combines the images into one image with exponentially higher levels of color gradation

Figure 24.15 High dynamic range of the scope increases the level of displayed color gradation, allowing pill identification on a low-contrast target. (Photos courtesy Keyence's VHX-1000 Digital Microscope.)

(Figure 24.15). The 16-bit data from this image can be used to emphasize certain characteristics of the image, including brightness, texture, contrast, and color. This can be useful in forensic applications, especially when examining targets with low levels of color and texture contrast.

Documentation and Measurement Tools

Many of the tools that would be needed for forensic documentation and labeling are available on the VHX-1000 unit itself. Split-screen comparisons are available for archived images as well as comparing a live image with an archived image (Figure 24.16). This tool is used

Figure 24.16 Four archived bullet casings are simultaneously compared in the split-screen mode of the scope. (Photos courtesy Keyence's VHX-1000 Digital Microscope.)

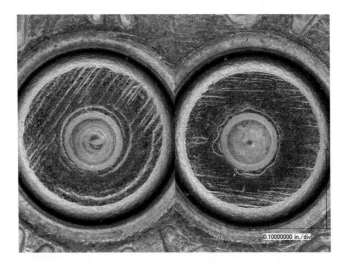

Figure 24.17 The VHX-1000 can be used as a comparison scope. Two archived hammer strike images can be compared using the split-screen function. (Photos courtesy Keyence's VHX-1000 Digital Microscope.)

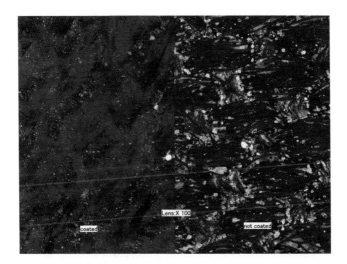

Figure 24.18 High-resolution imaging and split-screen capability show a clear difference between a coated and noncoated material. (Photos courtesy Keyence's VHX-1000 Digital Microscope.)

often for the comparison of questioned documents. Micro/macro shots of the sample can be shown and saved directly to the unit with any needed overlaid comments (Figure 24.17). In addition to these comment tools, measurements can be made directly on the image and can be stored within the image or exported as a CSV (comma-separated values) file. A CSV file is specially formatted to store spreadsheets or database-style information in a very simple format. A wide variety of measurements can be made on the image: point to point, radius, distance between two centers, parallel and perpendicular, and multipoint measurements (Figure 24.18). When comparing a hammer strike on one bullet casing to another bullet casing, one can measure how off center the strike is on the casing, easily quantifying some of the hammer strike characteristics. Distance between tool marks on the edges of a

Figure 24.19 These 54-megapixel three-CCD images reveal surface textures and properties of the bullet and tool marks that would otherwise go unobserved. (Photos courtesy Keyence's VHX-1000 Digital Microscope.)

bullet can be easily observed, measured, and recorded. The depth of the hammer strike can even be determined and documented using the 3D composition function (Figure 24.19).

3D Composition and Measurement

In an effort to better quantify some of the observations that are made in forensic applications, 3D profile composition and measurements can be made on a wide range of materials. Similar to the depth-up algorithm, the lens is scrolled through the different planes of focus, capturing only the focused pixels. By using the data on when the pixels came into focus, the VHX can construct a model of relative height topography (Figure 24.20).

When using the VH-S50 or VH-S15 motor, height data can be captured at an accuracy of 1 micron at ×1,000 magnification. Such 3D measurements as profile, distance, volume, and the like can be made with the VHX-H3M measurement software. Two 3D images can be compared simultaneously (Figure 24.21). An analyst can easily compare two hammer strikes on a bullet casing by comparing the 3D profiles, depth of the strike, or general 2D examination of how off center the strike was onto the bullet casing.

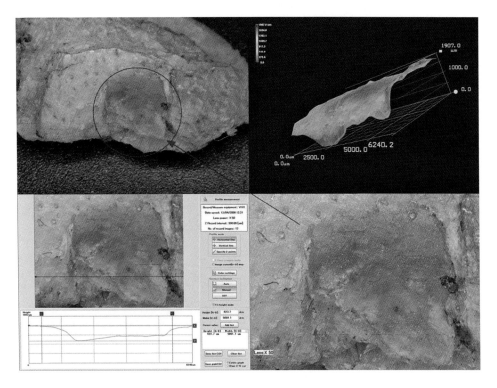

Figure 24.20 A skull fracture profile and 3D model can be made and observed simultaneously with the micro/macro shot of the fracture. (Photos courtesy Keyence's VHX-1000 Digital Microscope.)

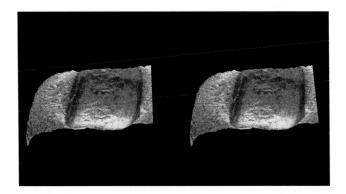

Figure 24.21 Two 3D models of a hammer strike can be compared side by side. (Photos courtesy Keyence's VHX-1000 Digital Microscope.)

SWGIT

25

Introduction

SWGIT is the Scientific Working on Imaging Technology. There are a number of scientific working groups (SWGs) (Figure 25.1).

Working Group	Web Site
• **SWGIT:** Imaging Technology	http://www.swgit.org
• **SWGDAM:** DNA Analysis Methods	None
• **SWGANTH:** Forensic Anthropology	http://www.swganth.org
• **SWGDE:** Digital Evidence	http://www.swgde.org/
• **SWGDOC:** Forensic Document Examination	None
• **SWGDRUG:** Analysis of Seized Drugs	http://www.swgdrug.org/
• **SWGFAST:** Friction Ridge Analysis, Study, and Technology	http://www.swgfast.org/
• **SWGGUN:** Firearms and Toolmarks	http://www.swggun.org/
• **SWGMAT:** Materials Analysis	http://www.swgmat.org/
• **SWGSTAIN:** Bloodstain Pattern Analysis	http://www.swgstain.org/
• **FISWG:** Facial Identification	http://www.fiswg.org/
• **SWGBRN:** Chemical, Biological, Radiological, and Nuclear Terrorism	None
• **SWGDVI:** Disaster Victim Identification	None
• **SWGFEX:** Fire and Explosives	None
• **SWGMAT:** Materials Analysis	http://www.swgmat.org
• **SWGGSR:** Gun Shot Residue	None
• **SWGTOX:** Forensic Toxicology	http://www.swg-tox.org
• **SWGTREAD:** Shoeprint and Tire Tread Evidence	http://www.swgtread.org
• **SWGIBR:** Illicit Business Records	None
• **SWGDOG:** Dogs and Orthogonal Detector Guidelines	http://www.swgdog.org

In the early 1990s, the Federal Bureau of Investigation (FBI) sponsored SWGs to improve common practices and create mutual agreements among federal, state, and local forensic practitioners.

The SWGIT consists of photographers, scientists, instructors, and managers from federal, state, local, and international law enforcement agencies as well as from the academic and research communities. All SWGIT documents represent the consensus opinion of this membership and should not be construed as the official policy of any of the represented agencies (SWGIT, Version 3.1 2007.06.08, 1.2).

The mission of the SWGIT is to facilitate the integration of imaging technologies and systems within the criminal justice system (CJS) by providing definitions and recommendations for the capture, storage, processing, analysis, transmission, and output of images (SWGIT, Version 3.1 2007.06.08, 1.1).

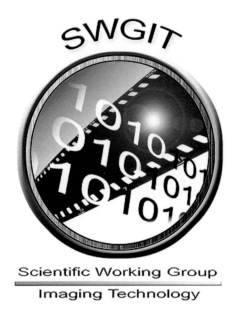

Figure 25.1 SWGIT logo.

The SWGIT document is broken down into 19 sections covering many of the areas of imaging in the criminal justice system.

Section 1: Overview of SWGIT and the Use of Imaging Technology in the Criminal Justice System (updated June 8, 2007)

Section 2: Considerations for Managers Migrating to Digital Imaging Technology (updated January 9, 2006)

Section 3: Guidelines for Field Applications of Imaging Technologies in the Criminal Justice System

Section 4: Recommendations and Guidelines for Using Closed-Circuit Television Security Systems in Commercial Institutions

Section 5: Guidelines for Image Processing (updated January 15, 2010)

Section 6: Guidelines and Recommendations for Training in Imaging Technologies in the Criminal Justice System

Section 7: Best Practices for Forensic Video Analysis (released January 16, 2009)

Section 8: General Guidelines for Capturing Latent Impressions Using a Digital Camera

Section 9: General Guidelines for Photographing Tire Impressions (updated January 15, 2010)

Section 10: General Guidelines for Photographing Footwear Impressions (updated January 15, 2010)

Section 11: Best Practices for Documenting Image Enhancement (updated January 15, 2010)

Section 12: Best Practices for Forensic Image Analysis

Section 13: Best Practices for Maintaining the Integrity of Digital Images and Digital Video (released June 4, 2007)

Section 14: Best Practices for Image Authentication (released June 4, 2007)

Section 15: Best Practices for Archiving Digital and Multimedia Evidence (DME) in the Criminal Justice System (released June 4, 2007)

Section 16: Best Practices for Forensic Photographic Comparison (released January 16, 2009)

Section 17: Digital Imaging Technology Issues for the Courts (updated June 5, 2009)

Section 18: Best Practices for Image Processing

Section 19: Issues Relating to Digital Image Compression and File Formats

The document was previously released as "Guidelines for the Use of Imaging Technologies in the Criminal Justice System" and "Definitions and Guidelines for the Use of Imaging Technologies in the Criminal Justice System" (SWGIT, Version 3.1 2007.06.08).

The document is a living document, changed to be current with recent court judicial decisions and laws. The committee meets twice a year to review and update the document.

There is a disclaimer for the document. (SWGIT, Version 3.1 2007.06.08)

Disclaimer

As a condition to the use of this document and the information contained herein, the SWGIT requests notification by e-mail before or contemporaneously to the introduction of this document, or any portion thereof, as a marked exhibit offered for or moved into evidence in any judicial, administrative, legislative, or adjudicatory hearing or other proceeding (including discovery proceedings) in the United States or any foreign country. Such notification shall include: 1) the formal name of the proceeding, including docket number or similar identifier; 2) the name and location of the body conducting the hearing or proceeding; 3) the name, mailing address (if available), and contact information of the party offering or moving the document into evidence. Subsequent to the use of this document in a formal proceeding, it is requested that SWGIT be notified as to its use and the outcome of the proceeding. Notifications should be sent to: SWGIT@yahoogroups.com.

Redistribution Policy

SWGIT grants permission for redistribution and use of all publicly posted documents created by SWGIT, provided that the following conditions are met:

1. Redistributions of documents, or parts of documents, must retain the SWGIT cover page containing the disclaimer.
2. Neither the name of SWGIT, nor the names of its contributors, may be used to endorse or promote products derived from its documents.

Any reference or quote from a SWGIT document must include the version number (or create date) of the document and mention if the document is in a draft status. (SWGIT, Version 3.1 2007.06.08)

The entire document is available online at http://www.theiai.org/guidelines/swgit. Since the document is constantly revised, I strongly advise that you visit the Web site for the most current version.

Bibliography

Authoring Organizations * Committee on Science, Technology, and Law (CSTL). Strengthening Forensic Science in the United States: A Path Forward. The National Academies Press. The National Academies Press, 2009. Web. 12 Oct. 2010. <http://www.nap.edu/catalog.php?record_id=12589>.

Criminalist Henry C. Lee to Present Continuing Professional Education Seminar. *The Mason Gazette*, Dec. 2006. Web. June 2009. <http://gazette.gmu.edu/>.

Daubert v. Merrell Dow Pharmaceuticals, 509 U.S. 579 (1993). LII Legal Information Institute at Cornell Law School. 30 Mar. 1993. Web. 12 Oct. 2010. <http://www.law.cornell.edu/supct/html/92-102.ZS.html>.

The *Frye* Opinion. Home. Web. 12 Oct. 2010. <http://www.daubertontheweb.com/frye_opinion.htm>.

Frye v. United States. 54 App. D. C. 46, 293 F. 1013. No. 3968. Court of Appeals of District of Columbia. Submitted November 7, 1923 December 3, 1923.

ID: Investigation Discovery: *Hollywood Crimes, Forensics, Murderers*. ID: Investigation Discovery. Web. 12 Oct. 2010. <http://investigation.discovery.com/>.

Merriam-Webster Dictionaries. Web. 12 Oct. 2010. <http://www.mobile-webster.com/>.

Miranda v. Arizona, 384 U. S. 436 :: Volume 384 :: 1966 :: Full Text." U.S. Supreme Court Cases from *Justia & Oyez*. US Supreme Court Cases, 1966. Web. 12 Oct. 2010. <http://supreme.justia.com/us/384/436/case.html>.

National Academies of Sciences (NAS). Strengthening forensic science in the United States: A path forward. Report to the U.S. Congress. 2009.

Nikon. "Http://www.nikonusa.com/Learn-And-Explore/Photography-Glossary/index.page?appendix=D." Http://www.nikonusa.com/Learn-And-Explore/Photography-Glossary/. Nikon, 2009. Web. 12 Oct. 2009. <http://www.nikonusa.com/>.

O.J Simpson. *The Times* | UK News, World News and Opinion. The Times | UK News, 12 Oct. 2008. Web. 2008. <http://www.thetimes.co.uk/tto/news/>.

Rule 16 Federal Rules of Civil Procedure - Notes to Rule 16 (LII 2009 Ed.). Rule 16 Legal Information Institute at Cornell Law School. Cornell Law School. Web. 12 Oct. 2009. <http://www.law.cornell.edu/rules/frcrmp/NRule16.htm>.

Rule 26 Federal Rules of Civil Procedure - Rule 26 (LII 2009 Ed.). Legal Information Institute at Cornell Law School. Cornell Law School. Web. 12 Oct. 2009. <http://www.law.cornell.edu/rules/frcrmp/Rule26.htm>.

Rule 30 Federal Rules of Civil Procedure - Rule 30 (LII 2009 Ed.). Legal Information Institute at Cornell Law School. Cornell Law School. Web. 12 Oct. 2009. <http://www.law.cornell.edu/rules/frcrmp/Rule30.htm>.

Rule 403 Federal Rules of Evidence (LII 2009 Ed.). Legal Information Institute at Cornell Law School. Cornell Law School. Web. 12 Oct. 2009. <http://www.law.cornell.edu/rules/fre/rules.htm>.

Rule 701. Federal Rules of Evidence (LII 2009 Ed.). Legal Information Institute at Cornell Law School. Cornell Law School, 1975. Web. 12 Oct. 2009. <http://www.law.cornell.edu/rules/fre/rules.htm>.

Rule 702. Federal Rules of Evidence (LII 2009 Ed.). Legal Information Institute at Cornell Law School. Cornell Law School, 2000. Web. 12 Oct. 2010. <http://www.law.cornell.edu/rules/fre/rules.htm>.

Rule 703. Federal Rules of Evidence (LII 2009 Ed.). Legal Information Institute at Cornell Law School. Cornell Law School, 2000. Web. 12 Oct. 2010. <http://www.law.cornell.edu/rules/fre/rules.htm>.

The Smithsonian. Encyclopedia Smithsonian: The Smithsonian from A to Z. Smithsonian Institution. The Smithsonian, 2009. Web. 12 Oct. 2010. <http://www.si.edu/encyclopedia_si/>.

SWGIT. The SWGIT Document. Scientific Working Group on Imaging Technology (SWGIT). SWGIT, 2010. Web. 12 Oct. 2010. <http://swgit.org/>.

Appendix A: Glossary

Note: All definitions are relative to imaging.

∞: Symbol for infinity.

archive image: Any image placed on media that is suitable for long-term storage.

artifact: A visual/aural aberration in an image, video, or audio recording resulting from a technical or operational limitation. Examples include speckles in a scanned picture or "blocking" in images compressed using the JPEG standard.

ASA: American Standard Association. Film speed or exposure index (EI) of film is described by a number using a system originally devised by the ASA. Now an obsolete system; film is described by its ISO value; the lower the number is, the slower the film will be.

aspect ratio: The ratio of height to width of a rectangle. Images with a wide aspect ratio are wider than they are tall. Images with a tall aspect ratio are taller than they are wide. For example, 35-mm film has an aspect ratio of 2:3 (24 × 36 mm and is sometimes called 1.5:1). Television usually has an aspect ratio of 4:3 (1.33:1), and some digital cameras use this aspect ratio as well.

authentication: The process of substantiating that the data is an accurate representation of what it purports to be.

autofocus: A setting that allows the camera to set the correct focus distance to the object imaged.

autofocus assist lamp: A light source, built into the camera, that provides light in low-light situations to assist in the autofocus mechanism of the camera.

beyond a reasonable doubt: The measurement used by jurors to convict an individual charged with a crime and brought to trial.

blackbody: An imaginary perfect emitter and absorber of radiation. Most light sources emit light that is a mixture of light with different wavelengths.

blooming: Distortion in an image that produces brightness and overexposure at the edges of objects.

bokeh: Selective "out-of-focus" areas of an image. The bokeh characteristics of a lens are important when using selective focus—making an object of interest sharp and the background softly out of focus.

bracketing: Taking a number of images of the same subject with different settings with the hope that one will be correct.

buffer: In a camera, the temporary memory area where the image is stored until it is written to the recording media used by the camera.

burst mode: A setting that will allow a number of images to be taken in a short period of time.

calibration: Using benchmark settings to set a device so that it works with a consistent output.

camera shake: Movement of the camera when slow shutter speeds are used, resulting in blurred images.

capture: The process of recording data, such as an image, video sequence, or audio stream.

capture device: A device used in the recording of data.

CCD: Charged coupled device.

CD/DCD: Optical disk formats designed to function as digital storage media. CD: compact disk; DCD: disk-caching disk.

chain of custody: The chronological documentation of the movement, location, and possession of evidence.

circle of confusion: Fuzzy disks that occur when a point of light is out of focus.

CMOS: Complementary metal-oxide semiconductor. A solid-state sensor that can capture an image.

color, neutral: A color containing equal parts of red, green, and blue; this then produces a gray color.

color correction: Adjusting the color of an image to become a more accurate representation of the original image.

color model, CYMK: Defining colors based on percentages of cyan, magenta, yellow, and black (k is black).

color model, RGB: Defining colors based on red, green, and blue.

color range: The range of colors that can be detected by a sensor.

colorimetry: The quantification of the color of an object.

compression: Making a file smaller by encoding, using fewer bits of information than the original image.

compression ratio: The size of a data file before compression divided by the file size after compression.

contrast: The range between the lightest and darkest tones in the image.

copy: An accurate reproduction of information.

demonstrative comparison: A method of presenting the similarities or differences among images or objects without rendering an opinion regarding identification or exclusion.

depth of field: A range of distance in an image in which the objects of interest are at least acceptably sharp.

diaphragm: An adjustable mechanism, in a camera, that can open similarly to the iris of a human eye; to open in f-stops.

digital evidence: Information of probative value that is stored or transmitted in a binary form.

digital image: An image that is represented by discrete numerical values organized in a two-dimensional array (Learn and Explore Photography, www.nikonusa.com). When viewed on a monitor or paper, it appears like a photograph.

digital processing chip: In a camera, a sold-state, silicon-based object that applies written code to process and store images.

diopter: An object used to make optical corrections in camera viewfinders.

direct lighting: Lighting coming from the direction of the camera. Also called front lighting.

directory listing: A list of files contained within an object. It may also contain other information, such as the size and dates of the files.

discovery: In a trial, at this point all information is exchanged by the prosecution and defense, including evidence, reports, images, and witness lists.

duplicate: An accurate and complete reproduction of all data objects independent of the physical media.

dynamic range: The difference between the brightest highlight and darkest value that a sensor (e.g., film or CCD) can detect and record in a single image.

enhancement techniques, traditional: Techniques that have direct counterparts in traditional darkrooms. They include brightness and contrast adjustment, color balancing, cropping, and dodging and burning.

evidence, exculpatory: Evidence that could be of benefit to the defense.

exposure: The amount of light allowed to reach the film sensor or film plane based on the amount of light, the lens opening, and the shutter speed.

exposure, correct: The amount of light allowed to reach the film sensor or film plane based on the amount of light, the lens opening, and the shutter speed—creating an image that truly and accurately depicts the original image.

exposure, over-: The amount of light allowed to reach the film sensor or film plane based on the amount of light, the lens opening, and the shutter speed—creating an image that does not truly and accurately depict the original image. The image is in fact dark.

exposure, under-: The amount of light allowed to reach the film sensor or film plane based on the amount of light, the lens opening, and the shutter speed—creating an image that does not truly and accurately depict the original image. The image is in fact light.

field: An element of a video signal containing alternate horizontal lines. For interlaced video, the scanning pattern is divided into two sets of spaced lines (odd and even) that are displayed sequentially. Each set of lines is called a field, and the interlaced set of the two sets of lines is a frame.

file format: The structure by which data are organized in a file.

film: In imaging, a device that is placed between the object to be imaged and the lens that effects the light reaching the film in some way.

filter, neutral density: In imaging, a device that is placed between the object to be imaged and the lens that retards the light reaching the sensing device or film. These are available in different densities, retarding the light in increments of ½ or 1 f-stop each. They may be stacked.

filter, polarizing: In imaging, a device that is placed between the object to be imaged and the lens that retards the light reaching the sensing device or film. They are most helpful, especially for reducing glare when imaging through glass.

flash, dedicated: A flash unit or strobe specifically designed for a specific camera make and model.

focal length: The distance between the sensor device or film and the optical center of the lens when the lens is focused on infinity (∞).

focal length, equivalent: A focal length of a digital camera translated to that of a 35-mm film camera.

focal plane: An imaginary line, perpendicular to the optical axis, that passes through the focal point, forming a plane of sharp focus, when the lens is set on infinity (∞).

focus, adjustable: A feature, available on many cameras, that allows the changing of the focus to make the object you wish to image in focus.

focus, fixed: A lens that cannot have its focus adjusted. Such cameras usually have lenses with small apertures that are permanently set to the hyperfocal distance.

focus lock: A feature available on many digital cameras that allows the focus to be "frozen" at a point where the object you wish to image is in focus.

forensic: As pertains to a court of law.

format, 35 mm: A small-format film and the most popular film format in use today, despite various attempts to dethrone it in the consumer field. The 35 mm refers to the width of the film; since the film has sprocket holes punched into the sides, the actual usable image area is nearly always 24 × 36 mm. (Some unusual cameras used half-size or half-frame image areas to pack more photographs into a single roll of 35-mm film.)

format, large: Film cameras that use large sheets of film rather than small rolls of film. These sheets are typically 4 × 5, 5 × 7, 8 × 10 inches and up. The negatives are so large that little, if any, enlarging is necessary to create a typical print. For this reason, large-format cameras offer photographs with the highest quality and finest grain of any type of camera.

format, medium: Medium-format film negatives are shot in a variety of aspect ratios depending on the camera body used. The most common aspect ratios are square (6 × 6 cm) and rectangular: 6 × 4.5, 6 × 7, 6 × 9, and 6 × 17 cm panoramic. The 6 × 4.5 cm format is commonly referred to as 645, and many cameras that use this format have 645 in the product name.

frame: Lines of spatial information of a video signal. For interlaced video, a frame consists of two fields, one of odd lines and one of even lines, displayed in sequence. For progressive scan (noninterlaced) video, the frame is written through successive lines that start at the top left of the picture and finish at the bottom right.

free space: Data storage areas available for use by the computer. The area may already contain previously stored information. Also referred to as unallocated space.

front lighting: *See* direct lighting

f-stop: Also f number. The relative aperture of a lens or the numbers used to indicate lens apertures, the amount of light that a lens lets in. These numbers are a relative number and are equivalent to the focal length of the lens divided by the size of the lens aperture. For example, if you were to take a 50-mm lens with a 6.25-mm diameter aperture, you would have a lens set to f/8. Generally, each increase or decrease in f-stop value either doubles or halves the aperture size. Since f-stop values are relative to the focal length, each camera lens should let the same amount of light through at the same f-stop value regardless of focal length.

gray card: A piece of cardboard of a medium gray color. This precisely determined shade of gray represents 18% gray in light intensity, or zone V on the zone system. Such gray cards can be useful for metering reflected light.

GSR: Gunshot reside, usually heavy metals used in manufacture of the primer, such as barium and antimony.

highlights: *Also* clipping. Area in a photograph where the lighting exceeds the maximum possible output.

hyperfocal distance: A point at which the depth of field (area of acceptable focus) extends from half the distance to the point all the way to infinity, the closest distance that is reasonably in focus if the lens is at infinity.

image comparison: The process of comparing images of questioned objects or persons to known objects or persons or images thereof and making an assessment of the correspondence between features in these images for rendering an opinion regarding identification or elimination.

image content analysis: The drawing of conclusions about an image. Targets for content analysis include, but are not limited to, the subjects or objects within an image; the conditions under which, or the process by which, the image was captured or created; the physical aspects of the scene (e.g., lighting or composition); or the provenance of the image.

image enhancement: Any process intended to improve the visual appearance of an image or specific features within an image.

image output: The means by which an image is presented for examination or observation.

image processing: Any activity that transforms an input image into an output image.

image-processing log: A record of the steps used in the processing of an image.

image rotation: Rotating the image 90, 180, or 270 degrees so that the top of the image corresponds to the top of the subject matter.

image synthesis: Any process that renders an image, using computer graphics techniques, for illustrative purposes (i.e., age progression, facial reconstruction, accident, or crime scene reconstruction).

image technology: Any system or method used to capture, store, process, analyze, transmit, or produce an image. Such systems include film, electronic sensors, cameras, video devices, scanners, printers, computers, and so on.

image transmission: The act of moving images from one location to another.

impeaching a witness: To discredit the testimony of a witness by proving that he or she has not told the truth or has been inconsistent by introducing contrary evidence, including statements made outside the courtroom in depositions or in statements of the witness heard by another.

integrity verification: The process of confirming that the data presented are complete and unaltered since time of acquisition.

intermediate storage: Any media or device on which data is temporarily stored for transfer to permanent or archival storage.

interpolation: 1. A method of image processing by which one pixel, block, or frame is displayed or stored based on the differences between the previous and subsequent pixel, block, or frame of information (Learn and Explore Photography. www. nikonusa.com). This is often done to increase the apparent clarity of an image. 2. Mathematical calculations used to determine what values a given pixel should have based on the values of its neighbors.

ISO: International Organization for Standardization, the Swiss-based international agency responsible for coordinating every kind of international standard imaginable, including film speed standards. Most exposure indices or film speeds today are described by the ISO system, which uses the same numeric values as the old ASA system (i.e., ISO 100, 400, 800). The slower the film is, the lower the number will be. By today's standards, ISO 100 is slow film, and ISO 800 or 1,600 is fast film.

ISO equivalent: Digital cameras do not use film and so cannot have film speed ratings as such. However, many digital cameras have adjustable light sensitivity levels, and these adjustable levels are stated as ISO film speed equivalents simply because the ISO film speed numbers are a well-understood and handy convention.

Joint Photographic Experts Group: An international committee of computer imaging experts. Pronounced "jay-peg."

JPEG: *Also* JPG. A digital image compression algorithm defined by the organization Joint Photographic Experts Group. JPEG pictures are (usually 24-bit) images on which lossy compression techniques have been applied to reduce dramatically the file size of a picture. JPEG images are used on the Web and by many digital cameras.

Kelvin (K): 1. The Kelvin scale is relevant to photography because color temperature is defined in kelvin. Apparently, it is technically inaccurate to refer to degrees kelvin; the unit alone is supposed to be used, although everyone still talks about degrees kelvin. Scientific temperature scale that is similar to celsius, only rather than defining zero as the freezing point of water, it defines zero as absolute zero—the coldest temperature that can theoretically be attained in the universe. Therefore, you cannot have negative kelvin units.

2. The unit of thermodynamic temperature, a base unit in SI is equal to the fraction 1/273.16 of the thermodynamic temperature of the triple point of water. The triple point of water is the unique combination of temperature and pressure at which water exists simultaneously as liquid, solid, and gas. The kelvin is also the basis of the Celsius temperature scale. The temperature in kelvin can be found by adding 273.15 to the temperature in degrees celsius.

lag time: Also "shutter-lag time." The time that elapses between the photographer pressing the shutter release and the camera actually opening the shutter and taking the photograph. On a purely mechanical film camera, there usually is not much lag time; you press the button or lever, and a mechanical action takes place instantly. The only delays are typically associated with moving the mirror out of the way on SLR cameras. But, with an automated film camera, there can be a split-second processing delay before the shutter is actually tripped. And with digital cameras, there can be a significant delay. Generally, expensive cameras have short lag times.

latitude: The range of camera exposures that produce acceptable images with a particular digital sensor or film.

leaf, shutter: A circular, multiblade shutter usually positioned within the lens (between the lens) itself, although some cameras position it inside the body near the lens mount. Either way, leaf shutters are not positioned near the film focal plane like rectangular or square focal plane shutters. Leaf shutters are round, and open and close like the aperture diaphragm on most lenses or like a mechanical approximation of the iris of the human eye.

lens, close up: *See* lens, macro

lens, fish-eye: A very wide-angle lens that does not correct straight lines; it exhibits extreme barrel distortion. Fish-eye lenses typically cover either 180 degrees vertically (8-mm fish-eye lenses for 35-mm film) or 180 degrees diagonally (15- to 16-mm fish-eye lenses for 35-mm film). The former cast circular images on the film, and the latter are full frame.

lens, macro: 1. Macro imaging is close-up imaging that does not involve microscopes. True macro imaging is generally considered to be 1:1 or greater. In other words, the subject is the same size as the final image (in the case of 35-mm film, 24×36 mm in size).

2. A lens capable of 1:1 or greater imaging.

lens, micro: Nikon's nomenclature for a macro lens. (*See* lens, macro)

lens, normal: A lens with a focal length equal to, or roughly equal to, the diagonal of the film format. The 50-mm lenses are called "normal" lenses on 35-mm cameras since the diagonal of 35-mm film is 42 mm. Larger film formats require longer focal lengths for normal lenses.

lens, telephoto: A lens that takes in a small area of the scene, it acts very similar to a telescope.

lens, wide angle: A lens that takes in a great deal of a scene owing to its wide coverage angle. The focal length of a wide-angle lens is always shorter than the diagonal of the film format. In the case of a 35-mm camera, any lens shorter than 42 mm or so is a wide angle.

light, additive: The act of using extra lamps, flash units, and the like to augment the existing or ambient light available.

light, ambient: The light that exists in the area around the subject matter.

light, available: Whatever light is available to a photographer without setting up extra lamps, turning on flash units, and so on. This can be natural sunlight, or it can be light from whatever artificial light sources happen to be around. Available light photography is therefore the art of taking photos in whatever light is there.

light, candle: Approximately 1,850–1.900 kelvin (color temperature).

light, daylight: Light that is considered equivalent to noonday sun, temperature typically 4,800–5,000 kelvin.

light, fill: Light supplementing the existing light or main light to fill in shadows and reduce harsh contrast.

light, fluorescent: Approximately 2,950 kelvin (color temperature).

light, incandescent (40 watt): Approximately 2,500 kelvin (color temperature).

light, mercury vapor: Approximately 4,000 kelvin (color temperature).

light, sodium vapor: Approximately 2,100 kelvin (color temperature).

light, subtractive: Using a panel of some dark light-absorbing material when lighting a subject to create shadows and the light. The effect of placing a dark panel next to a subject, just out of camera view. The panel prevents light from reflecting off walls and other objects back onto the subject, creating shadow.

light, white balance: *See* white balance

lighting, back-: A typical example is a photo of a person taken with the camera facing toward the sun. It is particularly difficult for automatic exposure camera systems to deal with backlighting since the range of light tends to be so extreme and lenses tend to flare.

lighting, bounce: Subject lighting that is performed by reflecting light from a light source off a larger surface. This is done to soften the light and is a commonly used technique with flash photography.

lighting, diffused: Light that is scattered by a translucent medium and is thus reflected or scattered in different directions. Diffuse light causes soft shadows rather than hard-edged ones because of all the different directions in which the lighting is traveling.

lighting, direct: Light coming from the camera. An image taken with a camera-mounted flash unit will produce extremely dark and hard-edged shadows on the wall behind the subject's head.

lighting, front: *See* lighting, direct

lighting, oblique: Light coming from 45 degrees while the camera is placed at 90 degrees. *See also* lighting, side

lighting, side: Light coming from either the left or right side of the subject.

lighting ratio: The ratio of the main light source to the secondary light source.

lossless compression: Compression in which no data are lost, and all data can be retrieved in their original form.

lossy compression: Compression in which data are lost and cannot be retrieved in their original form.

lossy image: In digital imaging when the compression algorithm used deletes some of the information to store the image (e.g., jpg is a lossy image format).

media: Objects on which data can be stored.

metadata: Data, frequently embedded within a file, that describes a file or directory, which can include the locations where the content is stored, dates and times, application-specific information, and permissions.

meter, averaging: *See* meter, center balanced

meter, center balanced: A light-metering system used by many cameras with internal light meters on many SLR cameras today. This system simply averages the exposure across the entire image frame but gives added emphasis (weight) to the central part of the image.

meter, center weighted: *See* meter, center balanced

meter, flash: A light meter capable of recording and metering the brief bursts of light from a flash unit.

meter, spot: Spot metering is the process of reading reflected light levels from a very small area, typically 1–3% of an image area. Most high-end SLR cameras have internal spot meters, which are particularly important for users of the zone system of light metering.

***Miranda* decision:** *Miranda v. Arizona* (consolidated with *Westover v. United States, Vignera v. New York,* and *California v. Stewart*), 384 U.S. 436 (1966), was a landmark 5–4 decision of the U.S. Supreme Court that was argued February 28–March 1, 1966, and decided June 13, 1966. The Court held that criminal suspects must be informed of their right to consult with an attorney and of their right against self-incrimination prior to questioning by police.

Mirandize: *See* Miranda decision

mirror lockup: SLR cameras contain mirrors that allow you to look through the lens while metering and focusing. When you take a photo, this reflex motor swings up out of the way, allowing a clear path from the lens to the surface of the film.

multimedia evidence: Analog or digital media, including, but not limited to, film, tape, magnetic and optical media, or the information contained therein.

noise: In communications theory, any disturbance that disrupts or affects or interferes with a signal in an unwanted fashion. In digital photography, noise is the appearance of random dots or changes in color value in an image, like "snow" that would appear on analog televisions.

nomenclature: A system of names assigned to objects or items in a particular science or art.

normal lens: A lens that allows items in the image to appear respectively the same as in the original area imaged. Usually about 45 degrees.

NTSC: National Television Standards Committee (European video format).

original image: An accurate and complete replica of the primary image, irrespective of media. For film and analog video, the primary image is the original image.

PAL: Phase alternation line (European Broadcast Union) (U.S. video format).

parallax error: Parallax error is a problem when you are using any camera system in which the viewfinder is a separate optical system from the actual taking lens. In an SLR camera, parallax is not a problem because when you look through the viewfinder you are looking through the same lens that takes the photo.

parallax shift: *See* parallax error

peer or technical review: An evaluation conducted by a second qualified individual of reports, notes, data, conclusions, and other documents.

photogrammetric analysis: The process of obtaining dimensional information regarding objects and people depicted in an image.

photogrammetry: The art, science, and technology of obtaining reliable information about physical objects and the environment through the processes of recording, measuring, and interpreting photographic images and patterns of electromagnetic radiant energy and other phenomena (Learn and Explore Photography, www.nikonusa.com).

In forensic applications, photogrammetry, sometimes called *mensuration*, most commonly is used to extract dimensional information from images, such as the height of subjects depicted in surveillance images and accident scene reconstruction. Other forensic photogrammetric applications include visibility and spectral analyses.

photometry: The measurement of light values of objects in an image.

physical copy: An accurate reproduction of information contained on the physical device.

primary image: The first instance in which an image is recorded onto any media that is a separate, identifiable object. Examples include a digital image recorded on a flash card or a digital image downloaded from the Internet.

processed image: Refers to the first instance in which an image is recorded onto any media that is a separate, identifiable object. Examples include a digital image recorded on a flash card or a digital image downloaded from the Internet.

proficiency test: A test to evaluate analysts, technical support personnel, and the quality performance of an agency. For example: (1) Open test: the analysts and technical support personnel are aware that they are being tested. (2) Blind test: the analysts and technical support personnel are not aware that they are being tested. (3) Internal test: Test conducted by the agency itself. (4) External test: Test conducted by an agency independent of the agency being tested.

proprietary file format: Any file format that is unique to a specific manufacturer or product.

qualitative image analysis: The process used to extract measurable data from an image.

quality assurance or QA: Planned and systematic actions necessary to provide sufficient confidence that the product or service of an agency or laboratory will satisfy given requirements for quality.

range finder: A type of focusing system or a direct-vision camera that uses such a system, which is based on principles of triangulation. A range-finder camera is one in which the scene in the viewfinder does not come through the taking lens. Instead, the viewfinder and taking lens have separate optical systems, linked or coupled in a complex fashion.

RAW: Files are not yet processed and ready to be printed. RAW files typically give the photographer the highest-quality output since no postprocessing has yet been applied to the image. For this reason, RAW files are frequently known as "digital negatives."

reliability: The extent to which you can depend on information.

reproducibility: The extent to which a process yields the same results in repeated trials.

resolution: The act, process, or capability of distinguishing between two separate but adjacent parts or stimuli, such as elements of detail in an image or similar colors (Learn and Explore Photography, www.nikonusa.com).

restoration: 1. The process of reversing damage done to an image due to a known cause (such as defocus or motion blur) so that the effects of the damage can be removed or reduced.

2. The process of restoring data from an image.

saturation: The purity or intensity of color. Color with low saturation looks washed out or pastel-like because it has a lot of white light. Completely unsaturated color is gray. Saturated color is intense and contains no white light.

shadow: Dark or poorly illuminated areas of a scene.

sharpening: Computer image-editing programs often support sharpening algorithms. Sharpening is the mathematical process of enhancing the apparent sharpness of an image by boosting the contrast of edges in images. Note that sharpening algorithms do not add any new information to the image; they simply enhance what is already there. And, it is easy to oversharpen an image, which results in ugly artifacts.

shutter: A movable physical barrier inside a camera or a lens that normally does not let light pass. However, when triggered, the shutter opens for a usually brief and precisely calibrated period of time before springing shut again.

shutter, focal plane: A camera shutter that lies inside the camera body, immediately in front of the film surface. Such shutters are rectangular and made of narrow blinds or curtains that move along, exposing the film surface to light. Most film SLR cameras have focal plane shutters, which are of the behind-the-lens kind. Not all cameras do, however. Other cameras place the shutter within the lens itself, called leaf shutters.

slave: Slave flashes are simply self-contained electronic flash units that respond to external triggers of some kind. Many slave flashes are triggered by light-optical slaves. They have small sensors built in or attached that detect the light pulse from another flash unit and then trigger immediately themselves. Since they respond so rapidly, the time delay between the trigger flash and the slave flash going off does not affect the exposure of the photo.

SLR: Single-lens reflex. An SLR camera views through the lens.

standard: A known with which to compare an unknown.

storage media: Any object on which data are preserved.

TIFF: Tagged image file format. A common raster image format.

time lapse: A sequence of photographs taken at predetermined time intervals.

TLR: Twin-lens reflex.

TTL: Through the lens.

validation: Techniques that have direct counterparts in traditional darkrooms. They include brightness and contrast adjustment, color balancing, cropping, and dodging and burning.

validation testing: An evaluation to determine if a tool, technique, or procedure functions correctly and as intended.

verification: 1. The process of confirming the accuracy of an item compared to its original. 2. Confirmation that a tool, technique, or procedure performs as expected.

voir dire: 1. From French "to see to speak," the questioning of prospective jurors by a judge and attorneys in court. Voir dire is used to determine if any juror is biased or cannot deal with the issues fairly or if there is cause not to allow a juror to serve (knowledge of the facts; acquaintanceship with parties, witnesses, or attorneys; occupation that might lead to bias; prejudice against the death penalty; or previous experiences such as having been sued in a similar case). Actually, one of the unspoken purposes of the voir dire is for the attorneys to get a feel for the personalities and likely views of the people on the jury panel. In some courts, the judge asks most of the questions, while in others the lawyers are given substantial latitude and time to ask questions. Some jurors may be dismissed for cause by the judge, and the attorneys may excuse others in "peremptory" challenges without stating any reason. 2. Questions asked to determine the competence of an alleged expert witness. 3. Any hearing outside the presence of the jury held during trial.

white balance: In digital photography, calibration of the white point. The assumed white point can vary depending on the light conditions; the concept of "white" is not an absolute thing. Most decent digital cameras let you specify whatever white point you want, usually by pointing the camera at a white object illuminated by the current light used by the imager. Some cameras also can detect the ambient light and determine the white point from that, termed automatic white balance.

witness: A person who sees something and answers questions posed to him or her by an attorney.

witness, expert: A person who sees something, has examined something, and answers questions posed to him or her by an attorney. This person has a great deal of training in the field in which he or she will testify. The person also has considerable education in the area and subject of testimony. He or she will also have experience in testifying concerning this field in a court of law. The expert witness may have published in the area in which he or she will testify. The judge will then make a determination and declare that this person is an expert witness. This person may give opinions.

witness, professional: A person who sees something in the course of his or her profession or job and answers questions posed by an attorney. This person can be a police officer, detective, security officer, or CSI. He or she has had training in the field in which he or she will testify but not to the point of being an expert.

work copy: A copy or duplicate of a recording or data that can be used for subsequent processing or analysis.

write block/write protect: Hardware or software methods of preventing modification of media content.

Appendix B: Photo I.D. Card*

PHOTO I.D. CARD

| Case Number: | Date / Time: |

Forensic Photographer:

CRIMINALISTICS

Roll ID

| R | G | B | C | M | Y |

* This image may be removed from the book and laminated for handy use.

Index